2450

Modern Critical Views

Henry Adams
Edward Albee
A. R. Ammons
Matthew Arnold
John Ashbery
W. H. Auden
Jane Austen
James Baldwin
Charles Baudelaire
Samuel Beckett
Saul Bellow
The Bible
Elizabeth Bishop
William Blake
Jorge Luis Borges
Elizabeth Bowen
Bertolt Brecht
The Brontës
Robert Browning
Anthony Burgess
George Gordon, Lord
   Byron
Thomas Carlyle
Lewis Carroll
Willa Cather
Cervantes
Geoffrey Chaucer
Kate Chopin
Samuel Taylor Coleridge
Joseph Conrad
Contemporary Poets
Hart Crane
Stephen Crane
Dante
Charles Dickens
Emily Dickinson
John Donne & the Seven-
   teenth-Century Meta-
   physical Poets
Elizabethan Dramatists
Theodore Dreiser
John Dryden
George Eliot
T. S. Eliot
Ralph Ellison
Ralph Waldo Emerson
William Faulkner
Henry Fielding
F. Scott Fitzgerald
Gustave Flaubert
E. M. Forster
Sigmund Freud
Robert Frost

Robert Graves
Graham Greene
Thomas Hardy
Nathaniel Hawthorne
William Hazlitt
Seamus Heaney
Ernest Hemingway
Geoffrey Hill
Friedrich Hölderlin
Homer
Gerard Manley Hopkins
William Dean Howells
Zora Neale Hurston
Henry James
Samuel Johnson and
   James Boswell
Ben Jonson
James Joyce
Franz Kafka
John Keats
Rudyard Kipling
D. H. Lawrence
John Le Carré
Ursula K. Le Guin
Doris Lessing
Sinclair Lewis
Robert Lowell
Norman Mailer
Bernard Malamud
Thomas Mann
Christopher Marlowe
Carson McCullers
Herman Melville
James Merrill
Arthur Miller
John Milton
Eugenio Montale
Marianne Moore
Iris Murdoch
Vladimir Nabokov
Joyce Carol Oates
Sean O'Casey
Flannery O'Connor
Eugene O'Neill
George Orwell
Cynthia Ozick
Walter Pater
Walker Percy
Harold Pinter
Plato
Edgar Allan Poe
Poets of Sensibility & the
   Sublime

Alexander Pope
Katherine Ann Porter
Ezra Pound
Pre-Raphaelite Poets
Marcel Proust
Thomas Pynchon
Arthur Rimbaud
Theodore Roethke
Philip Roth
John Ruskin
J. D. Salinger
Gershom Scholem
William Shakespeare
   (3 vols.)
   Histories & Poems
   Comedies
   Tragedies
George Bernard Shaw
Mary Wollstonecraft
   Shelley
Percy Bysshe Shelley
Edmund Spenser
Gertrude Stein
John Steinbeck
Laurence Sterne
Wallace Stevens
Tom Stoppard
Jonathan Swift
Alfred, Lord Tennyson
William Makepeace
   Thackeray
Henry David Thoreau
Leo Tolstoi
Anthony Trollope
Mark Twain
John Updike
Gore Vidal
Virgil
Robert Penn Warren
Evelyn Waugh
Eudora Welty
Nathanael West
Edith Wharton
Walt Whitman
Oscar Wilde
Tennessee Williams
William Carlos Williams
Thomas Wolfe
Virginia Woolf
William Wordsworth
Richard Wright
William Butler Yeats

These and other titles in preparation

Modern Critical Views

ERNEST HEMINGWAY

Modern Critical Views

ERNEST HEMINGWAY

Edited with an introduction by

Harold Bloom

Sterling Professor of the Humanities
Yale University

1985
CHELSEA HOUSE PUBLISHERS
New York

THE COVER:

Hemingway's personal myth as sportsman—big-game hunter, deep-sea fisherman, enthusiast for boxing and for bull-fighting—is an inalienable aspect of his art.—H.B.

PROJECT EDITORS: Emily Bestler, James Uebbing
ASSOCIATE EDITOR: Maria Behan
EDITORIAL COORDINATOR: Karyn Gullen Browne
EDITORIAL STAFF: Laura Ludwig, Linda Grossman, Peter Childers
DESIGN: Susan Lusk

Cover illustration by Robin Peterson. Picture courtesy of AP/Wide World and UPI/Bettman.

Printed and bound in the United States of America

10 9 8 7 6 5 4 3

Library of Congress Cataloging in Publication Data

Ernest Hemingway.
    (Modern critical views)
    Bibliography: p.
    Includes index.
    1. Hemingway, Ernest, 1899–1961—Criticism and
interpretation—Addresses, essays, lectures.   I. Bloom,
Harold.   II. Series.
PS3515.E37Z5865   1985   813029.52   85–5963
ISBN 0–87754–619–9

Chelsea House Publishers
95 Madison Avenue, New York, NY 10016
345 Whitney Avenue, New Haven, CT 06511
5068B West Chester Pike, Edgemont, PA 19028

Contents

Editor's Note

This volume gathers together a representative selection of the best literary criticism devoted to Hemingway's work during the last forty-five years. It is arranged in chronological sequence of publication (or revision).

The editor's "Introduction" seeks Hemingway's place in the American literary tradition. With the first two essays, by Lionel Trilling and Edmund Wilson, the relation of Hemingway to his contemporary readers begins to be explored. This relation is examined further in Robert Penn Warren's reading of A *Farewell to Arms*, in Harry Levin's classical analysis of Hemingway's style, and in Carlos Baker's biographical exegesis of the *ethos* of the author's work.

Mark Spilka's reconsideration of *The Sun Also Rises* is the last critical essay written during Hemingway's lifetime to be included in this volume. It is supplemented by Hemingway's famous interview with George Plimpton, which can be regarded as the novelist's own summing-up of his career.

Little of value was published about Hemingway in the decade after his suicide. The personal tribute by the novelist Reynolds Price records Hemingway's continued influence upon a new generation of American writers. This influence is examined again by Malcolm Cowley as he wryly reflects upon the defensive attempts to slay Hemingway's work posthumously. The essay by Steven K. Hoffman represents the several new emphases upon Hemingway's short stories that are now current, and is supplemented by Alfred Kazin's recent attempt at a retrospective view of all of Hemingway's work. Finally, John Hollander's reconsideration of the relation between style and idea in Hemingway briefly but illuminatingly opens up again the insights of Wallace Stevens and Robert Penn Warren that Hemingway essentially was a poet.

Introduction

Hemingway freely proclaimed his relationship to *Huckleberry Finn*, and there is some basis for the assertion, except that there is little in common between the rhetorical stances of Twain and of Hemingway. Kipling's *Kim*, in style and mode, is far closer to *Huckleberry Finn* than anything Hemingway wrote. The true accent of Hemingway's admirable style is to be found in an even greater and more surprising precursor:

> This grass is very dark to be from the white heads of old
>   mothers,
> Darker than the colorless beards of old men,
> Dark to come from under the faint red roofs of mouths.

Or again:

> I clutch the rails of the fence, my gore drips, thinn'd with
>   the ooze of my skin,
> I fall on the weeds and stones,
> The riders spur their unwilling horses, haul close,
> Taunt my dizzy ears and beat me violently over the head
>   with whip-stocks.
> Agonies are one of my changes of garments,
> I do not ask the wounded person how he feels, I myself
>   become the wounded person,
> My hurts turn livid upon me as I lean on a cane and observe.

Hemingway is scarcely unique in not acknowledging the paternity of Walt Whitman; T.S. Eliot and Wallace Stevens are far closer to Whitman than William Carlos Williams and Hart Crane were, but literary influence is a paradoxical and antithetical process, about which we continue to know all too little. The profound affinities between Hemingway, Eliot, and Stevens are not accidental, but are family resemblances due to the repressed but crucial relation each had to Whitman's work. Hemingway characteristically boasted (in a letter to Sara Murphy, February 27, 1936) that he had knocked Stevens down quite handily: ". . . for statistics sake Mr. Stevens is 6 feet 2 weighs 225 lbs. and . . . when he hits the ground it is highly spectaculous." Since this match between the two

...ace in Key West on February 19, 1936, I am moved, as a
...ian, for statistics' sake to point out that the victorious
...was born in 1899, and the defeated Stevens in 1879, so that
the ... st was then going on thirty-seven, and the poet verging on
fifty-seven. The two men doubtless despised one another, but in the
letter celebrating his victory, Hemingway calls Stevens "a damned fine
poet" and Stevens always affirmed that Hemingway was essentially a poet,
a judgment concurred in by Robert Penn Warren when he wrote that
Hemingway "is essentially a lyric rather than a dramatic writer." Warren
compared Hemingway to Wordsworth, which is feasible, but the resemblance to Whitman is far closer. Wordsworth would not have written: "I
am the man, I suffer'd, I was there," but Hemingway almost persuades us
he would have achieved that line had not Whitman set it down first.

II

It is now more than twenty years since Hemingway's suicide, and some
aspects of his permanent canonical status seem beyond doubt. Only a few
modern American novels seem certain to endure: *The Sun Also Rises*, *The
Great Gatsby*, *Miss Lonelyhearts*, *The Crying of Lot 49* and at least several
by Faulkner, including *As I Lay Dying*, *Sanctuary*, *Light in August*, *The
Sound and the Fury*, *Absalom, Absalom!* Two dozen stories by Hemingway
could be added to the group, indeed perhaps all of *The First Forty-Nine
Stories*. Faulkner is an eminence apart, but critics agree that Hemingway
and Fitzgerald are his nearest rivals, largely on the strength of their shorter
fiction. What seems unique is that Hemingway is the only American
writer of prose fiction in this century who, as a stylist, rivals the principal
poets: Stevens, Eliot, Frost, Hart Crane, aspects of Pound, W.C. Williams,
Robert Penn Warren, and Elizabeth Bishop. This is hardly to say that
Hemingway, at his best, fails at narrative or the representation of character. Rather, his peculiar excellence is closer to Whitman than to Twain,
closer to Stevens than to Faulkner, and even closer to Eliot than to
Fitzgerald, who was his friend and rival. He is an elegiac poet who mourns
the self, who celebrates the self (rather less effectively) and who suffers
divisions in the self. In the broadest tradition of American literature, he
stems ultimately from the Emersonian reliance on the god within, which
is the line of Whitman, Thoreau, and Dickinson. He arrives late and dark
in this tradition, and is one of its negative theologians, as it were, but as
in Stevens the negations, the cancellings, are never final. Even the most
ferocious of his stories, say "God Rest You Merry, Gentlemen" or "A

Natural History of the Dead," can be said to celebrate what we might call the Real Absence. Doc Fischer, in "God Rest You Merry, Gentlemen," is a precursor of Nathanael West's Shrike in *Miss Lonelyhearts*, and his savage, implicit religiosity prophesies not only Shrike's Satanic stance but the entire demonic world of Pynchon's explicitly paranoid or Luddite visions. Perhaps there was a nostalgia for a Catholic order always abiding in Hemingway's consciousness, but the cosmos of his fiction, early and late, is American Gnostic, as it was in Melville, who first developed so strongly the negative side of the Emersonian religion of self-reliance.

III

Hemingway notoriously and splendidly was given to overtly agonistic images whenever he described his relationship to canonical writers, including Melville, a habit of description in which he has been followed by his true ephebe, Norman Mailer. In a grand letter (September 6–7, 1949) to his publisher, Charles Scribner, he charmingly confessed: "Am a man without any ambition, except to be champion of the world, I wouldn't fight Dr. Tolstoi in a 20 round bout because I know he would knock my ears off." This modesty passed quickly, to be followed by: "If I can live to 60 I can beat him. (MAYBE)" Since the rest of the letter counts Turgenev, De Maupassant, Henry James, even Cervantes, as well as Melville and Dostoevsky, among the defeated, we can join Hemingway, himself, in admiring his extraordinary self-confidence. How justified was it, in terms of his ambitions?

It could be argued persuasively that Hemingway is the best short-story writer in the English language from Joyce's *Dubliners* until the present. The aesthetic dignity of the short story need not be questioned, and yet we seem to ask more of a canonical writer. Hemingway wrote *The Sun Also Rises* and not *Ulysses*, which is only to say that his true genius was for very short stories, and hardly at all for extended narrative. Had he been primarily a poet, his lyrical gifts would have sufficed: we do not hold it against Yeats that his poems, not his plays, are his principal glory. Alas, neither Turgenev nor Henry James, neither Melville nor Mark Twain provide true agonists for Hemingway. Instead, De Maupassant is the apter rival. Of Hemingway's intensity of style in the briefer compass, there is no question, but even *The Sun Also Rises* reads now as a series of epiphanies, of brilliant and memorable vignettes.

Much that has been harshly criticized in Hemingway, particularly in *For Whom the Bell Tolls*, results from his difficulty in adjusting his gifts to the demands of the novel. Robert Penn Warren suggests that Hemingway is successful when his "system of ironies and understatements is coherent." When incoherent, then Hemingway's rhetoric fails as persuasion, which is to say, we read *To Have and Have Not* or *For Whom the Bell Tolls* and we are all too aware that the system of tropes is primarily what we are offered. Warren believes this not to be true of *A Farewell to Arms*, yet even the celebrated close of the novel seems now a worn understatement:

> But after I had got them out and shut the door and turned off the light it wasn't any good. It was like saying good-by to a statue. After a while I went out and left the hospital and walked back to the hotel in the rain.

Contrast this to the close of "Old Man at the Bridge," a story only two and a half pages long:

> There was nothing to do about him. It was Easter Sunday and the Fascists were advancing toward the Ebro. It was a gray overcast day with a low ceiling so their planes were not up. That and the fact that cats know how to look after themselves was all the good luck that old man would ever have.

The understatement continues to persuade here because the stoicism remains coherent, and is admirably fitted by the rhetoric. A very short story concludes itself by permanently troping the mood of a particular moment in history. Vignette is Hemingway's natural mode, or call it hard-edged vignette: a literary sketch that somehow seems to be the beginning or end of something longer, yet truly is complete in itself. Hemingway's style encloses what ought to be unenclosed, so that the genre remains subtle yet trades its charm for punch. But a novel of three hundred and forty pages (*A Farewell to Arms*) which I have just finished reading again (after twenty years away from it) cannot sustain itself upon the rhetoric of vignette. After many understatements, too many, the reader begins to believe that he is reading a Hemingway imitator, like the accomplished John O'Hara, rather than the master himself. Hemingway's notorious fault is the monotony of repetition, which becomes a dulling litany in a somewhat less accomplished imitator like Nelson Algren, and sometimes seems self-parody when we must confront it in Hemingway.

Nothing is got for nothing, and a great style generates defenses in us, particularly when it sets the style of an age, as the Byronic Hemingway did. As with Byron, the color and variety of the artist's life becomes something of a veil between the work and our aesthetic apprehension of it. Hemingway's career included four marriages (and three divorces); service as an ambulance driver for the Italians in World War I (with an honorable wound); activity as a war correspondent in the Greek-Turkish War (1922), the Spanish Civil War (1937–39), the Chinese-Japanese War (1941) and the War against Hitler in Europe (1944–45). Add big-game hunting and fishing, safaris, expatriation in France and Cuba, bullfighting, the Nobel prize, and ultimate suicide in Idaho, and you have an absurdly implausible life, apparently lived in imitation of Hemingway's own fiction. The final effect of the work and the life together is not less than mythological, as it was with Byron, and with Whitman and with Oscar Wilde. Hemingway now is myth, and so is permanent as an image of American heroism, or perhaps more ruefully the American illusion of heroism. The best of Hemingway's work, the stories and *The Sun Also Rises*, are also a permanent part of the American mythology. Faulkner, Stevens, Frost, perhaps Eliot, and Hart Crane were stronger writers than Hemingway, but he alone in this American century has achieved the enduring status of myth.

LIONEL TRILLING

Hemingway and His Critics

Between *The Fifth Column*, the play
which makes the occasion for this large volume, and *The First Forty-Nine
Stories*, which make its bulk and its virtue, there is a difference of essence.
For the play is the work of Hemingway the "man" and the stories are by
Hemingway the "artist." This is a distinction which seldom enough means
anything in criticism, but now and then an author gives us, as Hemingway
gives us, writing of two such different kinds that there is a certain amount
of validity and at any rate a convenience in making it. Once made, the
distinction can better be elaborated than defined or defended. Hemingway
the "artist" is conscious, Hemingway the "man" is self-conscious; the
"artist" has a kind of innocence, the "man" a kind of naivety; the "artist"
is disinterested, the "man" has a dull personal ax to grind; the "artist" has
a perfect medium and tells the truth even if it be only *his* truth, but the
"man" fumbles at communication and falsifies. As Edmund Wilson said in
his "Letter to the Russians about Hemingway," which is the best estimate
of our author that I know,

> . . . something frightful seems to happen to Hemingway as soon as he
> begins to write in the first person. In his fiction, the conflicting elements
> of his personality, the emotional situations which obsess him, are exter-
> nalized and objectified; and the result is an art which is severe, intense,
> and deeply serious. But as soon as he talks in his own person, he seems to
> lose all his capacity for self-criticism and is likely to become fatuous or
> maudlin.

Mr. Wilson had in mind such specifically autobiographical and
polemical works as *Green Hills of Africa* (and obviously he was not

From *Partisan Review* 6 (Winter 1939). Copyright © 1939 by Lionel Trilling.

referring to the technical use of the first person in fictional narrative) but since the writing of the "Letter" in 1935, we may observe of Hemingway that the "man" has encroached upon the "artist" in his fiction. In *To Have and Have Not* and now in *The Fifth Column* the "first person" dominates and is the source of the failure of both works.

Of course it might be perfectly just to set down these failures simply to a lapse of Hemingway's talent. But there is, I think, something else to be said. For as one compares the high virtues of Hemingway's stories with the weakness of his latest novel and his first play, although one is perfectly aware of all that must be charged against the author himself, what forces itself into consideration is the cultural atmosphere which has helped to bring about the recent falling off. In so far as we can ever blame a critical tradition for a writer's failures, we must, I believe, blame American criticsm for the illegitimate emergence of Hemingway the "man" and the resultant inferiority of his two recent major works.

It is certainly true that criticism of one kind or another has played an unusually important part in Hemingway's career. Perhaps no American talent has so publicly developed as Hemingway's: more than any writer of our time he has been under glass, watched, checked up on, predicted, suspected, warned. One part of his audience took from him new styles of writing, of lovemaking, of very being; this was the simpler part, but its infatuate imitation was of course a kind of criticism. But another section of his audience responded negatively, pointing out that the texture of Hemingway's work was made up of cruelty, religion, anti-intellectualism, even of basic fascism, and looked upon him as the active proponent of evil. Neither part of such an audience could fail to make its impression upon a writer. The knowledge that he had set a fashion and become a legend may have been gratifying but surely also burdensome and depressing, and it must have offered no small temptation. Yet perhaps more difficult for Hemingway to support with equanimity, and, from our point of view, much more important, was the constant accusation that he had attacked good human values. For upon Hemingway were turned all the fine social feelings of the now passing decade, all the noble sentiments, all the desperate optimism, all the extreme rationalism, all the contempt of irony and indirection—all the attitudes which, in the full tide of the liberal-radical movement, became dominant in our thought about literature. There was demanded of him earnestness and pity, social consciousness, as it was called, something "positive" and "constructive" and literal. For is not life a simple thing and is not the writer a villain or a counterrevolutionary who does not see it so?

As if under the pressure of this critical tradition, which persisted in mistaking the "artist" for the "man," Hemingway seems to have undertaken to vindicate the "man" by showing that he, too, could muster the required "social" feelings in the required social way. At any rate, he now brought the "man" with all his contradictions and conflicts into his fiction. But "his ideas about life"—I quote Edmund Wilson again—

> or rather his sense of what happens and the way it happens, is in his stories sunk deep below the surface and is not conveyed by argument or preaching but by directly transmitted emotion: it is turned into something as hard as crystal and as disturbing as a great lyric. When he expounds this sense of life, however, in his own character of Ernest Hemingway, the Old Master of Key West, he has a way of sounding silly.

If, however, the failures of Hemingway "in his own character" were apparent to the practitioners of this critical tradition, they did not want Hemingway's virtues—the something "hard" and "disturbing." Indeed, they were in a critical tradition that did not want artists at all; it wanted "men," recruits, and its apologists were delighted to enlist Hemingway in his own character, with all his confusions and naivety, simply because Hemingway had now declared himself on the right side.

And so when *To Have and Have Not* appeared, one critic of the Left, grappling with the patent fact that the "artist" had failed, yet determined to defend the "man" who was his new ally, had no recourse save to explain that in this case failure was triumph because artistic fumbling was the mark of Hemingway's attempt to come to grips with the problems of modern life which were as yet too great for his art to encompass. Similarly, another critic of the Left, faced with the esthetic inferiority of Hemingway's first play, takes refuge in praising the personal vindication which the "man" has made by "taking sides against fascism." In other words, the "man" has been a sad case and long in need of regeneration; the looseness of thought and emotion, the easy and uninteresting idealism of the social feelings to which Hemingway now gives such sudden and literal expression, are seen as the grateful signs of a personal reformation.

But the disinterested reader does not have to look very deep to see that Hemingway's social feelings, whatever they may yet become, are now the occasion for indulgence in the "man." His two recent failures are failures not only in form but in feeling; one looks at *To Have and Have Not* and *The Fifth Column*, one looks at their brag, and their disconcerting forcing of the emotions, at their downright priggishness, and then one looks at the criticism which, as I conceive it, made these failures possible by demanding them and which now accepts them so gladly, and one is tempted to reverse the whole liberal-radical assumption about literature. One almost wishes to say to an author like Hemingway, "You have no duty, no responsibility. Literature, in a political sense, is not in the least important. Wherever the sword is drawn it is mightier than the pen. Whatever you can do as a man, you can win no wars as an artist."

Very obviously this would not be the whole truth, yet saying it might counteract the crude and literal theory of art to which, in varying measure, we have all been training ourselves for a decade. We have conceived the artist to be a man perpetually on the spot, who must always report to us his precise moral and political latitude and longitude. Not that for a moment we would consider shaping our own political ideas by his; but we who of course turn for political guidance to newspapers, theorists, or historians, create the fiction that thousands—not, to be sure, ourselves—are waiting on the influence of the creative artist, and we stand by to see if he is leading us as he properly should. We consider then that we have exalted the importance of art, and perhaps we have. But in doing so we have quite forgotten how complex and subtle art is and, if it is to be "used," how very difficult it is to use it.

One feels that Hemingway would never have thrown himself into his new and inferior work if the necessity had not been put upon him to justify himself before this magisterial conception of literature. Devoted to literalness, the critical tradition of the Left took Hemingway's symbols for his intention, saw in his stories only cruelty or violence or a calculated indifference, and turned upon him a barrage of high-mindedness—that liberal-radical high-mindedness that is increasingly taking the place of thought among the "progressive professional and middle-class forces" and that now, under the name of "good will," shuts out half the world. Had it seen what was actually in Hemingway's work, it would not have forced him out of his idiom of the artist and into the idiom of the man which he speaks with difficulty and without truth.

For what should have been always obvious is that Hemingway is a writer who, when he writes as an "artist," is passionately and aggressively concerned with truth and even with social truth. And with this in mind, one might begin the consideration of his virtues with a glance at Woodrow Wilson. Hemingway has said that all genuine American writing comes from the prose of Huckleberry Finn's voyage down the Mississippi, and certainly his own starts there. But Huck's prose is a sort of moral symbol. It is the antithesis to the Widow Douglas—to the pious, the respectable, the morally plausible. It is the prose of the free man seeing the world as it really is. And Woodrow Wilson was, we might say, Hemingway's Widow Douglas. To the sensitive men who went to war it was not, perhaps, death and destruction that made the disorganizing shock. It was perhaps rather that death and destruction went on at the instance and to the accompaniment of the fine grave words, of which Woodrow Wilson's speeches were the finest and gravest. Here was the issue of liberal theory; here in the bloated or piecemeal corpse was the outcome of the words of humanitarianism and ideals; this was the work of presumably careful men of good will, learned men, polite men. The world was a newspaper world, a state-paper world, a memorial-speech world. Words were trundled smoothly o'er the tongue—Coleridge had said it long ago—

> Like mere abstractions, empty sounds to which
> We join no feeling and attach no form
> As if the soldier died without a wound . . .
> Passed off to Heaven, translated and not killed.

Everyone in that time had feelings, as they called them; just as everyone has "feelings" now. And it seems to me that what Hemingway wanted first to do was to get rid of the "feelings," the comfortable liberal humanitarian feelings: and to replace them with the truth.

Not cynicism, I think, not despair, as so often is said, but this admirable desire shaped his famous style and his notorious set of admirations and contempts. The trick of understatement or tangential statement sprang from this desire. Men had made so many utterances in such fine language that it had become time to shut up. Hemingway's people, as everyone knows, are afraid of words and ashamed of them and the line from his stories which has become famous is the one that beings "Won't you please," goes on through its innumerable "pleases," and ends, "stop talking." Not only slain men but slain words made up the mortality of the war.

Another manifestation of the same desire in Hemingway was his devotion to the ideal of technique as an end in itself. A great deal can go down in the tumble but one of the things that stands best is a cleanly done job. As John Peale Bishop says in his admirable essay on Hemingway (which yet, I feel, contributes to the general misapprehension by asserting the evanescence of Hemingway's "compassion"), professional pride is one of the last things to go. Hemingway became a devotee of his own skill and he exploited the ideal of skill in his characters. His admired men always do a good job; and the proper handling of a rod, a gun, an *espada*, or a pen is a thing, so Hemingway seems always to be saying, which can be understood when speech cannot.

This does not mean that Hemingway attacks mind itself, a charge which has often been brought against him. It is perhaps safe to say that whenever he seems to be making such an attack, it is not so much *reason* as it is *rationalization* that he resists; "mind" appears simply as the complex of false feelings. And against "mind" in this sense he sets up what he believes to be the primal emotions, among others pain and death, met not with the mind but with techniques and courage. "Mind" he sees as a kind of castrating knife, cutting off people's courage and proper self-love, making them "reasonable," which is to say dull and false. There is no need to point out how erroneous his view would have been were it really mind that was in question, but in the long romantic tradition of the attitude it never really *is* mind that is in question but rather a dull overlay of mechanical negative proper feeling, or a falseness of feeling which people believe to be reasonableness and reasonable virtue. And when we think how quickly "mind" capitulates in a crisis, how quickly, for example, it accommodated itself to the war and served it and glorified it, revulsion from it and a turning to the life of action—reduced, to be sure, to athleticism: but skillful physical effort is perhaps something intellectuals too quickly dismiss as a form of activity—can be the better understood. We can understand too the insistence on courage, even on courage deliberately observed in its purity: that is, when it is at the service of the most sordid desires, as in "Fifty Grand."

This, then, was Hemingway's vision of the world. Was it a complete vision? Of course it was not. Was it a useful vision? That depended. If it was true, it was useful—if we knew how to use it. But the use of literature is not easy. In our hearts most of us are Platonists in the matter of art and we feel that we become directly infected by what we read; or at any rate we want to be Platonists, and we carry on a certain conviction from our Tom Swift days that literature provides chiefly a means of identification and emulation. The Platonist view is not wholly to be dismissed; we *do* in a degree become directly infected by art; but the position is too simple. And we are further Platonistic in our feeling that literature must be religious: we want our attitudes formulated by the tribal bard. This, of course, gives to literature a very important function. But it forgets that literature has never "solved" anything, though it may perhaps provide part of the data for eventual solutions.

With this attitude we asked, Can Hemingway's people speak only with difficulty? and we answered, Then it surely means that he thinks people should not speak. Does he find in courage the first of virtues? Then it surely means that we should be nothing but courageous. Is he concerned with the idea of death and of violence? Then it must mean that to him these are good things.

In short, we looked for an emotional leader. We did not conceive

Hemingway to be saying, Come, let us look at the world together. We supposed him to be saying, Come, it is your moral duty to be as my characters are. We took the easiest and simplest way of using the artist and decided that he was not the "man" for us. That he was a man and a Prophet we were certain; and equally certain that he was not the "man" we would want to be or the Prophet who could lead us. That, as artist, he was not concerned with being a "man" did not occur to us. We had, in other words, quite overlooked the whole process of art, overlooked style and tone, symbol and implication, overlooked the obliqueness and complication with which the artist may criticize life, and assumed that what Hemingway saw or what he put into his stories he wanted to have exist in the actual world.

In short, the criticism of Hemingway came down to a kind of moral-political lecture, based on the assumption that art is—or should be—the exact equivalent of life. The writer would have to be strong indeed who could remain unmoved by the moral pressure that was exerted upon Hemingway. He put away the significant reticences of the artist, opened his heart like "a man," and the flat literalness, the fine, fruity social idealism, of the latest novel and the play are the result.

The Fifth Column is difficult to speak of. Summary is always likely to be a critical treachery, but after consulting the summaries of those who admire the work and regard it as a notable event, it seems fair to say that it is the story of a tender-tough American hero with the horrors, who does counterespionage in Madrid, though everybody thinks he is just a playboy, who fears that he will no longer do his work well if he continues his liaison with an American girl chiefly remarkable for her legs and her obtuseness; and so sacrifices love and bourgeois pleasure for the sake of duty. Hemingway as a playwright gives up his tools of suggestion and tone and tells a literal story—an adventure story of the Spanish war, at best the story of the regeneration of an American Scarlet Pimpernel of not very good intelligence.

It is this work which has been received with the greatest satisfaction by a large and important cultural group as the fulfillment and vindication of Hemingway's career, as a fine document of the Spanish struggle, and as a political event of significance, "a sign of the times," as one reviewer called it. To me it seems none of these things. It does not vindicate Hemingway's career because that career in its essential parts needs no vindication; and it does not fulfill Hemingway's career because that career has been in the service of exact if limited emotional truth and this play is in the service of fine feelings. Nor can I believe that the Spanish war is represented in any good sense by a play whose symbols are so sentimentally personal and whose dramatic tension is so weak; and it seems to me that there is something even vulgar in making Spain serve as a kind of mental hospital for disorganized foreigners who, out of a kind of self-contempt, turn to the "ideal of the Spanish people." Nor, finally, can I think that Hemingway's statement of an antifascist position is of great political importance or of more than neutral virtue. It is hard to believe that the declaration of antifascism is nowadays any more a mark of sufficient grace in a writer than a declaration against disease would be in a physician or a declaration against accidents would be in a locomotive engineer. The admirable intention in itself is not enough and criticism begins and does not end when the intention is declared.

But I believe that judgments so simple as these will be accepted with more and more difficulty. The "progressive professional and middle-class forces" are framing a new culture, based on the old liberal-radical culture but designed now to hide the new anomaly by which they live their intellectual and emotional lives. For they must believe, it seems, that imperialist arms advance proletarian revolution, that oppression by the right people brings liberty. Like Hemingway's latest hero, they show one front to the world and another to themselves, know that within they are true proletarian men while they wrap themselves in Early American togas; they are enthralled by their own good will; they are people of fine feelings and they dare not think lest the therapeutic charm vanish. This is not a political essay and I am not here concerned with the political consequences of these things, bad though they be and worse though they will be, but only with the cultural consequences. For to prevent the anomaly from appearing in its genuine difficulty, emotion—of a very limited kind—has been apotheosized and thought has been made almost a kind of treachery; the reviewer of The Fifth Column to whom I have already referred cites as a virtue Hemingway's "unintellectual" partisanship of the Spanish cause. The piety of "good will" has become enough and Fascism is conceived not as a force which complicates the world but as a force which simplifies the world—and so it does for any number of people of good will (of a good will not to be doubted, I should say) for whom the existence of an absolute theological evil makes nonexistent any other evil.

It is this group that has made Hemingway its cultural hero and for reasons that need not be canvassed very far. Now that Hemingway has become what this group would call "affirmative" he has become insufficient; but insufficiency is the very thing this group desires. When Hemingway was in "negation" his themes of courage, loyalty, tenderness, and silence, tangentially used, suggested much; but now that they are used literally and directly they say far less than the situation demands. His stories showed a great effort of comprehension and they demand a considerable effort from their readers, that effort in which lies whatever teaching power there is in art; but now he is not making an effort to understand but to accept, which may indeed be the effort of the honest political man but not of the honest artist.

An attempt has been made to settle the problem of the artist's relation to politics by loudly making the requirement that he give up his base individuality and rescue humanity and his own soul by becoming the mouthpiece of a party, a movement, or a philosophy. That requirement has demonstrably failed as a solution of the problem; the problem, however, still remains. It may be, of course, that politics itself will settle the problem for us; it may be that in our tragic time art worthy the name cannot be produced and that we must live with the banalities of *The Fifth Column* or even with less. However, if the problem will be allowed to exist at all, it will not be solved in theory and on paper but in practice. And we have, after all, the practice of the past to guide us, at least with a few tentative notions. We can learn to stop pressing the writer with the demand for contemporaneity when we remember the simple fact that writers have always written directly to and about the troubles of their own time and for and about their contemporaries, some in ways to us more obvious than others but all responding inevitably to what was happening around them. We can learn too that the relation of an artist to his culture, whether that culture be national or the culture of a relatively small recusant group, is a complex and even a contradictory relation: the artist must accept his culture and be accepted by it, but also—so it seems—he must be its critic, correcting and even rejecting it according to his personal insight; his strength seems to come from the tension of this ambivalent situation and we must learn to welcome the ambivalence. Finally, and simplest of all, we learn not to expect a political, certainly not an immediately political, effect from a work of art; and in removing from art a burden of messianic responsibility which it never has discharged and cannot discharge we may leave it free to do whatever it actually can do.

EDMUND WILSON

Hemingway: Gauge of Morale

Ernest Hemingway's *In Our Time* was an odd and original book. It had the appearance of a miscellany of stories and fragments; but actually the parts hung together and produced a definite effect. There were two distinct series of pieces which alternated with one another: one a set of brief and brutal sketches of police shootings, bullfight crises, hangings of criminals, and incidents of the war; and the other a set of short stories dealing in its principal sequence with the growing-up of an American boy against a landscape of idyllic Michigan, but interspersed also with glimpses of American soldiers returning home. It seems to have been Hemingway's intention—'In Our Time'—that the war should set the key for the whole. The cold-bloodedness of the battles and executions strikes a discord with the sensitiveness and candor of the boy at home in the States; and presently the boy turns up in Europe in one of the intermediate vignettes as a soldier in the Italian army, hit in the spine by machine-gun fire and trying to talk to a dying Italian: 'Senta, Rinaldi. *Senta*,' he says, 'you and me, we've made a separate peace.'

But there is a more fundamental relationship between the pieces of the two series. The shooting of Nick in the war does not really connect two different worlds: has he not found in the butchery abroad the same world that he knew back in Michigan? Was not life in the Michigan woods equally destructive and cruel? He had gone once with his father, the doctor, when he had performed a Caesarean operation on an Indian squaw with a jackknife and no anaesthetic and had sewed her up with fishing leaders, while the Indian hadn't been able to bear it and had cut his throat in his bunk. Another time, when the doctor had saved the life of a squaw, her Indian had picked a quarrel with him rather than pay him in work. And Nick himself had sent his girl about her business when he had found out how terrible her mother was. Even fishing in Big Two-Hearted River—away and free in the woods—he had been conscious in a curious way of the cruelty inflicted on the fish, even of the silent agonies endured by the live bait, the grasshoppers kicking on the hook.

Not that life isn't enjoyable. Talking and drinking with one's friends is great fun; fishing in Big Two-Hearted River is a tranquil exhilaration. But the brutality of life is always there, and it is somehow bound up with the enjoyment. Bullfights are especially enjoyable. It is even exhilarating to build a simply priceless barricade and pot the enemy as they are trying to get over it. The condition of life is pain; and the joys of the most innocent surface are somehow tied to its stifled pangs.

The resolution of this dissonance in art made the beauty of Hemingway's stories. He had in the process tuned a marvelous prose. Out of the colloquial American speech, with its simple declarative sentences and its strings of Nordic monosyllables, he got effects of the utmost subtlety. F.M. Ford has found the perfect simile for the impression produced by this writing: 'Hemingway's words strike you, each one, as if they were pebbles fetched fresh from a brook. They live and shine, each in its place. So one of his pages has the effect of a brook-bottom into which you look down through the flowing water. The words form a tesellation, each in order beside the other.'

Looking back, we can see how this style was already being refined and developed at a time—fifty years before—when it was regarded in most literary quarters as hopelessly non-literary and vulgar. Had there not been the nineteenth chapter of *Huckleberry Finn?*—'Two or three nights went by; I reckon I might say they swum by; they slid along so quick and smooth and lovely. Here is the way we put in the time. It was a monstrous big river down there—sometimes a mile and a half wide,' and so forth. These pages, when we happen to meet them in Carl Van Doren's anthology of world literature, stand up in a striking way beside a passage of description from Turgenev; and the pages which Hemingway was later to write about American wood and water are equivalents to the transcriptions by Turgenev—the *Sportsman's Notebook* is much admired by Hemingway—of Russian forests and fields. Each has brought to an immense and wild country the freshness of a new speech and a sensibility not yet conventionalized by literary associations. Yet it *is* the European sensiblity which has come to Big Two-Hearted River, where the Indians are now obsolescent; in those solitudes it feels for the first time the cold current, the hot morning sun, sees the pine stumps, smells the sweet fern. And along with the mottled trout, with its 'clear water-over-gravel color,' the boy from the American Middle West fishes up a nice little masterpiece.

In the meantime there had been also Ring Lardner, Sherwood Anderson, Gertrude Stein, using this American language for irony, lyric poetry or psychological insight. Hemingway seems to have learned from them all. But he is now able to charge this naïve accent with a new complexity of emotion, a new shade of emotion: a malaise. The wholesale shattering of human beings in which he has taken part has given the boy a touch of panic.

II

The next fishing trip is strikingly different. Perhaps the first had been an idealization. It is possible to attain to such sensuous bliss merely through going alone into the woods: smoking, fishing, and eating, with no thought about anyone else or about anything one has ever done or will ever be obliged to do? At any rate, today, in *The Sun Also Rises*, all the things that are wrong with human life are there on the holiday, too—though one tries to keep them back out of the foreground and to occupy one's mind with the trout, caught now in a stream of the Pyrenees, and with the kidding of the friend from the States. The feeling of insecurity has deepened. The young American now appears in a seriously damaged condition: he has somehow been incapacitated sexually through wounds received in the war. He is in love with one of those international sirens who flourished in the cafés of the post-war period and whose ruthless and uncontrollable infidelities, in such a circle as that depicted by Hemingway, have made any sort of security impossible for the relations between women and men. The lovers of such a woman turn upon and rend one another because they are powerless to make themselves felt by *her*.

The casualties of the bullfight at Pamplona, to which these young people have gone for the *fiesta*, only reflect the blows and betrayals of demoralized human beings out of hand. What is the tiresome lover with whom the lady has just been off on a casual escapade, and who is unable to understand that he has been discarded, but the man who, on his way to the bull ring, has been accidentally gored by the bull? The young American who tells the story is the only character who keeps up standards of conduct, and he is prevented by his disability from dominating and directing the woman, who otherwise, it is intimated, might love him. Here the membrane of the style has been stretched taut to convey the vibrations of these qualms. The dry sunlight and the green summer landscapes have been invested with a sinister quality which must be new in literature. One enjoys the sun and the green as one enjoys suckling pigs and Spanish wine, but the uneasiness and apprehension are undruggable.

Yet one can catch hold of a code in all the drunkenness and the social chaos. 'Perhaps as you went along you did learn something,' Jake, the hero, reflects at one point. 'I did not care what it was all about. All I wanted to know was how to live in it. Maybe if you found out how to live in it you learned from that what it was all about.' 'Everybody behaves badly. Give them the proper chance,' he says later to Lady Brett.

' "You wouldn't behave badly." Brett looked at me.' In the end, she sends for Jake, who finds her alone in a hotel. She has left her regular lover for a young bullfighter, and this boy has for the first time inspired her with a respect which has restrained her from 'ruining' him: 'You know it makes one feel rather good deciding not to be a bitch.' We suffer and we make suffer, and everybody loses out in the long run; but in the meantime we can lose with honor.

This code still markedly figures, still supplies a dependable moral backbone, in Hemingway's next book of short stories, *Men Without Women*. Here Hemingway has mastered his method of economy in apparent casualness and relevance in apparent indirection, and has turned his sense of what happens and the way in which it happens into something as hard and clear as a crystal but as disturbing as a great lyric. Yet it is usually some principle of courage, of honor, of pity—that is, some principle of sportsmanship in its largest human sense—upon which the drama hinges. The old bullfighter in *The Undefeated* is defeated in everything except the spirit which will not accept defeat. You get the bull or he gets you: if you die, you can die game; there are certain things you cannot do. The burlesque show manager in *A Pursuit Race* refrains from waking his advance publicity agent when he overtakes him and realizes that the man has just lost a long struggle against whatever anguish it is that has driven him to drink and dope. 'They got a cure for that,' the manager had said to him before he went to sleep; ' "No," William Campbell said, "they haven't got a cure for anything." ' The burned major in *A Simple Enquiry*—that strange picture of the bedrock stoicism compatible with the abasement of war—has the decency not to dismiss the orderly who has rejected his proposition. The brutalized Alpine peasant who has been in the habit of hanging a lantern in the jaws of the stiffened corpse of his wife, stood in the corner of the woodshed till the spring will make it possible to bury her, is ashamed to drink with the sexton after the latter has found out what he has done. And there is a little sketch of Roman soldiers just after the Crucifixion:

'You see me slip the old spear into him?—You'll get into trouble doing that some day.—It was the least I could do for him. I'll tell you he looked pretty good to me in there today.'

This Hemingway of the middle twenties—*The Sun Also Rises* came out in '26—expressed the romantic disillusion and set the favorite pose for the period. It was the moment of gallantry in heartbreak, grim and nonchalant banter, and heroic dissipation. The great watchword was 'Have a drink'; and in the bars of New York and Paris the young people were getting to talk like Hemingway.

III

The novel, *A Farewell to Arms*, which followed *Men Without Women*, is in a sense not so serious an affair. Beautifully written and quite moving of course it is. Probably no other book has caught so well the strangeness of life in the army for an American in Europe during the war. The new places to which one was sent of which one had never heard, and the things that turned out to be in them; the ordinary people of foreign countries as one saw them when one was quartered among them or obliged to perform some common work with them; the pleasures of which one managed to cheat the war, intensified by the uncertainty and horror—and the uncertainty, nevertheless, almost become a constant, the horror almost taken for granted; the love affairs, always subject to being suddenly broken up and yet carried on while they lasted in a spirit of irresponsible freedom which derived from one's having forfeited control of all one's other actions—this Hemingway got into his book, written long enough after the events for them to present themselves under an aspect fully idyllic.

But *A Farewell to Arms* is a tragedy, and the lovers are shown as innocent victims with no relation to the forces that torment them. They themselves are not tormented within by that dissonance between personal satisfaction and the suffering one shares with others which it has been Hemingway's triumph to handle. *A Farewell to Arms*, as the author once said, is a *Romeo and Juliet*. And when Catherine and her lover emerge from the stream of action—the account of the Caporetto retreat is Hemingway's best sustained piece of narrative—when they escape from the alien necessities of which their romance has been merely an accident, which have been writing their story for them, then we see that they are not in themselves convincing as human personalities. And we are confronted with the paradox that Hemingway, who possesses so remarkable a mimetic gift in getting the tone of social and national types and in making his people talk appropriately, has not shown any very solid sense of character, or, indeed, any real interest in it. The people in his short stories are satisfactory because he has only to hit them off: the point of the story does not lie in personalities, but in the emotion to which a situation gives rise. This is true even in *The Sun Also Rises*, where the characters are sketched with wonderful cleverness. But in *A Farewell to Arms*, as soon as we are brought into real intimacy with the lovers, as soon as the author is obliged to see them through a searching personal experience, we find merely an idealized relationship, the abstractions of a lyric emotion.

With *Death in the Afternoon*, three years later, a new development for Hemingway commences. He writes a book not merely in the first person, but in the first person in his own character as Hemingway, and the results are unexpected and disconcerting. *Death in the Afternoon* has its value as an exposition of bullfighting; and Hemingway is able to use the subject as a text for an explicit statement of his conception of man eternally pitting himself—he thinks the bullfight a ritual of this—against animal force and the odds of death. But the book is partly infected by a queer kind of maudlin emotion, which sounds at once neurotic and drunken. He overdoes his glorification of the bravery and martyrdom of the bullfighter. No doubt the professional expert at risking his life single-handed is impressive in contrast to the flatness and unreality of much of the business of the modern world; but this admirable miniaturist in prose has already made the point perhaps more tellingly in the little prose poem called *Banal Story*. Now he offsets the virility of the bullfighters by anecdotes of the male homosexuals that frequent the Paris cafés, at the same time that he puts his chief celebration of the voluptuous excitement of the spectacle into the mouth of an imaginary old lady. The whole thing becomes a little hysterical.

The master of that precise and clean style now indulges in purple patches which go on spreading for pages. I am not one of those who admire the last chapter of *Death in the Afternoon*, with its rich, all too rich, unrollings of memories of good times in Spain, and with its what seem to me irrelevant reminiscences of the soliloquy of Mrs. Bloom in *Ulysses*. Also, there are interludes of kidding of a kind which Hemingway handles with skill when he assigns them to characters in his stories, but in connection with which he seems to become incapable of exercising good sense or good taste as soon as he undertakes them in his own person (the burlesque *Torrents of Spring* was an early omen of this). In short, we are compelled to recognize that, as soon as Hemingway drops the burning-glass of the disciplined and objective art with which he has learned to concentrate in a story the light of the emotions that flood in on him, he straightway becomes befuddled, slops over.

This befuddlement is later to go further, but in the meantime he publishes another volume of stories—*Winner Take Nothing*—which is almost up to its predecessor. In this collection he deals much more effectively than in *Death in the Afternoon* with that theme of contemporary decadence which is implied in his panegyric of the bullfighter. The first of these stories, *After the Storm*, is another of his variations—and one of the finest—on the theme of keeping up a code of decency among the hazards and pains of life. A fisherman goes out to plunder a wreck: he dives down to break in through a porthole, but inside he sees a woman with rings on her hands and her hair floating loose in the water, and he thinks about the passengers and crew being suddenly plunged to their deaths (he has almost been killed himself in a drunken fight the night before). He sees the cloud of sea birds screaming around, and he finds that he is unable to break the glass with his wrench and that he loses the anchor grapple with which he next tries to attack it. So he finally goes away and leaves the job to the Greeks, who blow the boat open and clean her out.

But in general the emotions of insecurity here obtrude themselves and dominate the book. Two of the stories deal with the hysteria of soldiers falling off the brink of their nerves under the strain of the experiences of the war, which here no longer presents an idyllic aspect; another deals with a group of patients in a hospital, at the same time crippled and hopeless; still another (a five-page masterpiece) with a waiter, who, both on his own and on his customers' account, is reluctant to go home at night, because he feels the importance of a 'clean well-lighted cafe' as a refuge from the 'nothing' that people fear. *God Rest You Merry, Gentlemen* repeats the theme of castration of *The Sun Also Rises*; and four of the stories are concerned more or less with male or female homosexuality. In the last story, *Fathers and Sons*, Hemingway reverts to the Michigan woods, as if to take the curse off the rest: young Nick had once enjoyed a nice Indian girl with plump legs and hard little breasts on the needles of the hemlock woods.

These stories and the interludes in *Death in the Afternoon* must have been written during the years that followed the stock-market crash. They are full of the apprehension of losing control of oneself which is aroused by the getting out of hand of a social-economic system, as well as of the fear of impotence which seems to accompany the loss of social mastery. And there is in such a story as *A Clean Well-Lighted Place* the feeling of having got to the end of everything, of having given up heroic attitudes and wanting only the illusion of peace.

IV

And now, in proportion as the characters in his stories run out of fortitude and bravado, he passes into a phase where he is occupied with building up his public personality. He has already now become a legend, as Mencken was in the twenties; he is the Hemingway of the handsome photographs with the sportsman's tan and the outdoor grin, with the ominous resemblance to Clark Gable, who poses with giant marlin which he has just hauled in off Key West. And unluckily—but for an American inevitably—the opportunity soon presents itself to exploit this personality for profit: he turns up delivering Hemingway monologues in well-paying and trashy magazines; and the Hemingway of these loose disquisitions, arrogant, belligerent and boastful, is certainly the worst-invented character to be found in the author's work. If he is obnoxious, the effect is somewhat mitigated by the fact that he is intrinsically incredible.

There would be no point in mentioning this journalism at all, if it did not seem somewhat to have contributed to the writing of certain unsatisfactory books. *Green Hills of Africa* (1935) owes its failure to falling between the two *genres* of personal exhibitionism and fiction. 'The writer has attempted,' says Hemingway, 'to write an absolutely true book to see whether the shape of a country and the pattern of a month's action can, if truly presented, compete with a work of the imagination.' He does try to present his own rôle objectively, and there is a genuine Hemingway theme—the connection between success at big-game hunting and sexual self-respect—involved in his adventures as he presents them. But the sophisticated technique of the fiction writer comes to look artificial when it is applied to a series of real happenings; and the necessity of sticking to what really happened makes impossible the typical characters and incidents which give point to a work of fiction. The monologues by the false, the publicity, Hemingway with which the narrative is interspersed are almost as bad as the ones that he has been writing for the magazines. He inveighs with much scorn against the literary life and against the professional literary man of the cities; and then manages to give the impression that he himself is a professional literary man of the touchiest and most self-conscious kind. He delivers a self-confident lecture on the high possibilities of prose writing; and then produces such a sentence as the following: 'Going downhill steeply made these Spanish shooting boots too short in the toe and there was an old argument, about this length of boot and whether the bootmaker, whose part I had taken, unwittingly first, only as interpreter, and finally embraced his theory patriotically as a

whole and, I believed, by logic, had overcome it by adding onto the heel.'
As soon as Hemingway begins speaking in the first person, he seems to lose
his bearings, not merely as a critic of life, but even as a craftsman.

In another and significant way, *Green Hills of Africa* is disappoint-
ing. *Death in the Afternoon* did provide a lot of data on bullfighting and
build up for us the bullfighting world; but its successor tells us little about
Africa. Hemingway keeps affirming—as if in accents of defiance against
those who would engage his attention for social problems—his passionate
enthusiasm for the African country and his perfect satisfaction with the
hunter's life; but he has produced what must be one of the only books ever
written which make Africa and its animals seem dull. Almost the only
thing we learn about the animals is that Hemingway wants to kill them.
And as for the natives, though there is one fine description of a tribe of
marvelous trained runners, the principle impression we get of them is that
they were simple and inferior people who enormously admired Hemingway.

It is not only that, as his critics of the Left had been complaining,
he shows no interest in political issues, but that his interest in his fellow
beings seems actually to be drying up. It is as if he were throwing himself
on African hunting as something to live for and believe in, as something
through which to realize himself; and as if, expecting of it too much, he
had got out of it abnormally little, less than he is willing to admit. The
disquiet of the Hemingway of the twenties had been, as I have said,
undruggable—that is, in his books themselves, he had tried to express it,
not drug it, had given it an appeasement in art; but now there sets in, in
the Hemingway of the thirties, what seems to be a deliberate self-drugging.
The situation is indicated objectively in *The Gambler, the Nun and the
Radio*, one of the short stories of 1933, in which everything from daily
bread to 'a belief in any new form of government' is characterized as 'the
opium of the people' by an empty-hearted patient in a hospital.

But at last there did rush into this vacuum the blast of the social
issue, which had been roaring in the wind like a forest fire.

Out of a series of short stories that Hemingway had written about a
Florida waterside character he decided to make a little epic. The result was
To Have and Have Not, which seems to me the poorest of all his stories.
Certainly some deep agitation is working upon Hemingway the artist.
Craftsmanship and style, taste and sense, have all alike gone by the board.
The negative attitude toward human beings has here become definitely
malignant: the hero is like a wooden-headed Punch, always knocking
people on the head (inferiors—Chinamen or Cubans); or, rather, he
combines the characteristics of Punch with those of Popeye the Sailor in
the animated cartoon in the movies. As the climax to a series of prodigies,

this stupendous pirate-smuggler named Harry Morgan succeeds, alone, unarmed, and with only a hook for one hand—though at the cost of a mortal wound—in outwitting and destroying with their own weapons four men carrying revolvers and a machine gun, by whom he has been shang-haied in a launch. The only way in which Hemingway's outlaw suffers by comparison with Popeye is that his creator has not tried to make him plausible by explaining that he does it all on spinach.

The impotence of a decadent society has here been exploited deliberately, but less successfully than in the earlier short stories. Against a background of homosexuality, impotence and masturbation among the wealthy holiday-makers in Florida, Popeye-Morgan is shown gratifying his wife with the same indefatigable dexterity which he has displayed in his other feats; and there is a choral refrain of praise of his *cojones*, which wells up in the last pages of the book when the abandoned Mrs. Popeye regurgitates Molly Bloom's soliloquy.

To be a man in such a world of maggots is noble, but it is not enough. Besides the maggots, there are double-crossing rats, who will get you if they are given the slightest chance. What is most valid in *To Have and Have Not* is the idea—conveyed better, perhaps, in the first of the series of episodes than in the final scenes of massacre and agony—that in an atmosphere (here revolutionary Cuba) in which man has been set against man, in which it is always a question whether your companion is not preparing to cut your throat, the most sturdy and straightforward American will turn suspicious and cruel. Harry Morgan is made to realize as he dies that to fight this bad world alone is hopeless. Again Heming-way, with his barometric accuracy, has rendered a moral atmosphere that was prevalent at the moment he was writing—a moment when social relations were subjected to severe tensions, when they seemed sometimes already disintegrating. But the heroic Hemingway legend has at this point invaded his fiction and, inflaming and inflating his symbols, has produced an implausible hybrid, half Hemingway character, half nature myth.

Hemingway had not himself particularly labored this moral of individualism *versus* solidarity, but the critics of the Left labored it for him and received his least creditable piece of fiction as the delivery of a new revelation. The progress of the Communist faith among our writers since the beginning of the depression has followed a peculiar course. That the aims and beliefs of Marx and Lenin should have come through to the minds of intellectuals who had been educated in the bourgeois tradition as great awakeners of conscience, a great light, was quite natural and entirely desirable. But the conception of the dynamic Marxist will, the exaltation of the Marxist religion, seized the members of the professional classes like a capricious contagion or hurricane, which shakes one and leaves his neighbor standing, then returns to lay hold on the second after the first has become quiet again. In the moment of seizure, each one of them saw a scroll unrolled from the heavens, on which Marx and Lenin and Stalin, the Bolsheviks of 1917, the Soviets of the Five-Year Plan, and the GPU of the Moscow trials were all a part of the same great purpose. Later the convert, if he were capable of it, would get over his first phase of snow blindness and learn to see real people and conditions, would study the development of Marxism in terms of nations, periods, personalities, instead of logical deductions from abstract propositions or—as in the case of the more naïve or dishonest—of simple incantatory slogans. But for many there was at least a moment when the key to all the mysteries of human history seemed suddenly to have been placed in their hands, when an infallible guide to thought and behavior seemed to have been given them in a few easy formulas.

Hemingway was hit pretty late. He was still in *Death in the Afternoon* telling the 'world-savers,' sensibly enough, that they should 'get to see' the world 'clear and as a whole. Then any part you make will represent the whole, if it's made truly. The thing to do is work and learn to make it.' Later he jibed at the literary radicals, who talked but couldn't take it; and one finds even in *To Have and Have Not* a crack about a 'highly paid Hollywood director, whose brain is in the process of outlasting his liver so that he will end up calling himself a Communist, to save his soul.' Then the challenge of the fight itself—Hemingway never could resist a physical challenge—the natural impulse to dedicate oneself to something bigger than big-game hunting and bullfighting, and the fact that the class war had broken out in a country to which he was romantically attached, seem to have combined to make him align himself with the Communists as well as the Spanish Loyalists at a time when the Marxist philosophy had been pretty completely shelved by the Kremlin, now reactionary as well as corrupt, and when the Russians were lending the Loyalists only help enough to preserve, as they imagined would be possible, the balance of power against Fascism while they acted at the same time as a police force to beat down the real social revolution.

Hemingway raised money for the Loyalists, reported the battle fronts. He even went so far as to make a speech at a congress of the League of American Writers, an organization rigged by the supporters of the Stalinist régime in Russia and full of precisely the type of literary revolutionists that he had been ridiculing a little while before. Soon the Stalinists had taken him in tow, and he was feverishly denouncing as Fascists other writers who criticized the Kremlin. It has been one of the expedients of the Stalin administration in maintaining its power and covering up its crimes to condemn on trumped-up charges of Fascist conspiracy, and even to kidnap and murder, its political opponents of the Left; and, along with the food and munitions, the Russians had brought to the war in Spain what the Austrian journalist Willi Schlamm called that diversion of doubtful value for the working class: 'Herr Vyshinsky's Grand Guignol.'

The result of this was a play, *The Fifth Column*, which, though it is good reading for the way the characters talk, is an exceedingly silly production. The hero, though an Anglo-American, is an agent of the Communist secret police, engaged in catching Fascist spies in Spain; and his principle exploit in the course of the play is clearing out, with the aid of a single Communist, an artillery post manned by seven Fascists. The scene is like a pushover and getaway from one of the cruder Hollywood Westerns. It is in the nature of a small boy's fantasy, and would probably be considered extravagant by most writers of books for boys.

The tendency on Hemingway's part to indulge himself in these boyish day-dreams seems to begin to get the better of his realism at the end of *A Farewell to Arms*, where the hero, after many adventures of fighting, escaping, love-making and drinking, rows his lady thirty-five kilometers on a cold and rainy night; and we have seen what it could do for Harry Morgan. Now, as if with the conviction that the cause and the efficiency of the GPU have added several cubits to his stature, he has let this tendency loose; and he has also found in the GPU's grim duty a pretext to give rein to the appetite for describing scenes of killing which has always been a feature of his work. He has progressed from grasshoppers and trout through bulls and lions and kudus to Chinamen and Cubans, and now to Fascists. Hitherto the act of destruction has given rise for him to complex emotions: he has indentified himself not merely with the injurer but also with the injured; there has been a masochistic comple-ment to the sadism. But now this paradox which splits our natures, and which has instigated some of Hemingway's best stories, need no longer present perplexities to his mind. The Fascists are dirty bastards, and to kill them is a righteous act. He who had made a separate peace, who had said farewell to arms, has found a reason for taking them up again in a spirit of rabietic fury unpleasantly reminiscent of the spy mania and the sacred anti-German rage which took possession of so many civilians and staff officers under the stimulus of the last war.

Not that the compensatory trauma of the typical Hemingway protagonist is totally absent even here. The main episode is the hero's brief love affair and voluntary breaking off with a beautiful and adoring girl whose acquaintance he has made in Spain. As a member of the Junior League and a graduate of Vassar, she represents for him—it seems a little hard on her—that leisure-class playworld from which he is trying to get away. But in view of the fact that from the very first scenes he treats her with more or less open contempt, the action is rather lacking in suspense as the sacrifice is rather feeble in moral value. One takes no stock at all in the intimation that Mr. Philip may later be sent to mortify himself in a camp for training Young Pioneers. And in the meantime he has fun killing Fascists.

In *The Fifth Column*, the drugging process has been carried further still: the hero, who has become finally indistinguishable from the false or publicity Hemingway, has here dosed himself not only with whiskey, but with a seductive and desirous woman, for whom he has the most admirable reasons for not taking any responsibility, with sacred rage, with the excitement of a bombardment, and with the indulgence in that headiest of sports, for which he has now the same excellent reasons: the bagging of human beings.

V

You may fear, after reading *The Fifth Column*, that Hemingway will never sober up; but as you go on to his short stories of this period, you find that your apprehensions were unfounded. Three of these stories have a great deal more body—they are longer and more complex—than the comparatively meager anecdotes collected in *Winner Take Nothing*. And here are his real artistic successes with the material of his adventures in Africa, which make up for the miscarried *Green Hills*: *The Short Happy Life of Francis Macomber* and *The Snows of Kilimanjaro*, which disengage, by dramatizing them objectively, the themes he had attempted in the earlier book but that had never really got themselves presented. And here is at least a beginning of a real artistic utilization of Hemingway's experience in Spain: an incident of the war in two pages which outweighs the whole of *The Fifth Column* and all his Spanish dispatches, a glimpse of an old man, 'without politics,' who has so far occupied his life in taking care of eight pigeons, two goats and a cat, but who has now been dislodged and separated from his pets by the advance of the Fascist armies. It is a story which takes its place among the war prints of Callot and Goya, artists whose union of elegance with sharpness has already been recalled by Hemingway in his earlier battle pieces: a story which might have been written about almost any war.

And here—what is very remarkable—is a story, *The Capital of the World*, which finds an objective symbol for, precisely, what is wrong with *The Fifth Column*. A young boy who has come up from the country and waits on table in a pension in Madrid gets accidentally stabbed with a meat knife while playing at bullfighting with the dishwasher. This is the simple anecdote, but Hemingway has built in behind it all the life of the pension and the city: the priesthood, the working-class movement, the grown-up bullfighters who have broken down or missed out. 'The boy Paco,' Hemingway concludes, 'had never known about any of this nor about what all these people would be doing on the next day and on other days to come. He had no idea how they really lived nor how they ended. He did not realize they ended. He died, as the Spanish phrase has it, full of illusions. He had not had time in his life to lose any of them, or even, at the end, to complete an act of contrition.' So he registers in this very fine piece the discrepancy between the fantasies of boyhood and the realities of the grown-up world. Hemingway the artist, who feels things truly and cannot help recording what he feels, has actually said good-bye to these fantasies at a time when the war correspondent is making himself ridiculous by attempting to hang on to them still.

The emotion which principally comes through in *Francis Macomber* and *The Snows of Kilimanjaro*—as it figures also in *The Fifth Column*—is a growing antagonism to women. Looking back, one can see at this point that the tendency has been there all along. In *The Doctor and the Doctor's Wife*, the boy Nick goes out squirrel-hunting with his father instead of obeying the summons of his mother; in *Cross Country Snow*, he regretfully says farewell to male companionship on a skiing expedition in Switzerland, when he is obliged to go back to the States so that his wife can have her baby. The young man in *Hills Like White Elephants* compels his girl to have an abortion contrary to her wish; another story, *A Canary for One*, bites almost unbearably but exquisitely on the loneliness to be endured by a wife after she and her husband shall have separated; the peasant of *An Alpine Idyll* abuses the corpse of his wife (these last three appear under the general title *Men Without Women*). Brett in *The Sun Also Rises* is an exclusively destructive force: she might be a better woman if she were mated with Jake, the American; but actually he is protected against her and is in a sense revenging his own sex through being unable to do anything for her sexually. Even the hero of *A Farewell to Arms* eventually destroys Catherine—after enjoying her abject devotion—by giving her a baby, itself born dead. The only women with whom Nick Adams' relations are perfectly satisfactory are the little Indian girls of his boyhood who are in a position of hopeless social disadvantage and have no power over the behavior of the white male—so that he can get rid of them the moment he has done with them. Thus in *The Fifth Column* Mr. Philip brutally breaks off with Dorothy—he has been rescued from her demoralizing influence by his enlistment in the Communist crusade, just as the hero of *The Sun Also Rises* has been saved by his physical disability—to revert to a little Moorish whore. Even Harry Morgan, who is represented as satisfying his wife on the scale of a Paul Bunyan, deserts her in the end by dying and leaves her racked by the cruelest desire.

And now this instinct to get the woman down presents itself frankly as a fear that the woman will get the man down. The men in both these African stories are married to American bitches of the most soul-destroying sort. The hero of *The Snows of Kilimanjaro* loses his soul and dies of futility on a hunting expedition in Africa, out of which he has failed to get what he had hoped. The story is not quite stripped clean of the trashy moral attitudes which have been coming to disfigure the author's work: the hero, a seriously intentioned and apparently promising writer, goes on a little sloppily over the dear early days in Paris when he was earnest, happy and poor, and blames a little hysterically the rich woman whom he has married and who has debased him. Yet it is one of Hemingway's remarkable stories. There is a wonderful piece of writing at the end when the reader is made to realize that what has seemed to be an escape by plane, with the sick man looking down on Africa, is only the dream of a dying man. The other story, *Francis Macomber*, perfectly realizes its purpose. Here the male saves his soul at the last minute, and then is actually shot down by his woman, who does not want him to have a soul. Here Hemingway has at last got what Thurber calls the war between men and women right out into the open and has written a terrific fable on the impossible civilized woman who despises the civilized man for his failure in initiative and nerve and then jealously tries to break him down as soon as he begins to exhibit any. (It ought to be noted, also, that whereas in *Green Hills of Africa* the descriptions tended to weigh down the narrative with their excessive circumstantiality, the landscapes and animals of *Francis Macomber* are alive and unfalteringly proportioned.)

Going back over Hemingway's books today, we can see clearly what an error of the politicos it was to accuse him of an indifference to society. His whole work is a criticism of society: he has responded to every pressure of the moral atmosphere of the time, as it is felt at the roots of human relations, with a sensitivity almost unrivaled. Even his preoccupation with licking the gang in the next block and being known as the best basketball player in high school has its meaning in the present epoch. After all, whatever is done in the world, political as well as athletic, depends on personal courage and strength. With Hemingway, courage and strength are always thought of in physical terms, so that he tends to give the impression that the bullfighter who can take it and dish it out is more of a man than any other kind of man, and that the sole duty of the revolutionary socialist is to get the counter-revolutionary gang before they get him.

But ideas, however correct, will never prevail by themselves: there must be people who are prepared to stand or fall with them, and the ability to act on principle is still subject to the same competitive laws which operate in sporting contests and sexual relations. Hemingway has expressed with genius the terrors of the modern man at the danger of losing control of his world, and he has also, within his scope, provided his own kind of antidote. This antidote, paradoxically, is almost entirely moral. Despite Hemingway's preoccupation with physical contests, his heroes are almost always defeated physically, nervously, practically: their victories are moral ones. He himself, when he trained himself stubbornly in his unconventional unmarketable art in a Paris which had other fashions, gave the prime example of such a victory; and if he has sometimes, under the menace of the general panic, seemed on the point of going to pieces as an artist, he has always pulled himself together the next moment. The principle of the Bourdon gauge, which is used to measure the pressure of liquids, is that a tube which has been curved into a coil will tend to straighten out in proportion as the liquid inside it is subjected to an increasing pressure.

The appearance of *For Whom the Bell Tolls* since this essay was written in 1939 carries the straightening process further. Here Hemingway has largely sloughed off his Stalinism and has reverted to seeing events in terms of individuals pitted against specific odds. His hero, an American teacher of Spanish who has enlisted on the side of the Loyalists, gives his life to what he regards as the cause of human liberation; but he is frustrated in the task that has been assigned him by the confusion of forces at cross-purposes that are throttling the Loyalist campaign. By the time that he comes to die, he has little to sustain him but the memory of his grandfather's record as a soldier in the American Civil War. The psychology of this young man is presented with a certain sobriety and detachment in comparison with Hemingway's other full-length heroes; and the author has here succeeded as in none of his earlier books in externalizing in plausible characters the elements of his own complex personality. With all this, there is an historical point of view which he has learned from his political adventures: he has aimed to reflect in this episode the whole course of the Spanish War and the tangle of tendencies involved in it.

The weaknesses of the book are its diffuseness—a shape that lacks the concision of his short stories, that sometimes sags and sometimes bulges; and a sort of exploitation of the material, an infusion of the operatic, that lends itself all too readily to the movies.

ROBERT PENN WARREN

Ernest Hemingway

In May, 1929, in *Scribner's Magazine*, the first installment of *A Farewell to Arms* appeared. The novel was completed in the issue of October, and was published in book form the same year. Ernest Hemingway was already regarded, by a limited literary public, as a writer of extraordinary freshness and power, as one of the makers, indeed, of a new American fiction. *A Farewell to Arms* more than justified the early enthusiasm of the connoisseurs for Hemingway, and extended his reputation from them to the public at large. Its great importance was at once acknowledged, and its reputation has survived through the changing fashions and interests of many years.

What was the immediate cause of its appeal? It told a truth about the First World War, and a truth about the generation who had fought it and whose lives, because of the war, had been wrenched from the expected pattern and the old values. Other writers had told or were to tell similar truths about this war. John Dos Passos in *Three Soldiers*, e.e. cummings in *The Enormous Room*, William Faulkner in *Soldiers's Pay*, Maxwell Anderson and Laurence Stallings in *What Price Glory?* All these writers had presented the pathos and endurance and gallantry of the individual caught and mangled in the great anonymous mechanism of a modern war fought for reasons that the individual could not understand, found insufficient to justify the event, or believed to be no reasons at all. And *A Farewell to Arms* was not the first book to record the plight of the men and women who, because of the war, had been unable to come to terms with life in the old way. Hemingway himself in *The Sun Also Rises*,

From *Robert Penn Warren: Selected Essays.* Copyright © 1966 by Robert Penn Warren. Charles Scribner's Sons, 1966.

1926, had given the picture of the dislocated life of young English and American expatriates in the bars of Paris, the "lost generation," as Gertrude Stein defined them. But before that, F. Scott Fitzgerald, who had been no nearer to the war than an officers' training camp, had written of the lost generation. For the young people about whom Fitzgerald wrote, even when they were not veterans and even when their love stories were enacted in parked cars, fraternity houses, and country clubs and not in the cafés and hotels of Paris, were like Hemingway's expatriates under the shadow of the war and were groping to find some satisfaction in a world from which the old values had been withdrawn. Hemingway's expatriates had turned their backs on the glitter of the Great Boom of the 1920's, and Fitzgerald's young men were usually drawn to the romance of wealth and indulgence, but this difference is superficial. If Hemingway's young men begin by repudiating the Great Boom, Fitzgerald's young men end with disappointment in what even success has to offer. "All the sad young men" of Fitzgerald—to take the title of one of his collections of stories—and the "lost generation" of Hemingway are seekers for landmarks and bearings in a terrain for which the maps have been mislaid.

A *Farewell to Arms*, which appeared ten years after the First World War and on the eve of the collapse of the Great Boom, seemed to sum up and bring to focus an inner meaning of the decade being finished. It worked thus, not because it disclosed the end results that the life of the decade was producing—the discontents and disasters that were beginning to be noticed even by unreflective people—but because it cut back to the beginning of the process, to the moment that had held within itself the explanation of the subsequent process.

Those who had grown up in the war, or in its shadow could look back nostalgically, as it were, to the lost moment of innocence of motive and purity of emotion. If those things had been tarnished or manhandled by the later business of living, they had, at least, existed, and on a grand scale. If they had been tarnished or manhandled, it was not through the fault of the individual who looked back to see the image of the old simple and heroic self in Frederick or Catherine, but through the impersonal grindings of the great machine of the universe. A *Farewell to Arms* served, in a way, as the great romantic alibi for a generation, and for those who aped and emulated that generation. It showed how cynicism or disillusionment, failure of spirit or the worship of material success, debauchery or despair, might have been grounded in heroism, simplicity, and fidelity that had met unmerited defeat. The early tragedy could cast a kind of flattering and extenuating afterglow over what had come later. The battlefields of A *Farewell to Arms* explained the bars of *The Sun Also*

Rises—and explained the young Krebs, of the story "Soldier's Home," who came back home to a Middle-Western town to accept his own slow disintegration.

This is not said in disparagement of *A Farewell to Arms*. It is, after all, a compliment to the hypnotic force of the book. For the hypnotic force of the book was felt from the first, and it is not unusual for such a book to be relished by its first readers for superficial reasons and not for the essential virtues that may engage those who come to it later.

In accounting for the immediate appeal of *A Farewell to Arms*, the history of the author himself is of some importance. In so far as the reader knew about Ernest Hemingway in 1929, he knew about a young man who seemed to typify in his own experience the central experience of his generation. Behind the story of *A Farewell to Arms* and his other books there was the shadow of his own story that could stamp his fiction with the authenticity of a document and, for the more impressionable, with the value of a revelation. He could give an ethic and a technique for living, even in the face of defeat or frustration, and yet his own story was the story that we have always loved: the American success story.

He was born in Oak Park, Illinois, in the Middle West—that region which it was fashionable to condemn (after Mencken and Sinclair Lewis) as romanceless, but which became endowed, paradoxically enough, with the romance of the American average. His father was a physician. There were two boys and four girls in the family. In the summers the family lived in northern Michigan, where there were Indians, and where lake, streams, and forests gave boyhood pursuits their appropriate setting. In the winters he went to school in Oak Park. He played football in high school, ran away from home, returned and, in 1917, graduated. After graduation he was for a short time a reporter on the *Kansas City Star*, but the war was on and he went to Italy as a volunteer ambulance driver. He was wounded and decorated, and after his recovery served in the Italian army as a soldier. For a time after the war he was a foreign correspondent for the *Toronto Star*, in the Near East.

In the years after the war Hemingway set about learning, quite consciously and with rigorous self-discipline, the craft and art of writing. During most of his apprenticeship he lived in Paris, one of the great number of expatriates who were drawn to the artistic capital of the world to learn to be writers, painters, sculptors, or dancers, or simply to enjoy on a low monetary exchange the freedom of life away from American or British conventions. "Young America," writes Ford Madox Ford, "from the limitless prairies leapt, released, on Paris. They stampeded with the madness of colts when you let down the slip-rails between dried pasture and green. The noise of their advancing drowned all sounds. Their innumerable forms hid the very trees on the boulevards. Their perpetual motion made you dizzy." And of Hemingway himself: "He was presented to me by Ezra [Pound] and Bill Bird and had rather the aspect of an Eton-Oxford, huskyish young captain of a midland regiment of His Britannic Majesty. . . . Into that animated din would drift Hemingway, balancing on the point of his toes, feinting at my head with hands as large as hams and relating sinister stories of Paris landlords. He told them with singularly choice words in a slow voice."

The originality and force of Hemingway's early stories, published in little magazines and in limited editions in France, were recognized from the first by many who made their acquaintance. The seeds of his later work were in those stories of In Our Time, concerned chiefly with scenes of inland American life and a boy's growing awareness of that life in contrast to vivid flashes of the disorder and brutality of the war years and the immediate post-war years in Europe. There are both contrast and continuity between the two elements of In Our Time. There is the contrast between the lyric rendering of one aspect of the boyhood world and the realistic rendering of the world of war, but there is also a continuity, because in the boyhood world there are recurring intimations of the blackness into which experience can lead even in the peaceful setting of Michigan.

With the publication of The Sun Also Rises, in 1926, Hemingway's work reached a wider audience, and at the same time defined more clearly the line his genius was to follow and his role as one of the spokesmen for a generation. But A Farewell to Arms gave him his first substantial popular success and established his reputation. It was a brilliant and compelling novel; it provided the great alibi; it crowned the success story of the American boy from the Middle West, who had hunted and fished, played football in high school, been a newspaper reporter, gone to war and been wounded and decorated, wandered exotic lands as a foreign correspondent, lived the free life of the Latin Quarter of Paris, and, at the age of thirty, written a best seller—athlete, sportsman, correspondent, soldier, adventurer, and author.

It would be possible and even profitable to discuss A Farewell to Arms in isolation from Hemingway's other work. But Hemingway is a peculiarly personal writer, and for all the apparent objectivity and self-suppression in his method as a writer, his work, to an uncommon degree, forms a continuous whole. One part explains and interprets another part. It is true that there have been changes between early and late work, that there has been an increasing self-consciousness, that attitudes and methods that in the beginning were instinctive and simple have become calculated and elaborated. But the best way to understand one of his books is, nevertheless, to compare it with both earlier and later pieces and seek to discern motives and methods that underlie all of his work.

Perhaps the simplest way into the whole question is to consider what kind of world Hemingway writes about. A writer may write about his special world merely because he happens to know that world, but he may also write about that special world because it best dramatizes for him the issues and questions that are his fundamental concerns—because, in other words, that special world has a kind of symbolic significance for him. There is often—if we discount mere literary fashion and imitation—an inner and necessary reason for the writer's choice of his characters and situations. What situations and characters does Hemingway write about?

They are usually violent. There is the hard-drinking and sexually promiscuous world of *The Sun Also Rises;* the chaotic and brutal world of war, as in *A Farewell to Arms, For Whom the Bell Tolls,* many of the inserted sketches of *In Our Time,* the play *The Fifth Column,* and some of the stories; the world of sport, as in "Fifty Grand," "My Old Man," "The Undefeated," "The Snows of Kilimanjaro"; the world of crime, as in "The Killers," "The Gambler, the Nun, and the Radio," and *To Have and Have Not.* Even when the situation of a story does not fall into one of these categories, it usually involves a desperate risk, and behind it is the shadow of ruin, physical or spiritual. As for the typical characters, they are usually tough men, experienced in the hard worlds they inhabit, and not obviously given to emotional display or sensitive shrinking—men like Rinaldi or Frederick Henry of *A Farewell to Arms,* Robert Jordan of *For Whom the Bell Tolls,* Harry Morgan of *To Have and Have Not,* the big-game hunter of "The Snows of Kilimanjaro," the old bullfighter of "The Undefeated," or the pugilist of "Fifty Grand." Or if the typical character is not of this seasoned order, he is a very young man, or boy, first entering the violent world and learning his first adjustment to it.

We have said that the shadow of ruin is behind the typical Hemingway situation. The typical character faces defeat or death. But out of defeat or death the character usually manages to salvage something. And here we discover Hemingway's special interest in such situations and characters. His heroes are not squealers, welchers, compromisers, or cowards, and when they confront defeat they realize that the stance they take, the stoic endurance, the stiff upper lip mean a kind of victory. If they are to be defeated they are defeated upon their own terms; some of them have even courted their defeat; and certainly they have maintained, even in the practical defeat, an ideal of themselves—some definition of how a man should behave, formulated or unformulated—by which they have lived. They represent some notion of a code, some notion of honor, that makes a man a man, and that distinguishes him from people who merely follow their random impulses and who are, by consequence, "messy."

In case after case, we can illustrate this "principle of sportsmanship," as Edmund Wilson has called it, at the center of a story or novel. Robert Jordan, in *For Whom the Bell Tolls*, is somehow happy as he lies, wounded, behind the machine gun that is to cover the escape of his friends and his sweetheart from Franco's Fascists. The old bullfighter, in "The Undefeated," continues his incompetent fight even under the jeers and hoots of the crowd, until the bull is dead and he himself is mortally hurt. Francis Macomber, the rich young sportsman who goes lion-hunting in "The Short, Happy Life of Francis Macomber," and who has funked it and bolted before a wounded lion, at last learns the lesson that the code of the hunter demands that he go into the bush after an animal he has wounded. Brett, the heroine of *The Sun Also Rises*, gives up Romero, the young bullfighter with whom she is in love, because she knows she will ruin him, and her tight-lipped remark to Jake, the newspaper man who is the narrator of the novel, might also serve as the motto of Hemingway's work: "You know it makes one feel rather good deciding not to be a bitch."

It is the discipline of the code that makes man human, a sense of style or good form. This applies not only in isolated, dramatic cases such as those listed above, but is a more pervasive thing that can give meaning, partially at least, to the confusions of living. The discipline of the soldier, the form of the athlete, the gameness of the sportsman, the technique of an artist can give some sense of the human order, and can achieve a moral significance. And here we see how Hemingway's concern with war and sport crosses his concern with literary style. If a writer can get the kind of style at which Hemingway, in *Green Hills of Africa*, professes to aim, then "nothing else matters. It is more important than anything else he can do." It is more important because, ultimately, it is a moral achievement. And no doubt for this reason, as well as for the reason of Henry James's concern with cruxes of a moral code, he is, as he says in *Green Hills of Africa*, an admirer of the work of Henry James, the devoted stylist.

But to return to the subject of Hemingway's world: the code and the discipline are important because they can give meaning to life that otherwise seems to have no meaning or justification. In other words, in a world without supernatural sanctions, in the God-abandoned world of modernity, man can realize an ideal meaning only in so far as he can define and maintain the code. The effort to do so, however limited and imperfect it may be, is the characteristically human effort and provides the tragic or pitiful human story. Hemingway's attitude on this point is much like that of Robert Louis Stevenson in "Pulvis et Umbra":

Poor soul, here for so little, cast among so many hardships, filled with desires so incommensurate and so inconsistent, savagely surrounded, savagely descended, irremediably condemned to prey upon his fellow lives: who should have blamed him had he been of a piece with his destiny and a being merely barbarous? And we look and behold him instead, filled with imperfect virtues . . . an ideal of decency, to which he would rise if it were possible; a limit of shame, below which, if it be possible, he will not stoop. . . . Man is indeed marked for failure in his effort to do right. But where the best consistently miscarry how tenfold more remarkable that all should continue to strive; and surely we should find it both touching and inspiriting, that in a field from which success is banished, our race should not cease to labor. . . . It matters not where we look, under what climate we observe him, in what stage of society, in what depth of ignorance, burthened with what erroneous morality; by campfires in Assiniboia, the snow powdering his shoulders, the wind plucking his blanket, as he sits, passing the ceremonial calumet and uttering his grave opinions like a Roman senator; on ships at sea, a man inured to hardship and vile pleasures, his brightest hope a fiddle in a tavern and a bedizened trull who sells herself to rob him, and he for all that, simple, innocent, cheerful, kindly like a child, constant to toil, brave to drown, for others; . . . in the brothel, the discard of society, living mainly on strong drink, fed with affronts, a fool, a thief, the comrade of thieves, and even here keeping the point of honor and the touch of pity, often repaying the world's scorn with service, often standing firm upon a scruple, and at a certain cost, rejecting riches:—everywhere some virtue cherished or affected, everywhere some decency of thought or carriage, everywhere the ensign of man's ineffectual goodness! . . . under every circumstance of failure, without hope, without help, without thanks, still obscurely fighting the lost fight of virtue, still clinging, in the brothel or on the scaffold, to some rag of honor, the poor jewel of their souls! They may seek to escape, and yet they cannot; it is not alone their privilege and glory, but their doom; they are condemned to some nobility. . . .

Hemingway's code is more rigorous than Stevenson's and perhaps he finds fewer devoted to it, but, like Stevenson, he can find his characteristic hero and characteristic story among the discards of society, and, like Stevenson, is aware of the touching irony of that fact. But for the moment the important thing in the parallel is that, for Stevenson, the world in which this drama of pitiful aspiration and stoic endurance is played out, is apparently a violent and meaningless world—"our rotary island loaded with predatory life and more drenched with blood . . . than ever mutinied ship, scuds through space."

Neither Hemingway nor Stevenson invented this world. It had already appeared in literature before their time, and that is a way of saying that this cheerless vision had already begun to trouble men. It is the world we find pictured (and denied) in Tennyson's "In Memoriam"—the world in which human conduct is a product of "dying Nature's earth and lime." It is the world pictured (and not denied) in Hardy and Housman, a world that seems to be presided over by blind Doomsters (if by anybody), as Hardy put it in his poem "Hap," or made by some brute and blackguard (if by anybody), as Housman put it in his poem "The Chestnut Casts Its Flambeaux." It is the world of Zola or Dreiser or Conrad or Faulkner. It is the world of, to use Bertrand Russell's phrase, "secular hurryings through space." It is the God-abandoned world, the world of Nature-as-all. We know where the literary men got this picture. They got it from the scientists of the nineteenth century. This is Hemingway's world, too, the world with nothing at center.

Over against this particular version of the naturalistic view of the world, there was, of course, an argument for Divine Intelligence and a Divine purpose, an argument that based itself on the beautiful system of nature, on natural law. The closely knit order of the natural world, so the argument ran, implies a Divine Intelligence. But if one calls Hemingway's attention to the fact that the natural world is a world of order, his reply is on record in a story called "A Natural History of the Dead." There he quotes from the traveler Mungo Park, who, naked and starving in an African desert, observed a beautiful little moss-flower and meditated thus:

> Can the Being who planted, watered, and brought to perfection, in this obscure part of the world, a thing which appears of so small importance, look with unconcern upon the situation and suffering of creatures formed after his own image? Surely not. Reflections like these would not allow me to despair: I started up and, disregarding both hunger and fatigue, travelled forward, assured that relief was at hand; and I was not disappointed.

And Hemingway continues:

> With a disposition to wonder and adore in like manner, as Bishop Stanley says [the author of A Familiar History of Birds], can any branch of Natural History be studied without increasing that faith, love and hope which we also, everyone of us, need in our journey through the wilderness of life? Let us therefore see what inspiration we may derive from the dead.

Then Hemingway presents the picture of a modern battlefield, where the bloated and decaying bodies give a perfect example of the natural order of chemistry—but scarcely an argument for faith, hope, and love. That picture is his answer to the argument that the order of nature implies meaning in the world.

In one of the stories, "A Clean, Well-Lighted Place," we find the best description of what underlies Hemingway's world of violent action. In the early stages of the story we see an old man sitting late in a Spanish café. Two waiters are speaking of him:

> "Last week he tried to commit suicide," one waiter said.
> "Why?"
> "He was in despair."
> "What about?"
> "Nothing."
> "How do you know it was nothing?"
> "He has plenty of money."

The despair beyond plenty of money—or beyond all the other gifts of the world: its nature becomes a little clearer at the end of the story when the older of the two waiters is left alone, reluctant too to leave the clean, well-lighted place:

> Turning off the electric light he continued the conversation with himself. It is the light of course but it is necessary that the place be clean and pleasant. You do not want music. Certainly you do not want music. Nor can you stand before a bar with dignity although that is all that is provided for these hours. What did he fear? It was not fear or dread. It was a nothing that he knew too well. It was all a nothing and a man was nothing too. It was only that and light was all it needed and a certain cleanness and order. Some lived in it and never felt it but he knew it all was nada y pues nada y nada y pues nada. Our nada who art in nada, nada be thy name thy kingdom nada thy will be nada in nada as it is in nada. Give us this nada our daily nada and nada us our nada as we nada our nadas and nada us not into nada but deliver us from nada; pues nada. Hail nothing full of nothing, nothing is with thee. He smiled and stood before a bar with a shining steam pressure coffee machine.
> "What's yours?" asked the barman.
> "Nada."

At the end the old waiter is ready to go home:

> Now, without thinking further, he would go home to his room. He would lie in bed and finally, with daylight, he would go to sleep. After all, he said to himself, it is probably only insomnia. Many must have it.

And the sleepless man—the man obsessed by death, by the meaninglessness of the world, by nothingness, by nada—is one of the recurring symbols in the work of Hemingway. In this phase Hemingway is a religious writer. The despair beyond plenty of money, the despair that makes a sleeplessness beyond insomnia, is the despair felt by a man who hungers for the sense of order and assurance that men seem to find in religious faith, but who cannot find grounds for his faith.

Another recurring symbol is the violent man. But the sleepless man and the violent man are not contradictory; they are complementary symbols. They represent phases of the same question, the same hungering for meaning in the world. The sleepless man is the man brooding upon nada, upon chaos, upon Nature-as-all. (For Nature-as-all equals moral chaos; even its bulls and lions and kudu are not admired by Hemingway as creatures of conscious self-discipline; their courage has a meaning only in so far as it symbolizes human courage.) The violent man is the man taking an action appropriate to the realization of the fact of nada. He is, in other words, engaged in the effort to discover human values in a naturalistic world.

Before we proceed with this line of discussion, it might be asked, "Why does Hemingway feel that the quest necessarily involves violence?" Now, at one level, the answer to this question would involve the whole matter of the bias toward violence in modern literature. But let us take it in its more immediate reference. The typical Hemingway hero is the man aware, or in the process of becoming aware, of nada. Death is the great nada. Therefore whatever code or creed the hero gets must, to be good, stick even in the face of death. It has to be good in the bull ring or on the battlefield and not merely in the study or lecture room. In fact, Hemingway is anti-intellectual, and has a great contempt for any type of solution arrived at without the testings of immediate experience.

So aside from the question of a dramatic sense that would favor violence, and aside from the mere matter of personal temperament (for Hemingway describes himself on more than one occasion as obsessed by death), the presentation of violence is appropriate in his work because death is the great nada. In taking violent risks man confronts in dramatic terms the issue of nada that is implicit in all of Hemingway's world.

But to return to our general line of discussion. There are two aspects to this violence that is involved in the quest of the Hemingway hero, two aspects that seem to represent an ambivalent attitude toward nature.

First, there is the conscious sinking into nature, as we may call it. On this line of reasoning we would find something like this: if there is at center only nada, then the only sure compensation in life, the only reality, is gratification of appetite, the relish of sensation.

Continually in the stories and novels one finds such sentences as this from Green Hills of Africa: ". . . drinking this, the first one of the day, the finest one there is, and looking at the thick bush we passed in the dark, feeling the cool wind of the night and smelling the good smell of Africa, I was altogether happy." What is constantly interesting in such sentences is the fact that happiness, a notion that we traditionally connect with a complicated state of being, with notions of virtue, of achievement, etc., is here equated with a set of merely agreeable sensations. For instance, in "Cross-Country Snow," one of the boys, George, says to the other, Nick, who in story after story is a sort of shadow of Hemingway himself, "Maybe we'll never go skiing again, Nick." And Nick replies, "We've got to. It isn't worth while if you can't." The sensations of skiing are the end of life. Or in another story, "Big Two-Hearted River: Part II," a story that is full of the sensation-as-happiness theme, we find this remark about Nick, who has been wading in a trout stream: "Nick climbed out onto the meadow and stood, water running down his trousers and out of his shoes, his shoes squelchy. He went over and sat on the logs. He did not want to rush his sensations any." The careful relish of sensation—that is what counts, always.

This intense awareness of the world of the senses is, of course, one of the things that made the early work of Hemingway seem, upon its first impact, so fresh and pure. Physical nature is nowhere rendered with greater vividness than in his work, and probably his only competitors in this department of literature are William Faulkner, among the modern, and Henry David Thoreau, among the older American writers. The meadows, forests, lakes, and trout streams of America, and the arid, sculpturesque mountains of Spain, appear with astonishing immediacy, an immediacy not dependent upon descriptive flourishes. But not only the appearance of landscape is important; a great deal of the freshness comes from the discrimination of sensation, the coldness of water in the "squelchy" shoes after wading, the tangy smell of dry sagebrush, the "cleanly" smell of grease and oil on a field piece. Hemingway's appreciation of the aesthetic qualities of the physical world is important, but a peculiar poignancy is implicit in the rendering of those qualities; the beauty of the physical world is a background for the human predicament, and the very relishing of the beauty is merely a kind of desperate and momentary compensation possible in the midst of the predicament.

This careful relishing of the world of the senses comes to a climax in drinking and sex. Drink is the "giant-killer," the weapon against man's thought of nada. And so is sex, for that matter, though when sexual attraction achieves the status of love, the process is one that attempts to achieve a meaning rather than to forget meaninglessness in the world. In terms of drinking and sex, the typical Hemingway hero is a man of monel-metal stomach and Homeric prowess in the arts of love. And the typical situation is love, with some drinking, against the background of nada—of civilization gone to pot, of war, or of death—as we get it in all of the novels in one form or another, and in many of the stories.

It is important to remember, however, that the sinking into nature, even at the level of drinking and mere sexuality, is a self-conscious act. It is not the random gratification of appetite. We see this quite clearly in *The Sun Also Rises* in the contrast between Cohn, who is merely a random dabbler in the world of sensation, who is merely trying to amuse himself, and the initiates like Jake and Brett, who are aware of the nada at the center of things and whose dissipations, therefore, have a philosophical significance. The initiate in Hemingway's world raises the gratification of appetite to the level of a cult and a discipline.

The cult of sensation, as we have already indicated, passes over very readily into the cult of true love, for the typical love story is presented primarily in terms of the cult of sensation. (*A Farewell to Arms*, as we shall see when we come to a detailed study of that novel, is closely concerned with this transition.) Even in the cult of true love it is the moment that counts, and the individual. There is never any past or future to the love stories, and the lovers are always isolated, not moving within the framework of obligations of an ordinary human society. The notion of the cult—a secret cult composed of those who have been initiated into the secret of nada—is constantly played up.

In *A Farewell to Arms*, for instance, Catherine and Frederick are two against the world, a world that is, literally as well as figuratively, an alien world. The peculiar relationship between Frederick and the priest takes on a new significance if viewed in terms of the secret cult. We shall come to this topic later, but for the moment we can say that the priest is a priest of Divine Love, the subject about which he and Frederick converse in the hospital and that Frederick himself is a kind of priest, one of the initiate in the end, of the cult of profane love. This same pattern of two against the world with an understanding confidant or interpreter, reappears in *For Whom the Bell Tolls*—with Pilar, the gipsy woman who understands "love," substituting for the priest of *A Farewell to Arms*.

The initiates of the cult of love are those who are aware of nada, but their effort, as members of the cult, is to find a meaning to put in place of the nada. That is, there is an attempt to make the relationship of love take on a religious significance in so far as it can give meaning to life. This general topic is not new with the work of Hemingway. It is one of the literary themes of the nineteenth century—and has, as a matter of fact, a longer history than that.

If the cult of love arises from and states itself in the language of the cult of sensation, it is an extension of the sinking-into-nature aspect of the typical Hemingway violence; but in so far as it involves a discipline and a search for a "faith," it leads us to the second aspect of the typical violence.

The violence, although in its first aspect it represents a sinking into nature, at the same time, in its second aspect, represents a conquest of nature, and of nada in man. It represents such a conquest, not because of the fact of violence, but because the violence appears in terms of a discipline, a style, and a code. It is, as we have already seen, in terms of a self-imposed discipline that the heroes make one gallant, though limited, effort to redeem the incoherence of the world: they attempt to impose some form upon the disorder of their lives, the technique of the bullfighter or sportsman, the discipline of the soldier, the fidelity of the lover, or even the code of the gangster, which, though brutal and apparently dehumanizing, has its own ethic. (Ole Anderson, in "The Killers," is willing to take his medicine without whining, and even recognizes some necessity and justice in his plight. Or the dying Mexican, in "The Gambler, the Nun, and the Radio," refuses to squeal despite the detective's argument: "One can, with honor, denounce one's assailant.")

If it is said that Frederick in A Farewell to Arms does not, when he deserts, exhibit the discipline of the soldier, the answer is simple: his obligation has been constantly presented as an obligation to the men in his immediate command, and he and the men in his command have never recognized an obligation to the total war—they recognize no meaning in the war and are bound together only by a squad sense and by their immediate respect for each other; when Frederick is separated from his men his obligation is gone. His true obligation then becomes the fidelity to Catherine.

The discipline, the form, is never quite capable of subduing the world, but fidelity to it is part of the gallantry of defeat. By fidelity to it the hero manages to keep one small place "clean" and "well-lighted," and manages to retain, or achieve for one last moment, his dignity. There should be, as the old Spanish waiter reflects, a "clean, well-lighted place" where one could keep one's dignity at the late hour.

We have said earlier that the typical Hemingway character is tough and, apparently, insensitive. But only apparently, for the fidelity to a code, to the discipline, may be the index to a sensitivity that allows the characters to see, at moments, their true plight. At times, and usually at times of stress, it is the tough man in the Hemingway world, the disciplined man, who is actually aware of pathos or tragedy. The individual toughness (which may be taken to be the private discipline demanded by the world) may find itself in conflict with the natural human reactions; but the Hemingway hero, though he may be aware of the claims of the natural reaction, the spontaneous human emotion, cannot surrender to it because he knows that the only way to hold on to the definition of himself, to "honor" or "dignity," is to maintain the discipline, the code. For example, when pity appears in the Hemingway world—as in "The Pursuit Race"—it does not appear in its maximum but in its minimum manifestation.

What this means in terms of style and method is the use of understatement. This understatement, stemming from the contrast between the sensitivity and the superimposed discipline, is a constant aspect of the work, an aspect that was caught in a cartoon in the *New Yorker*. The cartoon showed a brawny, muscle-knotted forearm and a hairy hand that clutched a rose. It was entitled "The Soul of Ernest Hemingway." Just as there is a margin of victory in the defeat of the Hemingway characters, so there is a little margin of sensitivity in their brutal and apparently insensitive world. Hence we have the ironical circumstance—a central circumstance in creating the pervasive irony of Hemingway's work—that the revelation of the values characteristic of his work arises from the most unpromising people and the most unpromising situations—the little streak of poetry or pathos in "The Pursuit Race," "The Killers," "My Old Man," "A Clean, Well-Lighted Place," or "The Undefeated." We have a perfect example of it in the last-named story. After the defeat of the old bullfighter, who is lying wounded on an operating table, Zurito, the picador, is about to cut off the old fellow's pigtail, the mark of his profession. But when the wounded man starts up, despite his pain, and says, "You couldn't do a thing like that," Zurito says, "I was joking." Zurito becomes aware that, after all, the old bullfighter is, in a way, undefeated, and deserves to die with his coleta on.

This locating of the poetic, the pathetic, or the tragic in the unpromising person or situation is not unique with Hemingway. It is something with which we are acquainted in a great deal of our literature since the Romantic Movement. In such literature, the sensibility is played down, and an antiromantic surface sheathes the work; the point is in the contrast. The impulse that led Hemingway to the simple character is akin to the one that drew Wordsworth to the same choice. Wordsworth felt that his unsophisticated peasants were more honest in their responses than the cultivated man, and were therefore more poetic. Instead of Wordsworth's peasant we have in Hemingway's work the bullfighter, the soldier, the revolutionist, the sportsman, and the gangster; instead of Wordsworth's children we have the young men like Nick, the person just on the verge of being initiated into the world. There are, of course, differences between the approach of Wordsworth and that of Hemingway, but there is little difference on the point of marginal sensibility. In one sense, both are anti-intellectual, and in such poems as "Resolution and Independence" or "Michael" one finds even closer ties.

I have just indicated a similarity between Wordsworth and Hemingway on the grounds of a romantic anti-intellectualism. But with Hemingway it is far more profound and radical than with Wordsworth. All we have to do to see the difference is to put Wordsworth's Preface to the *Lyrical Ballads* over against any number of passages from Hemingway. The intellectualism of the eighteenth century had merely put a veil of stereotyped language over the world and a veil of snobbism over a large area of human experience. That is Wordsworth's indictment. But Hemingway's indictment of the intellectualism of the past is that it wound up in the mire and blood of 1914 to 1918; that it was a pack of lies leading to death. We can put over against the Preface of Wordsworth, a passage from *A Farewell to Arms*:

> I was always embarrassed by the words sacred, glorious, and sacrifice and the expression in vain. We had heard them, sometimes standing in the rain almost out of earshot, so that only the shouted words came through, and had read them, on proclamations that were slapped up by billposters over other proclamations, now for a long time, and I had seen nothing sacred, and the things that were glorious had no glory and the sacrifices were like the stockyards at Chicago if nothing was done with the meat except to bury it. There were many words that you could not stand to hear and finally only the names of places had dignity. . . . Abstract words such as glory, honor, courage, or hallow were obscene beside the concrete names of villages, the numbers of roads, the names of rivers, the numbers of regiments and the dates.

I do not mean to say that the general revolution in style, and the revolt against the particular intellectualism of the nineteenth century, was a result of the First World War. As a matter of fact, that revolt was going on long before the war, but for Hemingway, and for many others, the war gave the situation a peculiar depth and urgency.

Perhaps we might scale the matter thus: Wordsworth was a revolutionist—he truly had a new view of the world—but his revolutionary view left great tracts of the world untouched; the Church of England, for instance. Arnold and Tennyson, a generation or so later, though not revolutionists themselves, are much more profoundly stirred by the revolutionary situation than ever Wordsworth was; that is, the area of the world involved in the debate was for them greater. Institutions are called into question in a more fundamental way. But they managed to hang on to their English God and their English institutions. With Hardy, the area of disturbance has grown greater, and what can be salvaged is much less. He, like the earlier Victorians, had a strong sense of community to sustain him in the face of the universe that was for him, as not finally for Arnold and Tennyson, unfriendly, or at least neutral and Godless. But his was a secret community, different from that of social institutions. It was a human communion that, as a matter of fact, was constantly being violated by institutions. Their violation of it is, in fact, a constant source of subject matter and a constant spring of irony. Nevertheless, Hardy could refer to himself as a meliorist. He could not keep company with Wordsworth or Tennyson or Arnold; and when Hardy, having been elected an Honorary Fellow of Magdalene College, Cambridge, was to be formally admitted, the Master, Doctor Donaldson (as we know from A.C. Benson's *Diary*) was much afraid that Hardy might dislike the religious service. The occasion, however, went off very well, even though Hardy, after impressing the Master with his knowledge or ecclesiastical music, did remark, "Of course it's only a sentiment to me now." Hardy listened to a sermon by the Archdeacon of Zanzibar, who declared that God was "a God of *desire*—who both hated and loved—not a mild or impersonal force." But even though Hardy could not accept the God of the Bishop of Zanzibar, he still had faith in the constructive power of the secret community.

Now, in Hemingway we see something very like Hardy's secret community, but one much smaller, one whose definition has become much more specialized. Its members are those who know the code. They recognize each other, they know the password and the secret grip, but they are few in number, and each is set off against the world like a wounded lion ringed round by waiting hyenas (*Green Hills of Africa* gives us the hyena symbol—the animal whose death is comic because it is all hideously "appetite": wounded, it eats its own intestines). Furthermore, this secret community is not constructive; Hemingway is no meliorist. In fact, there are hints that somewhere in the back of his mind, and in behind his work, there is a kind of Spenglerian view of history: our civilization is running down. We get this most explicitly in *Green Hills of Africa*:

> A continent ages quickly once we come. The natives live in harmony with it. But the foreigner destroys, cuts down the trees, drains the water, so that the water supply is altered and in a short time the soil, once the sod is turned under, is cropped out and, next, it starts to blow away as it has blown away in every old country and as I had seen it start to blow in

Canada. The earth gets tired of being exploited. A country wears out quickly unless man puts back in it all his residue and that of all his beasts. When he quits using beasts and uses machines, the earth defeats him quickly. The machine can't reproduce, nor does it fertilize the soil, and it eats what he cannot raise. A country was made to be as we found it. We are the intruders and after we are dead we may have ruined it but it will still be there and we don't know what the next changes are. I suppose they all end up like Mongolia.

I would come back to Africa but not to make a living from it. . . . But I would come back to where it pleased me to live; to really live. Not just let my life pass. Our people went to America because that was the place for them to go then. It had been a good country and we had made a bloody mess of it and I would go, now, somewhere else as we had always had the right to go somewhere else and as we had always gone. You could always come back. Let the others come to America who did not know that they had come too late. Our people had seen it at its best and fought for it when it was well worth fighting for. Now I would go somewhere else.

This is the most explicit statement, but the view is implicit in case after case. The general human community, the general human project, has gone to pot. There is only the little secret community of, paradoxically enough, individualists who have resigned from the general community, and who are strong enough to live without any of the illusions, lies, and big words of the herd. At least, this is the case up to the novel *To Have and Have Not*, which appeared in 1937. In that novel and in *For Whom the Bell Tolls*, Hemingway attempts to bring his individualistic hero back to society, to give him a common stake with the fate of other men.

But to return to the matter of Wordsworth and Hemingway. What in Wordsworth is merely simple or innocent is in Hemingway violent: the gangster or bullfighter replaces the leech-gatherer or the child. Hemingway's world is a more disordered world, and the sensibility of his characters is more ironically in contrast with their world. The most immediate consideration here is the playing down of the sensibility as such, the sheathing of it in the code of toughness. Gertrude Stein's tribute is here relevant: "Hemingway is the shyest and proudest and sweetest-smelling storyteller of my reading." But this shyness manifests itself in the irony. In this, of course, Hemingway's irony corresponds to the Byronic irony. But the relation to Byron is even more fundamental. The pity is valid only when it is wrung from the man who has been seasoned by experience. Therefore a premium is placed on the fact of violent experience. The "dumb ox" character, commented on by Wyndham Lewis, represents the Wordsworthian peasant; the character with the code of the tough guy, the initiate, the man cultivating honor, gallantry, and recklessness, represents the Byronic aristocrat.

The failures of Hemingway, like his successes, are rooted in this situation. The successes occur in those instances where Hemingway accepts the essential limitations of his premises—that is, when there is an equilibrium between the dramatization and the characteristic Hemingway "point," when the system of ironies and understatements is coherent. On the other hand, the failures occur when we feel that Hemingway has not respected the limitations of his premises—that is, when the dramatization seems to be "rigged" and the violence, therefore, merely theatrical. The characteristic irony, or understatement, in such cases, seems to be too self-conscious. For example, let us glance at Hemingway's most spectacular failure, *To Have and Have Not*. The point of the novel is based on the contrast between the smuggler and the rich owners of the yachts along the quay. But the irony is essentially an irony without any center of reference. It is superficial, for, as Philip Rahv indicates, the only difference between the smuggler and the rich is that the rich were successful in their buccaneering. The revelation that comes to the smuggler dying in his launch—"a man alone ain't got no . . . chance"—is a meaningless revelation, for it has no reference to the actual dramatization. It is, finally, a failure in intellectual analysis of the situation.

There is, I believe, a good chance that *For Whom the Bell Tolls* will not turn out to be Hemingway's best novel (an honor I should reserve for *A Farewell to Arms*) primarily because in this most ambitious of the novels Hemingway does not accept the limitations of his premises. I do not mean to imply that it is on a level with *To Have and Have Not*. There is a subtler irony in the later novel. I have pointed out that the irony in *To Have and Have Not* is that of the contrast between the smuggler and the rich in the yachts along the pier; that is, it is a simple irony, in direct line with the ostensible surface direction of the story. But the irony in *For Whom the Bell Tolls* runs counter to the ostensible surface direction of the story. As surface, we have a conflict between the forces of light and the forces of darkness, freedom versus fascism, etc. Hero and heroine are clearly and completely and romantically aligned on the side of light. We are prepared to see the Fascist atrocities and the general human kindness of the Loyalists. It happens to work out the other way. The scene of horror is the massacre by the Loyalists, not by the Fascists. Again, in the attack on El Sordo's hill by the Fascists, we are introduced to a young Fascist lieutenant, whose bosom friend is killed in the attack. We are suddenly given this little human glimpse—against the grain of the surface. But this incident, we discover later, is preparation for the very end of the novel. We leave the hero lying wounded, preparing to cover the retreat of his friends. The man who is over the sights of the machine gun as the book ends is the Fascist lieutenant, whom we have been made to know as a man, not as a monster. This general ironical conditioning of the overt story line is reflected also in the attitude of Anselmo, who kills but cannot believe in killing. In other words, the irony here is much more functional, and more complicated, than that of *To Have and Have Not*; the irony affirms that the human values may transcend the party lines.

Much has been said to the effect that *To Have and Have Not* and *For Whom the Bell Tolls* represent a basic change of point of view, an enlargement of what I have called the secret community. Now no doubt that is the intention behind both books, but the temper of both books, the good one and the bad one, is the old temper, the cast of characters is the old cast, and the assumptions lying far below the explicit intention are the old assumptions.

The monotony and self-imitation, into which Hemingway's work sometimes falls, are again an effect of a failure in dramatization. Hemingway, apparently, can dramatize his "point" in only one basic situation and with only one set of characters. He has, as we have seen, only two key characters, with certain variations from them by way of contrast or counterpoint. His best women characters, by the way, are those who most nearly approximate the men; that is, they embody the masculine virtues and point of view characteristic of Hemingway's work.

But the monotony is not merely a monotony deriving from the characters as types; it derives, rather, from the limitations of the author's sensibility, which seems to come alive in only one issue. A more flexible sensibility, one capable of making nicer discriminations, might discover great variety in such key characters and situations. But Hemingway's successes are due, in part at least, to the close co-ordination that he sometimes achieves between the character and the situation, and the sensibility as it reflects itself in the style.

The style characteristically is simple, even to the point of monotony. The characteristic sentence is simple, or compound; and if compound, there is no implied subtlety in the co-ordination of the clauses. The paragraph structure is, characteristically, based on simple sequence. There is an obvious relation between this style and the characters and situations with which the author is concerned—a relation of dramatic decorum. (There are, on the other hand, examples, especially in the novels, of other, more fluent, lyrical effects, but even here this fluency is founded on the conjunction *and*; it is a rhythmical and not a logical fluency. And the lyrical quality is simply a manifestation of that marginal sensibility, as can be demonstrated by an analysis of the occasions on which it appears.)

But there is a more fundamental aspect of the question, an aspect that involves not the sensibility of the characters, but the sensibility of the author. The short, simple rhythms, the succession of co-ordinate clauses, the general lack of subordination—all suggest a dislocated and ununified world. The figures who live in this world live a sort of hand-to-mouth existence perceptually, and conceptually they hardly live at all. Subordination implies some exercise of discrimination—the sifting of reality through the intellect. But in Hemingway we see a romantic anti-intellectualism.

In Wordsworth, too, we see this strain of anti-intellectualism. He, too, wishes to clear away the distorting sophistications of the intellect, and to keep his eye on the object. The formulations of the intellect create the "veil of familiarity" that he would clear away. His mode, too, was to take unpromising material and reveal in it the lyric potentiality. He, too, was interested in the margin of sensibility. He, too, wished to respect the facts, and could have understood Hemingway's rejection of the big abstract words in favor of "the concrete names of villages, the numbers of roads, the names of rivers, the numbers of regiments and the dates."

The passage from A Farewell to Arms from which the above quotation comes is, of course, the passage most commonly used to explain the attitude behind Hemingway's style. But we can put with it other passages of a similar import, and best of all a sentence from the story "Soldier's Home." Krebs, the boy who has been through the war and who comes back home to find himself cut off from life, had "acquired the nausea in regard to experience that is the result of untruth or exaggeration." He is a casualty, not of bullet or bayonet, but of the big, abstract words. Hemingway's style is, in a way, an attempt to provide an antidote for that "nausea."

A Farewell to Arms is a love story. It is a compelling story at the merely personal level, but it is much more compelling and significant when we see the figures of the lovers silhouetted against the flame-streaked blackness of war, of a collapsing world, of nada. For there is a story behind the love story. That story is the quest for meaning and certitude in a world that seems to offer nothing of the sort. It is, in a sense, a religious book; if it does not offer a religious solution it is nevertheless conditioned by the religious problem.

The very first scene of the book, though seemingly casual, is important if we are to understand the deeper motivations of the story. It is the scene at the officers' mess where the captain baits the priest. "Priest every night five against one," the captain explains to Frederick. But

Frederick, we see in this and later scenes, takes no part in the baiting. There is a bond between him and the priest, a bond that they both recognize. This becomes clear when, after the officers have advised Frederick where he should go on his leave to find the best girls, the priest turns to him and says that he would like to have him to go to Abruzzi, his own province:

"There is good hunting. You would like the people and though it is cold it is clear and dry. You could stay with my family. My father is a famous hunter."

"Come on," said the captain. "We go whorehouse before it shuts."

"Goodnight," I said to the priest.

"Goodnight," he said.

In this preliminary contrast between the officers, who invite the hero to go the brothel, and the priest, who invites him to go to the cold, clear, dry country. we have in its simplest form the issue of the novel.

Frederick does go with the officers that night, and on his leave he does go to the cities, "to the smoke of cafés and nights when the room whirled and you needed to look at the wall to make it stop, nights in bed, drunk, when you knew that that was all there was, and the strange excitement of waking and not knowing who it was with you, and the world all unreal in the dark and so exciting that you must resume again unknowing and not caring in the night, sure that this was all and all and all and not caring." Frederick, at the opening of the novel, lives in the world of random and meaningless appetite, knowing that it is all and all and all, or thinking that he knows that. But behind that there is a dissatisfaction and disgust. Upon his return from his leave, sitting in the officers' mess, he tries to tell the priest how he is sorry that he had not gone to the clear, cold, dry country—the priest's home, which takes on the shadowy symbolic significance of another kind of life, another view of the world. The priest had always known that other country.

He had always known what I did not know and what, when I learned it, I was always able to forget. But I did not know that then, although I learned it later.

What Frederick learns later is the story behind the love story of the book.

But this theme is not merely stated at the opening of the novel and then absorbed into the action. It appears later, at crucial points, to define the line of meaning in the action. When, for example, Frederick is wounded, the priest visits him in the hospital. Their conversation makes even plainer the religious background of the novel. The priest has said that he would like to go back after the war to the Abruzzi. He continues:

> "It does not matter. But there in my country it is understood that a man may love God. It is not a dirty joke."
> "I understand."
> He looked at me and smiled.
> "You understand but you do not love God."
> "No."
> "You do not love Him at all?" he asked.
> "I am afraid of him in the night sometimes."
> "You should love Him."
> "I don't love much."
> "Yes," he said. "You do. What you tell me about in the nights. That is not love. That is only passion and lust. When you love you wish to do things for. You wish to sacrifice for. You wish to serve."
> "I don't love."
> "You will. I know you will. Then you will be happy."

We have here two important items. First, there is the definition of Frederick as the sleepless man, the man haunted by nada. Second, at this stage in the novel, the end of Book I, the true meaning of the love story with Catherine has not yet been defined. It is still at the level of appetite. The priest's role is to indicate the next stage of the story, the discovery of the true nature of love, the "wish to do things for." And he accomplishes this by indicating a parallel between secular love and Divine Love, a parallel which implies Frederick's quest for meaning and certitude. And to emphasize further this idea, Frederick, after the priest leaves, muses on the high, clean country of the Abruzzi, the priest's home that has already been endowed with the symbolic significance of the religious view of the world.

In the middle of Book II (chapter XVIII), in which the love story begins to take on the significance that the priest had predicted, the point is indicated by a bit of dialogue between the lovers.

> "Couldn't we be married privately some way? Then if anything happened to me or if you had a child."
> "There's no way to be married except by church or state. We are married privately. You see, darling, it would mean everything to me if I had any religion. But I haven't any religion."
> "You gave me the Saint Anthony."
> "That was for luck. Some one gave it to me."
> "Then nothing worries you?"
> "Only being sent away from you. You're my religion. You're all I've got."

Again, toward the end of Book IV (chapter XXXV), just before Frederick and Catherine make their escape into Switzerland, Frederick is talking with a friend, the old Count Greffi, who has just said that he thought H.G. Wells's novel *Mr. Britling Sees It Through* a very good study of the English middle-class soul. But Frederick twists the word *soul* into another meaning.

"I don't know about the soul."
"Poor boy. We none of us know about the soul. Are you *Croyant?*"
"At night."

Later in the same conversation the Count returns to the topic:

"And if you ever become devout pray for me if I am dead. I am asking several of my friends to do that. I had expected to become devout myself but it has not come." I thought he smiled sadly but I could not tell. He was so old and his face was very wrinkled, so that a smile used so many lines that all gradations were lost.
"I might become very devout," I said. "Anyway, I will pray for you."
"I had always expected to become devout. All my family died very devout. But somehow it does not come."
"It's too early."
"Maybe it is too late. Perhaps I have outlived my religious feeling."
"My own comes only at night."
"Then too you are in love. Do not forget that is a religious feeling."

So here we find, again, Frederick defined as the sleepless man, and the relation established between secular love and Divine Love.

In the end, with the death of Catherine, Frederick discovers that the attempt to find a substitute for universal meaning in the limited meaning of the personal relationship is doomed to failure. It is doomed because it is liable to all the accidents of a world in which human beings are like the ants running back and forth on a log burning in a campfire and in which death is, as Catherine says just before her own death, "just a dirty trick." But this is not to deny the value of the effort, or to deny the value of the discipline, the code, the stoic endurance, the things that make it true—or half true—that "nothing ever happens to the brave."

This question of the characteristic discipline takes us back to the beginning of the book, and to the context from which Frederick's effort arises. We have already mentioned the contrast between the officers of the mess and the priest. It is a contrast between the man who is aware of the issue of meaning in life and those who are unaware of it, who give themselves over to the mere flow of accident, the contrast between the disciplined and the undisciplined. But the contrast is not merely between the priest and the officers. Frederick's friend, the surgeon Rinaldi, is another who is on the same "side" of the contrast as the priest. He may go to the brothel with his brother officers, he may even bait the priest a little, but his personal relationship with Frederick indicates his affiliations; he is one of the initiate. Furthermore, he has the discipline of his profession, and, as we have seen, in the Hemingway world, the discipline that seems to be merely technical, the style of the artist or the form of the athlete or bullfighter, may be an index to a moral value. "Already," Rinaldi says, "I am only happy when I am working." (Already the seeking of pleasure in sensation is inadequate for Rinaldi.) This point appears more sharply in the remarks about the doctor who first attends to Frederick's wounded leg. He is incompetent and does not wish to take the responsibility for a decision.

> Before he came back three doctors came into the room. I have noticed that doctors who fail in the practice of medicine have a tendency to seek one another's company and aid in consultation. A doctor who cannot take out your appendix properly will recommend to you a doctor who will be unable to remove your tonsils with success. These were three such doctors.

In contrast with them there is Doctor Valentini, who is competent, who is willing to take responsibility, and who, as a kind of mark of his role, speaks the same lingo, with the same bantering, ironical tone, as Rinaldi—the tone that is the mark of the initiate.

So we have the world of the novel divided into two groups, the initiate and the uninitiate, the aware and the unaware, the disciplined and the undisciplined. In the first group are Frederick, Catherine, Rinaldi, Valentini, Count Greffi, the old man who cut the paper silhouettes "for pleasure," and Passini, Manera, and the other ambulance men in Frederick's command. In the second group are the officers of the mess, the incompetent doctors, the "legitimate hero" Ettore, and the "patriots"—all the people who do not know what is really at stake, who are deluded by the big words, who do not have the discipline. They are the messy people, the people who surrender to the flow and illusion of things. It is this second group who provide the context of the novel, and more especially the context from which Frederick moves toward his final complete awareness.

The final awareness means, as we have said, that the individual is thrown back upon his private discipline and his private capacity to endure. The hero cuts himself off from the herd, the confused world, which symbolically appears as the routed army at Caporetto. And, as Malcolm Cowley has pointed out, the plunge into the flooded Tagliamento, when Frederick escapes from the battle police, has the significance of a rite. By this "baptism" Frederick is reborn into another world; he comes out into the world of the man alone, no longer supported by and involved in society.

> Anger was washed away in the river along with my obligation. Although that ceased when the carabiniere put his hands on my collar. I would like to have had the uniform off although I did not care much about the outward forms. I had taken off the stars, but that was for convenience. It was no point of honor. I was not against them. I was through. I wished them all the luck. There were the good ones, and the brave ones, and the calm ones and the sensible ones, and they deserved it. But it was not my show any more and I wished this bloody train would get to Maestre and I would eat and stop thinking.

So Frederick, by a decision, does what the boy Nick does as the result of the accident of a wound. He makes a "separate peace." And from the waters of the flooded Tagliamento arises the Hemingway hero in his purest form, with human history and obligation washed away, ready to enact the last phase of his appropriate drama, and learn from his inevitable defeat the lesson of lonely fortitude.

This is not the time to attempt to give a final appraisal of Hemingway's work as a whole or even of this particular novel—if there is ever a time for a "final" appraisal. But we may touch on some of the objections which have been brought against his work.

First, there is the objection that his work is immoral or dirty or disgusting. This objection appeared in various quarters against A Farewell to Arms at the time of its first publication. For instance, Robert Herrick wrote that if suppression were to be justified at all it would be justified in this case. He said that the book had no significance, was merely a "lustful indulgence," and smelled of the "boudoir," and summarized his view by calling it "garbage." That objection has, for the most part, died out, but its echoes can still be occasionally heard, and now and then at rare intervals some bigot or high-minded but uninstructed moralist will object to the inclusion of A Farewell to Arms in a college course.

The answer to this moralistic objection is fundamentally an answer to the charge that the book has no meaning. The answer would seek to establish the fact that the book does deal seriously with a moral and philosophical issue, which, for better or worse, does exist in the modern world in substantially the terms presented by Hemingway. This means that the book, even if it does not end with a solution that is generally acceptable, still embodies a moral effort and is another document of the human effort to achieve ideal values. As for the bad effect it may have on some readers, the best answer is perhaps to be found in a quotation from Thomas Hardy, who is now sanctified but whose most famous novels, *Tess of the D'Urbervilles* and *Jude the Obscure*, once suffered the attacks of the dogmatic moralists, and one of whose books was burned by a bishop:

> Of the effects of such sincere presentation on weak minds, when the courses of the characters are not exemplary and the rewards and punishments ill adjusted to deserts, it is not our duty to consider too closely. A novel which does moral injury to a dozen imbeciles, and has bracing results upon intellects of normal vigor, can justify its existence; and probably a novel was never written by the purest-minded author for which there could not be found some moral invalid or other whom it was capable of harming.

Second, there is the objection that Hemingway's work, especially of the period before *To Have and Have Not*, has no social relevance, that it is off the main stream of modern life, and that it has no concern with the economic structure of society. Critics who hold this general view regard Hemingway, like Joseph Conrad and perhaps like Henry James, as an exotic. There are several possible lines of retort to this objection. One line is well stated in the following passage by David Daiches if we substitute the name of Hemingway for Conrad:

> Thus it is no reproach to Conrad that he does not concern himself at all with the economic and social background underlying human relationships in modern civilization, for he never sets out to study those relationships. The Marxists cannot accuse him of cowardice or falsification, because in this case the charge is not relevent [though it might be relevant to *To Have and Have Not* or to *For Whom the Bell Tolls*]. That, from the point of view of the man with a theory, there are accidents in history, no one can deny. And if a writer chooses to discuss those accidents rather than the events which follow the main stream of historical causation, the economic, or other, determinist can only shrug his shoulder and maintain that these events are less instructive to the students than are the major events which he chooses to study; but he cannot accuse the writer of falsehood or distortion.

That much is granted by one of the ablest critics of the group who would find Hemingway an exotic. But a second line of retort would fix on the word *instructive* in the foregoing passage, and would ask what kind of instruction, if any, is to be expected of fiction, as fiction. Is the kind of instruction expected of fiction in direct competition, at the same level, with the kind of instruction offered in Political Science I or Economics II? If that is the case, then out with Shakespeare and Keats and in with Upton Sinclair.

Perhaps *instruction* is not a relevant word, after all, for this case. This is a very thorny and debatable question, but it can be ventured that what good fiction gives us is the stimulation of a powerful image of human nature trying to fulfill itself, and not instuction in an abstract sense. The economic man and political man are important aspects of human nature and may well constitute part of the *materials* of fiction. Neither the economic nor the political man is the complete man; other concerns may still be important enough to engage the attention of a writer—such concerns as love, death, courage, the point of honor, and the moral scruple. A man has to live with other men in terms not only of economic and political arrangements but also of moral arrangements; and he has to live with himself, he has to define himself. It can truly be said that these concerns are all interrelated in fact, but it might be dangerously dogmatic to insist that a writer should not bring one aspect into sharp, dramatic focus.

And it might be dangerously dogmatic to insist that Hemingway's ideas are not relevant to modern life. The mere fact that they exist and have stirred a great many people is a testimony to their relevance. Or to introduce a variation on that theme, it might be dogmatic to object to his work on the ground that he has few basic ideas. The history of literature seems to show that good artists may have very few *basic* ideas. They may have many ideas, but the ideas do not lead a life of democratic give-and-take, of genial camaraderie. No, there are usually one or two basic, obsessive ones. Like Savonarola, the artist may well say: *"Le mie cose erano poche e grandi."* And the ideas of the artist are grand simply because they are intensely felt, intensely realized—not because they are, by objective standards, by public, statistical standards, "important." No, that kind of public, statistical importance may be a condition of their being grand but is not of the special essence of their grandeur. (Perhaps not even the condition—perhaps the grandeur inheres in the fact that the artistic work shows us a parable of meaning—how idea is felt and how passion becomes idea through order.)

An artist may need few basic ideas, but in assessing his work we must introduce another criterion in addition to that of intensity. We must introduce the criterion of area. An artist's basic ideas do not operate in splendid isolation; to a greater or lesser degree, they prove themselves by their conquest of other ideas. Or again differently, the focus is a focus of experience, and the area of experience involved gives us another criterion of condition, the criterion of area. Perhaps an example would be helpful here. We have said that Hemingway is concerned with the scruple of honor, that this is a basic idea in his work. But we find that he applies this idea to a relatively small area of experience. In fact, we never see a story in which the issue involves the problem of definition of the scruple, nor do we ever see a story in which honor calls for a slow, grinding, day-to-day conquest of nagging difficulties. In other words, the idea is submitted to the test of a relatively small area of experience, to experience of a hand-picked sort, and to characters of a limited range.

But within that range, within the area in which he finds congenial material and in which competing ideas do not intrude themselves too strongly, Hemingway's expressive capacity is very powerful and the degree of intensity is very great. He is concerned not to report variety of human nature or human situation, or to analyze the forces operating in society, but to communicate a certain feeling about, a certain attitude toward, a special issue. That is, he is essentially a lyric rather than a dramatic writer, and for the lyric writer virtue depends upon the intensity with which the personal vision is rendered rather than upon the creation of a variety of characters whose visions are in conflict among themselves. And though Hemingway has not given—and never intended to give—a documented diagnosis of our age, he has given us one of the most compelling symbols of a personal response to our age.

HARRY LEVIN

Observations on the Style
of Ernest Hemingway

"The most important author living to-day, the outstanding author since the death of Shakespeare," is Ernest Hemingway. So we have lately been assured by John O'Hara in *The New York Times Book Review*. We should have to know what Mr. O'Hara thinks of the various intervening authors, of Shakespeare himself, and indeed of literature, in order to get the full benefit of this evaluation. It might be inferred, from his view of *Across the River and into the Trees*, that he holds them well on this side of idolatry. Inasmuch as Hemingway's latest novel tends regrettably to run certain attitudes and mannerisms to the ground, merely to describe it—if I may use an unsportsmanlike simile—is like shooting a sitting bird. Mr. O'Hara's gallant way of protecting this vulnerable target is to charge the air with invidious comparisons. His final encomium should be quoted in full, inasmuch as it takes no more than two short words, which manage to catch the uncertainty of the situation as well as the strident unsteadiness of Mr. O'Hara's tone: "Real class." That interesting phrase, which could be more appropriately applied to a car or a girl, carries overtones of petty snobbery; it seems to look up toward an object which, it admits in wistful awe, transcends such sordid articles of the same commodity as ordinarily fall within its ken. To whistle after Hemingway in this fashion is doubtless a sincerer form of flattery than tributes which continue to be inhibited by the conventions of literary discourse. Had Mr. O'Hara been a French symbolist poet, he might have said: *Tout le reste est littérature.*

Yet Hemingway too, one way or another, is literature. If his preoccupation has been mortality, his ambition—spurred perhaps by having easily won such rewards as contemporaries offer—is nothing less than immortality. He doesn't speak of building a monument or even burning a candle, but he sometimes refers to playing in the big league or writing something that will not soon go bad. Shakespeare, as Colonel Cantwell acknowledges in *Across the River*, is "the winner and still the undisputed champion." But Mr. O'Hara's buildup seems to suggest that Hemingway is training for the title bout. At least there are confirmatory signs, to state the matter in milder and more bookish terms, that he is becoming a classic in his time. He has just become the subject of "a critical survey" which should be welcomed as the first of its kind, with the expectation that its shortcomings will probably be made good by a long shelf of future volumes devoted to *Hemingwayforschung*. Since the present volume has been pasted together from other publications, it does not pretend to originality; it offers a readable and typical selection of twenty-one reviews and articles. This sort of symposium, especially when it concentrates upon so compact a body of material, is bound to cross and recross familiar territory. It is no discredit to the contributors—in fact it reinforces their positions—that they do not diverge from each other more variously. However, it raises questions reflecting upon the judgment and knowledge of the anthologist.

He does not seem to have cast a very wide net. Given the scope and impact of his author, we might fairly expect international representation. But, except for one Soviet contribution, the table of contents is one hundred per cent American, thereby excluding such significant essays as the almost classical polemic of Wyndham Lewis or the more recent appreciation of Claude-Edmonde Magny. Closer to home, it is hard to see how the editor—whose introduction strives to counterbalance the negative emphasis of so much criticism—could have overlooked the handsome tribute and prescient revaluation by Robert Penn Warren, which appeared in *The Kenyon Review* (Winter, 1947). Yet sins of omission, with anthologies, should always be considered venial; and we need not question the individual merits of the editor's inclusions. Some of them justify their place by being too little known and not readily accessible: notably Lincoln Kirstein's sensitive review of *Death in the Afternoon* and Edward Fenimore's informative article on the language of *For Whom the Bell Tolls*. But others, though not less notable, are not so readily justified: chapters from volumes still in print by Edmund Wilson, Alfred Kazin, and W.M. Frohock. It should also be pointed out that Malcolm Cowley has published better pieces on Hemingway than the profile that Mr. McCaffery reprints from

Life. The editor might have done a more useful job by collecting Hemingway's unreprinted writings. These are not touched upon by the bibliography, which is therefore inadequate; and there are no notes to identify the contributors, though several of them require identification. Since the chronological arrangement is based on dates of books, rather than periodical publication, it is somewhat misleading.

Yet when these cavils have been duly registered, it should be acknowledged that the book remains faithful to its protagonist. Its qualities and defects, like his, are journalistic—and I use that term in no deprecatory spirit, for journalism has more often than not been the school of our ablest writers, from Mark Twain to Hemingway himself. I simply refer to the losing race that fiction runs against fact, the hot pursuit of immediate reality in which the journalist outstrips the novelist, and also the risks—artistic as well as physical—that the imaginative writer takes by competing on the reporter's ground. For one thing, the successful reporter is seldom content to remain a good observer; give him a by-line, and he starts writing about himself; and he ends by making news for his professional colleagues, the gossip columnists. From all accounts, including his own, it would seem that, as a correspondent in the last war, Hemingway saw action in more ways than one. It may be that his refusal to draw the line between actor and spectator is one of the secrets of his vitality. Herein it is reported by John Groth that "Hemingway's jeep driver knew him as Hemingway the guy, rather than Hemingway the famous writer." And Mr. McCaffery devotes his particular enthusiasm to "Hemingway as a man among men." We see him plain; we hear and applaud his feats as soldier, traveler, sportsman, athlete, and playboy; and sooner or later we find ourselves asking why this consummate extrovert should have taken the trouble to become a famous writer.

If he was, as we are informed, "an okay joe" to his comrades in arms, he is something more complex to his fellow writers. Their collected opinions range from grudging admiration to fascinated suspicion. Though most of them make their separate peace with him, they leave a total impression which is fairly consistent and surprisingly hostile. The exception that proves the rule, in this case Elliot Paul, is the warm admirer who demonstrates his loyalty by belaboring Hemingway's critics. Few of them are able to maintain the distinction, premised by Mr. McCaffery's subtitle, between "the man" and "his work." Curiously enough, the single essay that undertakes to deal with craftsmanship is the one that emanates from Marxist Russia. The rest, though they incidentally contain some illuminating comments on technique, seem more interested in recapitulating the phases of Hemingway's career, in treating him as the spokesman of his generation, or in coming to grips with a natural phenomenon. All this is an impressive testimonial to the force of his personality. Yet what is personality, when it manifests itself in art, if not style? It is not because of the figure he cuts in the rotogravure sections, or for his views on philosophy and politics, that we listen to a leading *Heldentenor*. No contemporary voice has excited more admiration and envy, stimulated more imitation and parody, more admiration and envy, stimulated more imitation and parody and had more effect on the rhythms of our speech than Hemingway's has done. Ought we not then, first and last, to be discussing the characteristics of his prose, when we talk about a man who—as Archibald MacLeish has written—"whittled a style for his time"?

II

Mr. Hemingway, in his turn, would hardly be himself—which he is, of course, quite as consciously as any writer could be—if he did not take a dim view of criticism. This is understandable and, as he would say, right: since criticism, ever seeking perspective, moves in the very opposite direction from his object, which has been immediacy. His ardent quest for experience has involved him in a lifelong campaign against everything that tends to get in its way, including those more or less labored efforts to interpret and communicate it which may be regarded—if not disregarded—as academic. Those of us who live in the shelter of the academy will not be put off by his disregard; for most of us have more occasion than he to be repelled by the encrustations of pedantry; and many of us are predisposed to sympathize with him, as well as with ourselves, when he tells us what is lacking in critics and scholars. That he continues to do so is a mark of attention which ought not to go unappreciated. Thus currently, in introducing a brilliant young Italian novelist to American readers, he departs from his subject to drive home a critical contrast:

> The Italy that [Elio Vittorini] learned and the America that the American boys learned [writes Ernest Hemingway, making a skillful transition] has little to do with the Academic Italy or America that periodically attacks all writing like a dust storm and is always, until everything shall be completely dry, dispersed by rain.

Since Hemingway is sparing in his use of metaphors, the one he introduces here is significant. "Dryasdust" has long been the layman's stock epithet for the results of scholarly inquiry; while drouth, as evoked by T.S. Eliot, has become a basic symbol of modern anxiety. The country that seems to interest Hemingway most, Spain, is in some respects a literal wasteland; and his account of it—memorably his sound track for the Joris Ivens film, *The Spanish Earth*—emphasizes its dryness. Water, the contrasting element, for Hemingway as for his fellow men, symbolizes the purification and renewal of life. Rain beats out a cadence which runs through his work: through *A Farewell to Arms*, for example, where it lays the dust raised by soldiers' boots at the outset, accompanies the retreat from Caporetto, and stays with the hero when the heroine dies—even providing the very last word at the end. It is rain which, in a frequently quoted paragraph, shows up the unreality of "the words sacred, glorious, and sacrifice and the expression in vain." In the present instance, having reduced the contemporary situation to a handful of dust, as it were, Hemingway comes back to that sense of reality which he is willing to share with Vittorini. In the course of a single sentence, utilizing a digressive Ciceronian device, paraleipsis, he has not only rounded up such writers as he considers academic; he has not only accused them of sterility, by means of that slippery logical short cut which we professors term an enthymeme; but, like the veteran strategist he is, he has also managed to imply that they are the attackers and that he is fighting a strictly defensive action.

The conflict advances into the next paragraph, which opens on the high note that closed the previous one and then drops down again anticlimactically:

> Rain to an academician is probably, after the first fall has cleared the air,
> H_2O with, of course, traces of other things.

Even the ultimate source of nature's vitality is no more than a jejune scientific formula to us, if I may illustrate Hemingway's point by paraphrasing his sentence. Whereas—and for a moment it seems as if the theme of fertility would be sounded soon again—but no, the emphasis waxes increasingly negative:

> To a good writer, needing something to bring the dry country alive so that it will not be a desert where only such cactus as New York literary reviews grow dry and sad, inexistent without the watering of their benefactors, feeding on the dried manure of schism and the dusty taste of disputed dialectics, their only flowering a desiccated criticism as alive as stuffed birds, and their steady mulch the dehydrated cuds of fellow critics; . . .

There is more to come, but we had better pause and ruminate upon this particular mouthful. Though we may or may not accept Hemingway's opinion, we must admit that he makes us taste his distaste. Characteristically, he does not countercriticize or state the issue in intellectual terms.

Instead he proceeds from agriculture to the dairy, through an atmosphere calculated to make New Yorkers uncomfortable, elaborating his earthy metaphor into a barnyard allegory which culminates in a scatological gesture. The gibe about benefactors is a curious one, since it appears to take commercial success as a literary criterion, and at the same time to identify financial support with spiritual nourishment. The hopeful adjective "alive," repeated in this deadening context, is ironically illustrated by a musty ornithological specimen: so much for criticism! Such a phrase as "disputed dialectics," which is unduly alliterative, slightly tautological, and—like "cactus"—ambiguously singular or plural, touches a sphere where the author seems ill at ease. He seems more sure of his ground when, after this muttered parenthesis, he returns to his starting point, turns the prepositional object into a subject, and sets out again toward his predicate, toward an affirmation of mellow fruitfulness:

> . . . such a writer finds rain to be made of knowledge, experience, wine, bread, oil, salt, vinegar, bed, early mornings, nights, days, the sea, men, women, dogs, beloved motor cars, bicycles, hills and valleys, the appearance and disappearance of trains on straight and curved tracks, love, honor and disobey, music, chamber music and chamber pots, negative and positive Wassermanns, the arrival and non-arrival of expected munitions and/or reinforcements, replacements or your brother.

These are the "other things" missed by the academician and discerned by the "good writer"—whether he be Vittorini or Hemingway. It is by no means a casual inventory; each successive item, artfully chosen, has its meaningful place in the author's scheme of things. Knowledge is equated with experience, rendered concrete by the staple fare of existence, and wet down by essential liquids redolent of the Mediterranean; bed, with its double range of elementary associations, initiates a temporal cycle which revolves toward the timeless sea. Men, women, and dogs follow each other in unrelieved sequence; but the term of endearment, "beloved," is reserved for motor cars; while wavering alternatives suggest the movement of other vehicles over the land. Then come the great abstractions, love and honor, which are undercut by a cynical negation of the marriage ceremony, "disobey." Since chamber music sounds high-brow, it must be balanced against the downright vulgarity of chamber pots. The pangs of sex are scientifically neutralized by the reference to Wassermann tests, and the agonies of war are deliberately stated in the cool and/or colorless jargon of military dispatches. The final choice, "replacements or your brother," possibly echoes a twist of Continental slang (*et ton frère!*); but, more than that, it suddenly replaces a strategic loss with a personal bereavement.

The sentence, though extended, is not periodic: instead of suspending its burden, it falls back on anacoluthon, the rhetoric of the gradual breakdown and the fresh start. Hence, the first half is an uncharacteristic and unsuccessful endeavor to complete an elaborate grammatical structure which soon gets out of control. The second half thereupon brings the subject as quickly and simply as possible to its object, which opens up at once into the familiar Hemingway catalogue, where effects can be gained seriatim by order rather than by construction. After the chain of words has reached its climactic phrase, "your brother," it is rounded out by another transitional sentence:

> All these are a part of rain to a good writer along with your hated or beloved mother, may she rest in peace or in pieces, porcupine quills, cock grouse drumming on a basswood log, the smell of sweet grass and fresh-smoked leather and Sicily.

This time love dares to appear in its primary human connection, but only in ambivalence with hatred, and the hazards of sentimentality are hysterically avoided by a trite pun. And though the final images resolve the paragraph by coming back to the Sicilian locale of Vittorini's novel, they savor more of the northern woods of Hemingway's Upper Peninsula. Meanwhile the digression has served its purpose for him and for ourselves; it has given us nothing less than his definition of knowledge—not book knowledge, of course, but the real thing. Thus Robert Jordan decides to write a book about his adventures in Spain: "But only about the things he knew, truly, and about what he knew." Such a book is Hemingway's novel about him, *For Whom the Bell Tolls*; and what he knew, there put into words, is already one remove away from experience. And when Hemingway writes about Vittorini's novel, unaccustomed though he is to operating on the plane of criticism, he is two removes away from the objects he mentions in his analysis—or should I call it a hydroanalysis? Critics—and I have in mind Wyndham Lewis—have called his writing "the prose of reality." It seems to come closer to life than other prose, possibly too close for Mr. Lewis, yet for better or worse it happens to be literature. Its effectiveness lies in virtually persuading us that it is not writing at all. But though it may feel like walks in the rain or punches in the jaw, to be literal, it consists of words on the page. It is full of half-concealed art and self-revealing sacrifice. Since Hemingway is endlessly willing to explicate such artful and artificial pursuits as bullfighting and military tactics, he ought not to flinch under technical scrutiny.

III

Hemingway's hatred for the profession of letters stems quite obviously from a lover's quarrel. When Richard Gordon is reviled by his dissatisfied wife in *To Have and Have Not*, her most embittered epithet is "you writer." Yet Hemingway's writing abounds in salutes to various fellow writers, from the waitress's anecdote about Henry James in *Torrents of Spring* to Colonel Cantwell's spiritual affinity with D'Annunzio. And from Nick Adams, who takes Meredith and Chesterton along on fishing trips, to Hemingway himself, who arranges to be interviewed on American literature in *Green Hills of Africa*, his heroes do not shy away from critical discussion. His titles, so often quoted from books by earlier writers, have been so apt that they have all but established a convention. He shows an almost academic fondness, as well as a remarkable flair, for epigraphs: the Colonel dies with a quotation on his lips. Like all of us, Hemingway has been influenced by T.S. Eliot's taste for Elizabethan drama and metaphysical poetry. Thus Hemingway's title, "In Another Country," is borrowed from a passage he elsewhere cites, which he might have found in Marlowe's *Jew of Malta* or possibly in Eliot's "Portrait of a Lady." A *Farewell to Arms*, which echoes Lovelace's title, quotes in passing from Marvell's "To His Coy Mistress," echoed more recently by Robert Penn Warren, which is parodied in *Death in the Afternoon*. Hemingway is no exception to the rule that makes parody the starting point for realistic fiction. Just as Fielding took off from Richardson, so Hemingway takes off from Sherwood Anderson—indeed his first novel, *Torrents of Spring*, which parodies Anderson's *Dark Laughter*, is explicit in its acknowledgments to *Joseph Andrews*. It has passages, however, which read today like a pastiche of the later Hemingway:

> Yogi was worried. There was something on his mind. It was spring, there was no doubt of that now, and he did not want a woman. He had worried about it a lot lately. There was no question about it. He did not want a woman. He couldn't explain it to himself. He had gone to the Public Library and asked for a book the night before. He looked at the librarian. He did not want her. Somehow she meant nothing to him.

A recoil from bookishness, after a preliminary immersion in it, provided Fielding's master, Cervantes, with the original impetus for the novel. In "A Banal Story" Hemingway provides us with his own variation on the theme of *Don Quixote*, where a writer sits reading about romance in a magazine advertisement, while in far-off Madrid a bullfighter dies and is buried. The ironic contrast—romantic preconception exploded by contact with harsh reality—is basic with Hemingway, as it has been with all novelists who have written effectively about war. The realism of his generation reacted, not only against Wilsonian idealism, but against Wilsonian rhetoric. Hence the famous paragraph from the Caporetto episode describing Frederic Henry's embarrassment before such abstract words as "glory" and "honor," which seem to him obscene beside the concrete names of places and numbers of roads. For a Spaniard, Hemingway notes in *Death in the Afternoon*, the abstraction may still have concreteness: honor may be "as real a thing as water, wine, or olive oil." It is not so for us: "All our words from loose using have lost their edge." And "The Gambler, The Nun, and The Radio" brings forward a clinching example: "Liberty, what we believed in, now the name of a Macfadden publication." That same story trails off in a litany which reduces a Marxist slogan to meaninglessness: "the opium of the people" is everything and nothing. Even more desolating, in "A Clean, Well-Lighted Place," is the reduction of the Lord's prayer to nothingness: "Our nada who art in nada . . ." Since words have become inflated and devalued, Hemingway is willing to recognize no values save those which can be immediately felt and directly pointed out. It is his verbal skepticism which leads toward what some critics have called his moral nihilism. Anything serious had better be said with a smile, stranger. The classic echo, "irony and pity," jingles through *The Sun Also Rises* like a singing commercial.

There is something in common between this attitude and the familiar British habit of understatement. "No pleasure in anything if you mouth it too much," says Wilson, the guide in "The Short Happy Life of Francis Macomber." Yet Jake, the narrator of *The Sun Also Rises*, protests—in the name of American garrulity—that the English use fewer words than the Eskimos. Spanish, the language of Hemingway's preference, is at once emotive and highly formal. His Spanish, to judge from *Death in the Afternoon*, is just as ungrammatical as his English. In "The Undefeated" his Spanish bullfighters are made to speak the slang of American prize fighters. Americanisms and Hispanisms, archaic and polyglot elements, are so intermingled in *For Whom the Bell Tolls* that it calls to mind what Ben Jonson said of *The Faerie Queene*: "Spenser writ no language." Hemingway offers a succinct example by translating "*Eras mucho caballo*" as "Thou wert plenty of horse." It is somewhat paradoxical that a writer, having severely cut down his English vocabulary, should augment it by continual importation from other languages, including the Swahili. But this is a facet of the larger paradox that a writer so essentially American should set the bulk of his work against foreign backgrounds. His characters, expatriates for the most part, wander through the ruins of

Babel, smattering many tongues and speaking a demotic version of their own. Obscenity presents another linguistic problem, for which Hemingway is not responsible; but his coy ways of circumventing the taboos of censorship are more of a distraction than the conventional blanks. When he does permit himself an expression not usually considered printable, in *Death in the Afternoon*, the context is significant. His interlocutor, the Old Lady, requests a definition and he politely responds: "Madam, we apply the term now to describe unsoundness in abstract conversation or, indeed, any overmetaphysical tendency in speech."

For language, as for literature, his feeling is strongly ambivalent. Perhaps it could be summed up by Pascal's maxim: *"La vraie éloquence se moque de l'éloquence."* Like the notorious General Cambronne, Hemingway feels that one short spontaneous vulgarism is more honest than all those grandiloquent slogans which rhetoricians dream up long after the battle. The disparity between rhetoric and experience, which became so evident during the First World War, prompted the twenties to repudiate the genteel stylistic tradition and to accept the American vernacular as our norm of literary discourse. "Literary" is a contradiction in terms, for the resultant style is basically oral; and when the semiliterate speaker takes pen in hand, as Hemingway demonstrates in "One Reader Writes"—as H.L. Mencken demonstrated in "A Short View of Gamalielese"—the result is even more artificial than if it had been written by a writer. A page is always flat, and we need perspective to make it convey the illusion of life in the round. Yet the very fact that words means so much less to us than the things they represent in our lives is a stimulus to our imaginations. In "Fathers and Sons" young Nick Adams reads that Caruso has been arrested for "mashing," and asks his father the meaning of that expression.

> "It is one of the most heinous of crimes," his father answered. Nick's imagination pictured the great tenor doing something strange, bizarre, and heinous with a potato masher to a beautiful lady who looked like the pictures of Anna Held on the inside of cigar boxes. He resolved, with considerable horror, that when he was old enough he would try mashing at least once.

The tone of this passage is not altogether typical of Hemingway. Rather, as the point of view detaches itself affectionately and ironically from the youth, it approximates the early Joyce. This may help to explain why it suggests a more optimistic approach to language than the presumption that, since phrases can be snares and delusions, their scope should be limited to straight denotation. The powers of connotation, the possibilities of oblique suggestion and semantic association, are actually grasped by Hemingway as well as any writer of our time. Thus he can retrospectively endow a cheap and faded term like "mashing" with all the promise and poetry of awakening manhood. When Nick grows up, foreign terms will hold out the same allure to him; like Frederic Henry, he will seek the actuality that resides behind the names of places; and Robert Jordan will first be attracted to Spain as a professional philologist. But none of them will find an equivalence between the word and the thing; and Hemingway, at the end of *Death in the Afternoon*, laments that no book is big enough to do final justice to its living subject. "There was so much to write," the dying writer realizes in "The Snows of Kilimanjaro," and his last thoughts are moving and memorable recollections of some of the many things that will now go unwritten. Walt Whitman stated this challenge and this dilemma, for all good writers, when he spoke of expressing the inexpressible.

IV

The inevitable compromise, for Hemingway, is best expressed by his account of Romero's bullfighting style: "the holding of his purity of line through the maximum of exposure." The maximum of exposure—this throws much light upon the restlessness of Hemingway's career, but here we are primarily concerned with the holding of his purity of line. It had to be the simplest and most flexible of lines in order to accommodate itself to his desperate pursuit of material. His purgation of language has aptly been compared, by Robert Penn Warren, to the revival of diction that Wordsworth accomplished with *Lyrical Ballads*. Indeed the question that Coleridge afterward raised might once again be asked: why should the speech of some men be more real than that of others? Today that question restates itself in ideological terms: whether respect for the common man necessitates the adoption of a commonplace standard. Everyone who writes faces the same old problems, and the original writers—like Wordsworth or Hemingway—are those who develop new ways of meeting them. The case of Wordsworth would show us, if that of Hemingway did not, that those who break down conventions tend to substitute conventions of their own. Hemingway's prose is not without precedents; it is interesting to recall that his maiden effort, published by *The Double Dealer* in 1922, parodied the King James Bible. He has his forerunners in American fiction, from Cooper to Jack London, whose conspicuous lack was a style as dynamic as their subject matter. The ring-tailed roarers of the frontier, such as Davy Crockett, were colonel Cantwell's brothers under the skin;

but, as contrasted with the latter's tragic conception of himself, they were mock-heroic and seriocomic figures, who recommend themselves to the reader's condescension. Mark Twain has been the most genuine influence, and Hemingway has acknowledged this by declaring—with sweeping generosity—that *Huckleberry Finn* is the source of all modern American literature.

But Mark Twain was conducting a monologue, a virtual tour de force of impersonation, and he ordinarily kept a certain distance between his narrative role and his characters. And among Hemingway's elder contemporaries, Ring Lardner was a kind of ventriloquist, who made devastating use of the vernacular to satirize the vulgarity and stupidity of his dummies. It remained for Hemingway—along with Anderson—to identify himself wholly with the lives he wrote about, not so much entering into them as allowing them to take possession of him, and accepting—along with their sensibilities and perceptions—the limitations of their point of view and the limits of their range of expression. We need make no word count to be sure that his literary vocabulary, with foreign and technical exceptions, consists of relatively few and short words. The corollary, of course, is that every word sees a good deal of hard use. Furthermore, his syntax is informal to the point of fluidity, simplifying as far as possible the already simple system of English inflections. Thus "who" is normally substituted for "whom," presumably to avoid school-marmish correctness; and "that," doing duty for "which," seems somehow less prophetic of complexity. Personal pronouns frequently get involved in what is stigmatized, by teachers of freshman composition, as faulty reference; there are sentences in which it is hard to tell the hunter from his quarry or the bullfighter from the bull. "When his father died he was only a kid and his manager buried him perpetually." So begins, rather confusingly, "The Mother of a Queen." Sometimes it seems as if Hemingway were taking pains to be ungrammatical, as do many educated people out of a twisted sense of *noblesse oblige*. Yet when he comes closest to pronouncing a moral, the last words of Harry Morgan—the analphabetic hero of *To Have and Have Not*—seem to be half-consciously fumbling toward some grammatical resolution: "A man . . . ain't got no hasn't got any can't really isn't any way out. . . ."

The effectiveness of Hemingway's method depends very largely upon his keen ear for speech. His conversations are vivid, often dramatic, although he comes to depend too heavily upon them and to scant the other obligations of the novelist. Many of his wisecracks are quotable out of context, but as Gertrude Stein warned him: "Remarks are not literature." He can get his story told, and still be as conversational as he pleases, by telling it in the first person. "Brother, that was some storm," says the narrator, and the reader hears the very tone of his voice. In one of Hemingway's critical digressions, he declares that he has always sought "the real thing, the sequence of motion and fact which made [sic] the emotion. . . ." This seems to imply the clear-cut mechanism of verbal stimulus and psychological response that Eliot formulates in his theory of the objective correlative. In practice, however, Hemingway is no more of a behaviorist than Eliot, and the sharp distinction between motion and emotion is soon blurred. Consider his restricted choice of adjectives, and the heavy load of subjective implication carried by such uncertain mono-syllables as "fine" and "nice." From examples on nearly every page, we are struck by one which helps to set the scene for A Farewell to Arms: "The town was very nice and our house was very fine." Such descriptions—if we may consider them descriptions—are obviously not designed for pictorial effect. When the Colonel is tempted to call some fishing boats pictur-esque, he corrects himself: "The hell with picturesque. They are just damned beautiful." Where "picturesque" might sound arty and hence artificial, "beautiful"—with "damned" to take off the curse—is permissible because Hemingway has packed it with his own emotional charge. He even uses it in For Whom the Bell Tolls to express his esthetic apprecia-tion of gunfire. Like "fine" and "nice," or "good" and "lovely," it does not describe; it evaluates. It is not a stimulus but a projected response, a projection of the narrator's euphoria in a given situation. Hemingway, in effect, is saying to the reader: Having wonderful time. Wish you were here.

In short, he is communicating excitement; and if this communica-tion is received, it establishes a uniquely personal relationship; but when it goes astray, the diction goes flat and vague. Hemingway manages to sustain his reputation for concreteness by an exploring eye for the inciden-tal detail. The one typescript of his that I have seen, his carbon copy of "The Killers" now in the Harvard College Library, would indicate that the arc light and the tipped-back derby hat were later observations than the rest. Precision at times becomes so arithmetical that, in "The Light of the World," it lines up his characters like a drill sergeant: "Down at the station there were five whores waiting for the train to come in, and six white men and four Indians." Numbers enlarge the irony that concludes the opening chapter of A Farewell to Arms when, after a far from epic invocation, a casual introduction to the landscape, and a dusty record of troops falling back through the autumn, rain brings the cholera which kills off "only seven thousand." A trick of multiplication, which Heming-way may have picked up from Gertrude Stein, is to generalize the specific episode: "They always picked the finest places to have the quarrels."

When he offers this general view of a restaurant—"It was full of smoke and drinking and singing"—he is an impressionist if not an abstractionist. Thence to expressionism is an easy step: ". . . the room whirled." It happens that, under pressure from his first American publishers, the author was compelled to modify the phrasing of "Mr. and Mrs. Elliott." In the original version, subsequently restored, the title characters "try to have a baby." In the modified version they "think of having a baby." It could be argued that, in characterizing this rather tepid couple, the later verb is more expressive and no more euphemistic than the earlier one; that "think," at any rate, is not less precise or effectual than "try." But, whereas the sense of effort came naturally, the cerebration was an afterthought.

If we regard the adjective as a luxury, decorative more often than functional, we can well understand why Hemingway doesn't cultivate it. But, assuming that the sentence derives its energy from the verb, we are in for a shock if we expect his verbs to be numerous or varied or emphatic. His usage supports C.K. Ogden's argument that verb forms are disappearing from English grammar. Without much self-deprivation, Hemingway could get along on the so-called "operators" of Basic English, the sixteen monosyllabic verbs that stem from movements of the body. The substantive verb *to be* is predominant, characteristically introduced by an expletive. Thus the first story of *In Our Time* begins, and the last one ends, with the storyteller's gambit: "there was," "there were." In the first two pages of *A Farewell to Arms* nearly every other sentence is of this type, and the third page employs the awkward construction, "there being." There is—I find the habit contagious—a tendency to immobilize verbs by transposing them into gerunds. Instead of writing *they fought* or *we did not feel*, Hemingway writes "there was fighting" and "there was not the feeling of a storm coming." The subject does little more than point impersonally at its predicate: an object, a situation, an emotion. Yet the idiom, like the French *il y a*, is ambiguous; inversion can turn the gesture of pointing into a physical act; and the indefinite adverb can indicate, if not specify, a definite place. Contrast, with the opening of *A Farewell to Arms*, that of "In Another Country": "In the fall the war was always there, but we did not go to it any more." The negative is even more striking, when Frederic Henry has registered the sensations of his wound, and dares to look at it for the first time, and notes: "My knee wasn't there." The adverb is *there* rather than *here*, the verb is *was* rather than *is*, because we—the readers— are separated from the event in space and time. But the narrator has lived through it, like the Ancient Mariner, and now he chooses his words to grip and transfix us. *Lo!* he says. *Look! I was there.*

V

Granted, then, that Hemingway's diction is thin; that, in the technical sense, his syntax is weak; and that he would rather be caught dead than seeking the *mot juste* or the balanced phrase. Granted that his adjectives are not colorful and his verbs not particularly energetic. Granted that he commits as many literary offenses as Mark Twain brought to book with Fenimore Cooper. What is behind his indubitable punch, the unexampled dynamics of Hemingway's style? How does he manage, as he does, to animate this characteristic sentence from "After the Storm"?

> I said "Who killed him?" and he said "I don't know who killed him but he's dead all right," and it was dark and there was water standing in the street and no lights and windows broke and boats all up in the town and trees blown down and everything all blown and I got a skiff and went out and found my boat where I had her inside of Mango Key and she was all right only she was full of water.

Here is a good example of Hemingway's "sequence of motion and fact." It starts from dialogue and leads into first-person action; but the central description is a single clause, where the expletive takes the place of the observer and his observations are registered one by one. Hence, for the reader, it lives up to Robert Jordan's intention: "you . . . feel that all that happened to you." Hemingway puts his emphasis on nouns because, among parts of speech, they come closest to things. Stringing them along by means of conjunctions, he approximates the actual flow of experience. For him, as for Marion Tweedy Bloom, the key word is *and*, with its renewable promise of continuity, occasionally varied by *then* and *so*. The rhetorical scheme is polysyndeton—a large name for the childishly simple habit of linking sentences together. The subject, when it is not taken for granted, merely puts us in touch with the predicate: the series of objects that Hemingway wants to point out. Even a preposition can turn this trick, as "with" does in this account of El Sordo waiting to see the whites of his enemy's eyes:

> Come on, Comrade Voyager . . . Keep on coming with your eyes forward . . . Look. With a red face and blond hair and blue eyes. With no cap on and his moustache is yellow. With blue eyes. With pale blue eyes. With pale blue eyes with something wrong with them. With pale blue eyes that don't focus. Close enough. Too close. Yes, Comrade Voyager. Take it, Comrade Voyager.

Prose gets as near as it can to physical conflict here. The figure enlarges as it advances, the quickening impression grows clear and sharp and almost unbearable, whereupon it is blackened out by El Sordo's rifle. Each clipped sentence, each prepositional phrase, is like a new frame in a strip of film; indeed the whole passage, like so many others, might have been filmed by the camera and projected on the screen. The course of Harry Morgan's launch speeding through the Gulf Stream, or of Frederic Henry's fantasy ascending the elevator with Catherine Barkley, is given this cinematographic presentation. *Green Hills of Africa* voices the long-range ambition of obtaining a fourth and fifth dimension in prose. Yet if the subordinate clause and the complex sentence are the usual ways for writers to obtain a third dimension, Hemingway keeps his writing on a linear plane. He holds the purity of his line by moving in one direction, ignoring sidetracks and avoiding structural complications. By presenting a succession of images, each of which has its brief moment when it commands the reader's undivided attention, he achieves his special vividness and fluidity. For what he lacks in structure he makes up in sequence, carefully ordering visual impressions as he sets them down and ironically juxtaposing the various items on his lists and inventories. "A Way You'll Never Be" opens with a close-up showing the debris on a battlefield, variously specifying munitions, medicaments, and leftovers from a field kitchen, then closing in on the scattered papers with this striking montage effect: ". . . group postcards showing the machine-gun unit standing in ranked and ruddy cheerfulness as in a football picture for a college annual; now they were humped and swollen in the grass. . . ." It is not surprising that Hemingway's verse, published by *Poetry* in 1923, is recognizably imagistic in character—and perhaps his later heroics are foreshadowed by the subject of one of those poems, Theodore Roosevelt.

In her observant book, *L'Age du roman américain*, Claude-Edmonde Magny stresses Hemingway's "exaltation of the instant." We can note how this emphasis is reflected in his timing, which—after his placing has bridged the distance from *there* to *here*—strives to close the gap between *then* and *now*. Where Baudelaire's clock said "remember" in many languages, Robert Jordan's memory says: "Now, *ahora, maintenant, heute.*" When death interrupts a dream, in "The Snows of Kilimanjaro," the ultimate reality is heralded by a rising insistence upon the word "now." It is not for nothing that Hemingway is the younger contemporary or Proust and Joyce. Though his time is neither *le temps perdu* nor the past nostalgically recaptured, he spends it gathering roses while he can, to the ever-accelerating rhythm of headlines and telegrams and loud-speakers. The act, no sooner done than said, becomes simultaneous with the word, no sooner said than felt. Hemingway goes so far, in "Fathers and Sons," as to render a sexual embrace by an onomatopoetic sequence of adverbs.

But, unlike Damon Runyon and Dickens, he seldom narrates in the present tense, except in such sporting events as "Fifty Grand." Rather, his timeliness expresses itself in continuous forms of the verb and in his fondness for all kinds of participial constructions. These, compounded and multiplied, create an ambience of overwhelming activity, and the epithets shift from El Sordo's harassed feelings to the impact of the reiterated bullets, as Hemingway recounts "the last lung-aching, leg-dead, mouth-dry, bullet-spatting, bullet-cracking, bullet-singing run up the final slope of the hill." More often the meaning takes the opposite turn, and moves from the external plane into the range of a character's senses, proceeding serially from the visual to the tactile, as it does when the "Wine of Wyoming" is sampled: "It was very light and clear and good and still tasted of the grapes."

When Nick Adams goes fishing, the temperature is very tangibly indicated: "It was getting hot, the sun hot on the back of his neck." The remark about the weather is thereby extended in two directions, toward the distant source of the heat and toward its immediate perception. Again in "Big Two-Hearted River," Nick's fatigue is measured by the weight of his pack: ". . . it was heavy. It was much too heavy." As in the movies, the illusion of movement is produced by repeating the same shot with further modification every time. Whenever a new clause takes more than one step ahead, a subsequent clause repeats it in order to catch up. Repetition, as in "Up in Michigan," brings the advancing narrative back to an initial point of reference. "Liz liked Jim very much. She liked it the way he walked over from the shop and often went to the kitchen door to watch him start down the road. She liked it about his moustache. She liked it about how white his teeth were when he smiled." The opaque verb "like," made increasingly transparent, is utilized five more times in this paragraph; and the fumbling preposition "about" may be an acknowl-edgment of Hemingway's early debt to Gertrude Stein. The situation is located somewhere between a subjective Liz and an objective Jim. The theme of love is always a test of Hemingway's objectivity. When Frederic kisses Catherine, her responses are not less moving because they are presented through his reflexes; but it is her sentimental conversation which leaves him free to ask himself: "What the hell?" At first glance, in a behavioristic formula which elsewhere recurs, Colonel Cantwell seems so hard-boiled that motions are his only emotions: "He saw that his hand was trembling." But his vision is blurred by conventionally romantic tenderness when he contemplates a heroine whose profile "could break your . . . or anyone else's heart." Hemingway's heroines, when they aren't bitches, are fantasies—or rather, the masculine reader is invited to supply his own, as with the weather in Mark Twain's *American Claimant*. They are pin-up girls.

If beauty lies in the eye of the beholder, Hemingway's purpose is to make his readers beholders. This is easily done when the narration is conducted in the first person; we can sit down and drink, with Jake Barnes, and watch Paris walk by. The interpolated chapters of *In Our Time*, most of them reminiscences from the army, employ the collective *we*; but, except for "My Old Man," the stories themselves are told in the third person. Sometimes, to strengthen the sense of identification, they make direct appeal to the second person; the protagonist of "Soldier's Home" is "you" as well as "he"—and, more generally, "a fellow." With the exception of Jake's confessions, that is to say *The Sun Also Rises*, all of Hemingway's novels are written in the *style indirect libre*—indirect discourse which more or less closely follows the consciousness of a central character. An increasing tendency for the author to intrude, commenting in his own person, is one of the weaknesses of *Across the River*. He derives his strength from a power to visualize episodes through the eyes of those most directly involved; for a page, in "The Short Happy Life of Francis Macomber," the hunt is actually seen from the beast's point of view. Hemingway's use of interior monologue is effective when sensations from the outer world are entering the stream of a character's consciousness, as they do with such a rush at El Sordo's last stand. But introspection is not Hemingway's genre, and the night thoughts of *To Have and Have Not* are among his least successful episodes. His best are events, which are never far to seek; things are constantly happening in his world; his leg-man, Nick Adams, happens to be the eyewitness of "The Killers." The state of mind that Hemingway communicates to us is the thrill that Nick got from skiing in "Cross Country Snow," which "plucked Nick's mind out and left him only the wonderful, flying, dropping sensation in his body."

VI

If psychological theories could be proved by works of fiction, Hemingway would lend his authority to the long-contested formula of William James, which equates emotion with bodily sensation. Most other serious writers, however, would bear witness to deeper ranges of sensibility and more complex processes of motivation than those he sees fit to describe. Some of them have accused Hemingway of aggressive anti-intellectualism: I am thinking particularly of Aldous Huxley. But Huxley's own work is so pure an example of all that Hemingway has recoiled from, so intellectual in the airiest sense, and so unsupported by felt experience, that the argument has played into Hemingway's hands. We have seen enough of the latter to know that he doesn't really hate books—himself having written a dozen, several of which are, and will remain, the best of their kind. As for his refusal to behave like a man of letters, he reminds us of Hotspur, who professes to be a laconic philistine and turns out—with no little grandiloquence—to be the most poetic character in Shakespeare's play. Furthermore, it is not Hemingway, but the sloganmongers of our epoch, who have debased the language; he has been attempting to restore some decent degree of correspondence between words and things; and the task of verification is a heavy one, which throws the individual back on his personal resources of awareness. That he has succeeded within limits, and with considerable strain, is less important than that he has succeeded, that a few more aspects of life have been captured for literature. Meanwhile the word continues to dematerialize, and has to be made flesh all over again; the firsthand perception, once it gets written down, becomes the secondhand notation; and the writer, who attains his individuality by repudiating literary affectation, ends by finding that he has struck a new pose and founded another school.

It is understandable why no critique of Hemingway, including this one, can speak for long of the style without speaking of the man. Improving on Buffon, Mark Schorer recently wrote: "[Hemingway's] style is not only his subject, it is his view of life." It could also be called his way of life, his *Lebenstil*. It has led him to live his books, to brave the maximum of exposure, to tour the world in an endless search for wars and their moral equivalents. It has cast him in the special role of our agent, our plenipotentiary, our roving correspondent on whom we depend for news from the fighting fronts of modern consciousness. Here he is, the man who was there. His writing seems so intent upon the actual, so impersonal in its surfaces, that it momentarily prompts us to overlook the personality behind them. That would be a serious mistake; for the point of view, though brilliantly intense, is narrowly focused and obliquely angled. We must ask: who is this guide to whom we have entrusted ourselves on intimate terms in dangerous places? Where are his limitations? What are his values? We may well discover that they differ from our assumptions, when he shows us a photograph of a bullfighter close to a bull, and comments: "If there is no blood on his belly afterwards you ought to get your money back." We may be ungrateful to question such curiosity, when we are indebted to it for many enlargements of our vicarious knowledge; and it may well spring from the callowness of the tourist rather than the morbidity of the voyeur, from the American zest of the fan who pays his money to reckon the carnage. When Spain's great poet García Lorca celebrated the very same theme, averting his gaze from the spilling of the blood, his refrain was *"Que no quiero verla!"* ("I do not want to see it!")

Yet Hemingway wants to see everything—or possibly he wants to be in a position to tell us that he has seen everything. While the boy Nick, his seeing eye, eagerly watches a Caesarean childbirth in "Indian Camp," the far from impassive husband turns away; and it is later discovered that he has killed himself. "He couldn't stand things . . ." so runs the diagnosis of Nick's father, the doctor. This, for Nick, is an initiation to suffering and death; but with the sunrise, shortly afterward, youth and well-being reassert themselves; and the end of the story reaffirms the generalization that Hazlitt once drew: "No young man ever thinks he shall die." It is easy enough for such a young man to stand things, for he is not yet painfully involved in them; he is not a sufferer but a wide-eyed onlooker, to whom the word "mashing" holds out mysterious enticements. Hemingway's projection of this attitude has given his best work perennial youthfulness; it has also armed his critics with the accusation that, like his Robert Cohn, he is "a case of arrested development." If this be so, his plight is generalized by the Englishman Wilson, who observes that "Americans stay little boys . . . all their lives." And the object of Wilson's observation, Francis Macomber, would furnish a classic case history for Adler, if not for Freud—the masculine sense of inferiority which seeks to overcome itself by acts of prowess, both sanguinary and sexual. Despite these two sources of excitement, the story is a plaintive modulation of two rather dissonant themes: *None but the brave deserves the fair* and *The female of the species is deadlier than the male.* After Francis Macomber has demonstrated his manhood, the next step is death. The world that remains most alive to Hemingway is that stretch between puberty and maturity which is strictly governed by the ephebic code: a world of mixed apprehension and bravado before the rite of passage, the baptism of fire, the introduction to sex.

Afterward comes the boasting, along with such surviving ideals as Hemingway subsumes in the word *cojones*—the English equivalent sounds more skeptical. But for Jake Barnes, all passion spent in the First World War, or for Colonel Cantwell, tired and disgruntled by the Second, the aftermath can only be elegiac. The weather-beaten hero of *Across the River*, which appears in 1950, is fifty years old and uneasily conscious of that fact; whereas "the childish, drunken heroics" of *The Sun Also Rises* took place just about twenty-five years ago. From his spectacular arrival in the twenties, Hemingway's course has paralleled that of our century; and now, at its mid-point, he balks like the rest of us before the responsibilities of middle age. When, if ever, does the *enfant du siècle*, that *enfant terrible*, grow up? (Not necessarily when he grows a beard and calls himself "Mr. Papa.") Frederic Henry plunges into the Po much as Huck Finn dived into the Mississippi, but emerges to remind us even more pointedly of Fabrice del Dongo in Stendhal's *Chartreuse de Parme*, and of our great contemporary shift from transatlantic innocence to Old-World experience. Certain intimations of later years are present in Hemingway's earlier stories, typically Ad Francis, the slap-happy ex-champ in "The Battler." Even in "Fifty Grand," his most contrived tale, the beat-up prizefighter suffers more than he acts and wins by losing—a situation which has its corollary in the title of Hemingway's third collection, *Winner Take Nothing*. The ultimate article of his credo, which he shares with Malraux and Sartre, is the good fight for the lost cause. And the ultimate protagonist is Jesus in "Today Is Friday," whose crucifixion is treated like an athletic feat, and whose capacity for taking punishment rouses a fellow feeling in the Roman soldiers. The stoic or masochistic determination to take it brings us back from Hemingway to his medium, which—although it eschews the passive voice—is essentially a receiving instrument, especially sensitized for recording a series of violent shocks.

The paradox of toughness and sensitivity is resolved, and the qualities and defects of his writing are reconciled, if we merely remember that he was—and still is—a poet. That he is not a novelist by vocation, if it were not revealed by his books, could be inferred from his well-known retort to F. Scott Fitzgerald. For Fitzgerald the rich were different—not quantitatively, because they had more money, but qualitatively, because he had a novelistic interest in manners and morals. Again, when we read André Gide's reports from the Congo, we realize what *Green Hills of Africa* lacks in the way of social or psychological insight. As W. M. Frohock has perceived, Hemingway is less concerned with human relations than with his own relationship to the universe—a concern which might have spontaneously flowered into poetry. His talents come out most fully in the texture of his work, whereas the structure tends to be episodic and uncontrived to the point of formlessness. *For Whom the Bell Tolls*, the only one of his six novels that has been carefully constructed, is in some respects an overexpanded short story. Editors rejected his earliest stories on the grounds that they were nothing but sketches and anecdotes, thereby paying incidental tribute to his sense of reality. Fragments of truth, after all, are the best that a writer can offer; and, as Hemingway has said, ". . . Any part you make will represent the whole if it's made truly." In periods as confusing as the present, when broader and maturer representations are likely to falsify, we are fortunate if we can find authenticity in the lyric cry, the adolescent mood, the tangible feeling, the trigger response. If we think of Hemingway's temperamental kinship with e.e. cummings, and of cummings's "Buffalo Bill" or "Olaf glad and big," it is easy to think of Hemingway as a poet. After the attractions and distractions of timeliness have been outdated, together with categorical distinctions between the rich and the poor, perhaps he will be remembered for a poetic vision which renews our interrupted contact with the timeless elements of man's existence: bread, wine, bed, music, and a few more concrete-universals. When El Sordo raises his glance from the battlefield, he looks up at the identical patch of blue sky that Henry Fleming saw in *The Red Badge of Courage* and that looked down on Prince Andrey in *War and Peace*.

CARLOS BAKER

The Way It Was

*"The job of the last twenty-five years was for the writer or artist to get
what there was to be got (artistically) out of the world extant."*

— EZRA POUND

"A writer's job is to tell the truth,"
said Hemingway in 1942. He had believed it for twenty years and he
would continue to believe it as long as he lived. No other writer of our
time had so fiercely asserted, so pugnaciously defended, or so consistently
exemplified the writer's obligation to speak truly. His standard of truth-
telling remained, moreover, so high and so rigorous that he was ordinarily
unwilling to admit secondary evidence, whether literary evidence or evidence picked up from other sources than his own experience. "I only
know what I have seen," was a statement which came often to his lips and
pen. What he had personally done, or what he knew unforgettably by
having gone through one version of it, was what he was interested in
telling about. This is not to say that he refused to invent freely. But he
always made it a sacrosanct point to invent in terms of what he actually
knew from having been there.

The primary intent of his writing, from first to last, was to seize
and project for the reader what he often called "the way it was." This is a
characteristically simple phrase for a concept of extraordinary complexity,
and Hemingway's conception of its meaning subtly changed several times
in the course of his career—always in the direction of greater complexity.
At the core of the concept, however, one can invariably discern the

operation of three esthetic instruments: the sense of place, the sense of fact, and the sense of scene.

The first of these, obviously a strong passion with Hemingway, is the sense of place. "Unless you have geography, background," he once told George Antheil, "you have nothing." You have, that is to say, a dramatic vacuum. Few writers have been more place-conscious. Few have so carefully charted out the geographical groundwork of their novels while managing to keep background so conspicuously unobtrusive. Few, accordingly, have been able to record more economically and graphically the way it is when you walk through the streets of Paris in search of breakfast at a corner café. Or when your footfalls echo among surrounding walls on the ancient cobblestones of early morning Venice, heading for the market-place beside the Adriatic. Or when, at around six o'clock of a Spanish dawn, you watch the bulls running from the corrals at the Puerta Rochapea through the streets of Pamplona towards the bullring.

"When I woke it was the sound of the rocket exploding that announced the release of the bulls from the corrals at the edge of town. . . . Down below the narrow street was empty. All the balconies were crowded with people. Suddenly a crowd came down the street. They were all running, packed close together. They passed along and up the street toward the bullring and behind them came more men running faster, and then some stragglers who were really running. Behind them was a little bare space, and then the bulls, galloping, tossing their heads up and down. It all went out of sight around the corner. One man fell, rolled to the gutter, and lay quiet. But the bulls went right on and did not notice him. They were all running together."

This scene is as morning-fresh as a design in India ink on clean white paper. First is the bare white street, seen from above, quiet and empty. Then one sees the first packed clot of runners. Behind these are the thinner ranks of those who move faster because closer to the bulls. Then the almost comic stragglers, who are "really running." Brilliantly behind these shines the "little bare space," a desperate margin for error. Then the clot of running bulls—closing the design, except of course for the man in the gutter making himself, like the designer's initials, as inconspicuous as possible.

The continuing freshness of such occasions as this might be associated with Hemingway's lifelong habit of early waking. More likely, the freshness arises because Hemingway loves continental cities, makes it almost a fetish to know them with an artist's eye, and has trained himself rigorously to see and retain those aspects of a place that make it *that place*, even though, with an odd skill, he manages at the same time to render these aspects generically.

As with the cities—and Hemingway's preference is for the Latin cities—so with the marshes, rivers, lakes, troutstreams, gulfstreams, groves, forests, hills, and gullies, from Wyoming to Tanganyika, from the Tagliamento to the Irati, and from Key West to the Golden Horn. "None can care for literature itself," said Stevenson, somewhere, "who do not take a special pleasure in the sound of names." Hemingway's love of names is obvious. It belongs to his sense of place. But like the rest of his language, it is under strict control. One never finds, as so often happens in the novels of Thomas Wolfe or the poetry of Carl Sandberg, the mere riot and revel of place-names, played upon like guitar-strings for the music they contain. Hemingway likes the words *country* and *land*. It is astonishing how often they recur in his work without being obtrusive. He likes to move from place to place, and to be firmly grounded, for the time being, in whatever place he has chosen. It may be the banks of the Big Two-Hearted River of northern Michigan or its Spanish equivalent above Burguete. It may be the Guadarrama hilltop where El Sordo died, or the Veneto marshes where Colonel Cantwell shot his last mallards from a duckblind. Wherever it is, it is solid and permanent, both in itself and in the books.

The earliest of his published work, descriptively speaking, shows an almost neoclassical restraint. Take a sample passage from *The Sun Also Rises*, not his earliest but fairly representative. This one concerns the Irati Valley fishing-trip of Jake Barnes and Bill Gorton.

> It was a beech wood and the trees were very old. Their roots bulked above the ground and the branches were twisted. We walked on the road between the thick trunks of the old beeches and the sunlight came through the leaves in light patches on the grass. The trees were big, and the foliage was thick but it was not gloomy. There was no undergrowth, only the smooth grass, very green and fresh, and the big gray trees were well spaced as though it were a park. "This is country," Bill said.

It is such country as an impressionist might paint almost exactly in the terms, and the subdued colors, which Hemingway employs. More than this, however, is the fact that in such a paragraph Dr. Samuel Johnson's Imlac could find little to criticize. Even the arrangement of the beech trees themselves, like the choice of the words, is clean and classical. The foliage is thick, but there is no gloom. Here is neither teeming undergrowth nor its verbal equivalent. The sage of Johnson's *Rasselas* advises all aspirant poets against numbering the streaks of the tulip or describing in detail the different shades of the verdure of the forest. Young Hemingway, still an aspirant poet, follows the advice. When he has finished, it is possible to say (and we supply our own inflection for Bill Gorton's words): "This is country."

For all the restraint, the avoidance of color-flaunting adjectives, and the plainsong sentences (five compound to one complex), the paragraph is loaded with precisely observed fact: beech wood, old trees, exposed roots, twisted branches, thick trunks, sunpatches, smooth green grass, foliage which casts a shade without excluding light. One cannot say that he has been given a generalized landscape—there are too many exact factual observations. On the other hand, the uniquenesses of the place receive no special emphasis. One recognizes easily the generic type of the clean and orderly grove, where weeds and brush do not flourish because of the shade, and the grass gets only enough light to rise to carpet-level. Undoubtedly, as in the neoclassical esthetic, the intent is to provide a generic frame within which the reader is at liberty to insert his own uniquenesses—as many or as few as his imagination may supply.

Along with the sense of place, and as a part of it, is the sense of fact. Facts march through all his pages in a stream as continuous as the refugee wagons in Thrace or the military camions on the road from the Isonzo. Speculation, whether by the author or by the characters, is ordinarily kept to a minimum. But facts, visible or audible or tangible facts, facts baldly stated, facts without verbal paraphernalia to inhibit their striking power, are the stuff of Hemingway's prose.

Sometimes, especially in the early work, the facts seem too many for the effect apparently intended, though even here the reader should be on guard against misconstruing the intention of a given passage. It is hard to discover, nevertheless, what purpose beyond the establishment of the sense of place is served by Barnes's complete itinerary of his walk with Bill Gorton through the streets of Paris. The direction is from Madame Lecomte's restaurant on the Île St. Louis across to the left bank of the Seine, and eventually up the Boulevard du Port Royal to the Café Select. The walk fills only two pages. Yet it seems much longer and does not further the action appreciably except to provide Jake and Bill with healthy after-dinner exercise. At Madame Lecomte's (the facts again), they have eaten "a roast chicken, new green beans, mashed potatoes, a salad, and some apple pie and cheese." To the native Parisian, or a foreigner who knows the city, the pleasure in the after-dinner itinerary would consist in the happy shock of recognition. For others, the inclusion of so many of the facts of municipal or gastronomic geography—so many more than are justified by their dramatic purpose—may seem excessive.

Still, this is the way it was that time in Paris. Here lay the bridges and the streets, the squares and the cafés. If you followed them in the prescribed order, you came to the café where Lady Brett Ashley sat on a high stool at the bar, her crossed legs stockingless, her eyes crinkling at the corners.

If an imaginative fusion of the sense of place and the sense of fact is to occur, and if, out of the fusing process, dramatic life is to arise, a third element is required. This may be called the sense of scene. Places are less than geography, facts lie inert and uncoordinated, unless the imagination runs through them like a vitalizing current and the total picture moves and quickens. How was it, for example, that second day of the San Fermin fiesta in the Pamplona bullring after Romero had killed the first bull?

"They had hitched the mules to the dead bull and then the whips cracked, the men ran, and the mules, straining forward, their legs pushing, broke into a gallop, and the bull, one horn up, his head on its side, swept a swath smoothly across the sand and out the red gate."

Here are a dead bull, men, mules, whips, sand, and a red gate like a closing curtain—the place and the facts. But here also, in this remarkably graphic sentence, are the seven verbs, the two adverbs, and the five adverbial phrases which fuse and coordinate the diverse facts of place and thing and set them in rapid motion. If one feels that the sentence is very satisfying as a scene, and wishes to know why, the answer might well lie where it so often lies in a successful lyric poem—that is, in our sense of difficulty overcome. Between the inertness of the dead bull when he is merely *hitched* (a placid verb) and the smooth speed with which the body finally *sweeps* across the sand and out of sight, come the verbs of sweating effort: *crack, run, strain,* and *break.* It is precisely at the verb *broke* that the sentence stops straining and moves into the smooth glide of its close. The massing, in that section of the sentence, of a half-dozen s's, compounded with the *th* sounds of *swath* and *smoothly,* can hardly have been inadvertent. They ease (or grease) the path of the bull's departure.

The pattern in the quoted passage is that of a task undertaken, striven through, and smoothly completed: order and success. For another graphic sentence, so arranged as to show the precise opposites—total disorder and total failure—one might take the following example from *Death in the Afternoon.* The protagonist is a "phenomenon," a bullfighter who has lost his nerve.

"In your mind you see the phenomenon, sweating, white-faced, and sick with fear, unable to look at the horn or go near it, a couple of swords on the ground, capes all around him, running in at an angle on the bull hoping the sword will strike a vital spot, cushions sailing down into the ring and the steers ready to come in."

In this passage, place has become predicament. The facts, thrown in almost helter-skelter, imply the desperate inward fear which is responsible for the creation of the outward disorder. Verbs are held to a minimum, and their natural naked power is limited with qualifications. The phenomenon is *unable to look*, and *hoping to strike*, not *looking* and *striking*. He runs, but it is at a bad angle. The disorder of the swords on the ground and the capes all around is increased by the scaling-in of seat-cushions from the benches, the audience's insult to gross cowardice. The author-spectator's crowning insult is the allusion to the steers, who by comparison with the enraged bull are bovine, old-womanly creatures. On being admitted to the ring, they will quiet and lead away the bull the phenomenon could not kill.

The sense of place and the sense of fact are indispensable to Hemingway's art. But the true craft, by which diversities are unified and compelled into graphic collaboration, comes about through the operation of the sense of scene. Often, moving through the Latin language countries, watching the crowd from a café table or a barrera bench, Hemingway seems like a lineal descendant of Browning's observer in *How It Strikes a Contemporary*.

> You saw go up and down Valladolid
> A man of mark, to know next time you saw . . .
> Scenting the world, looking it full in face.

WHAT HAPPENED

Although they are clearly fundamental to any consideration of Hemingway's esthetic aims, place, fact, and scene are together no more than one phase of a more complex observational interest. The skillful writer can make them work in harmony, with place and fact like teamed horses under the dominance of the sense of scene. The result is often as striking and satisfactory to watch as a good chariot race. But the event is, after all, mainly an extrinsic matter. These are not Plato's horses of the soul.

The complementary phase is inward: a state of mind causally related to the extrinsic events and accurately presented in direct relation to those events. When Samuel Putnam asked Hemingway in the late twenties for a definition of his aims, the answer was: "Put down what I see and what I feel in the best and simplest way I can tell it." Taken as absolute standards, of course, bestness and simplicity will often be at variance, a fact of which Hemingway at that date was apparently becoming more and more conscious. But his aim from the beginning had been to show, if he could, the precise relationship between what he saw and what he felt.

It is characteristic of Hemingway, with his genuine scorn for overintellectualized criticism, that he has himself refused to employ critical jargon in the presentation of his esthetic ideas. It is also evident, however, that early in his career, probably about 1922, he had evolved an esthetic principle which might be called "the discipline of double perception." The term is not quite exact, since the aim of double perception is ultimately a singleness of vision. This is the kind of vision everyone experiences when his two eyes, though each sees the same set of objects from slightly disparate angles, work together to produce a unified picture with a sense of depth to it. According to Hemingway, he was trying very hard for this double perception about the time of his return from the Near East in the fall of 1922. Aside from knowing "truly" what he "really" felt in the presence of any given piece of action, he found that his greatest difficulty lay in putting down on paper "what really happened in action; what the actual things were which produced the emotion" felt by the observer. No wonder that he was finding it hard to get "the real thing, the sequence of motion and fact which made the emotion." Whatever that real thing was, if you stated it "purely" enough and were likewise lucky, there was a chance that your statement of it would be valid, esthetically and emotionally valid, forever.

Fundamental to the task is the deletion of one's own preconceptions. Such and such was the way it *ought* to be, the way you *assumed* it was. But "oughts" and "assumptions" are dangerous ground for a man to stand on who wishes to take the word of no one else, and to achieve in esthetics what René Descartes thought he had achieved in philosophy, namely, a start at the start. The hope was that the genuinely serious and determined writer-observer might be able in time to penetrate behind the illusions which all our preconceptions play upon the act of clear seeing.

It would then become his task to perfect himself in the discipline of double perception. To make something so humanly true that it will outlast the vagaries of time and change, yet will still speak directly to one's own changing time, he must somehow reach a state of objective awareness between two poles, one inward-outward and the other outward-inward. The first need (though not always first in order of time) is the ability to look within and to describe that complex of mixed emotions which a given set of circumstances has produced in the observer's mind.

The other necessity is to locate and to state factually and exactly that outer complex of motion and fact which produced the emotional reaction.

This second class of things and circumstances, considered in their relations to the emotional complexes of the first class, would be precisely what T.S. Eliot called "objective correlatives." His statement calls them variously "a set of objects, a situation, a chain of events which shall be the formula of that particular emotion; such that when the external facts, which must terminate in sensory experience, are given, the emotion is immediately evoked." He states further that the idea of artistic "inevitability" consists in the "complete adequacy of the external to the emotion." Mr. Eliot's generic description fits Hemingway's customary performance. Yet it may be noticed that Eliot's most frequent practice, as distinguished from his theoretical formulation, is to fashion his objective correlatives into a series of complex *literary* symbols. These are designed to elicit a more or less controlled emotional response from the reader (like the Wagnerian passage in *The Waste Land*), depending to some degree on the extent of his cultural holdings. With Hemingway, on the other hand, the objective correlatives are not so much inserted and adapted as observed and encompassed. They are to be traced back, not to anterior literature and art objects, but to things actually seen and known by direct experience of the world.

Hemingway's method has this special advantage over Eliot's—that one's ability to grasp the emotional suggestions embodied in an objective correlative depends almost solely on two factors: the reader's sensitivity to emotional suggestion, and the degree of his imaginative and sympathetic involvement in the story which is being told. With Eliot these two factors are likewise emphatically present, but a third is added. This third, which in a measure controls and delimits the first two, is the factor of "literary" experience. One's emotional response to the Wagnerian passage cannot be really full unless he knows its origin, can see it in both its original and its new and secondary context, and can make certain quick comparisons between the two. Some, though not all, of Eliot's correlatives accordingly show a "twice-removed" quality which in a measure pales and rarefies them. They cannot always achieve the full-bloodedness and immediacy of correlatives taken directly from the actual set of empirical circumstances which produced in the author the emotion which he is seeking to convey to the reader.

The objective correlatives in Hemingway appear to be of two main types, arbitrarily separable though always working together in a variety of ways. The first may be called *things-in-context:* that particular arrangement of facts in their relations to one another which constitutes a static field of perception. The second type may be called *things-in-motion*, since the arrangement of facts in their relations one to another is almost never wholly static. One might call any combination of the two types by the generic term of *what happened*, where the idea of happening implies a sequence of events in a certain order in time, though any event in the sequence can be arrested to form a static field of observation. If you have *what happened* in this special sense, you will have a chance of reproducing, in a perspective with depth, "the way it was."

To write for permanence, therefore, is to find and set down those things-in-context and things-in-motion which evoked a reaction in the writer as observer. Yet even the presence of both of these correlatives will not suffice to produce the total effect unless one also knows and says what he "really felt" in their presence. The important corollary idea of selection, meaning the elimination of the irrelevant and the unimportant at both poles, is clearly implied in Hemingway's phrase, "stated purely enough." During the five years of his early apprenticeship and the next five in which he developed his skills with such remarkable rapidity, the discipline of double perception was for Hemingway the leading esthetic principle. It is hard to imagine a better—or more difficult—task for the young writer to attempt. Although other principles later arose to supplement this first one, it still continued to occupy one whole side of his attention.

TRUTH AND FALLACY

The basis of Hemingway's continuing power, and the real backbone of his eminence, is in practical esthetics. "Pure" or theoretical esthetics, of that special bloodless order which can argue to all hours without a glance at concretions, holds little interest for an artist of so pragmatic and empirical a cast of mind. One might even doubt that theoretical esthetics is of real interest to any genuine artist, unless in his alter ego he happens also to be a philosophical critic. If that is true, his artistic life is always in some danger, as Hemingway's is not. In esthetics as in his personal philosophy, he strove very hard to stay free of the wrong kind of illusion, and out from under the control of any cut-and-dried system, always trying instead to keep his eye trained on the thing in itself and the effect of the thing in himself. The actual, he wrote in 1949, is "made of knowledge, experience, wine, bread, oil, salt, vinegar, bed, early mornings, nights, days, the sea, men, women, dogs, beloved motor cars, bicycles, hills and valleys, the appearance and disappearance of trains on straight and curved tracks . . . cock grouse drumming on a basswood log, the smell of sweet grass and fresh-smoked leather and Sicily." Given the knowledge and experience of these and their unnamed equivalents, the artist can be at home in the world. If he is a practical esthetician whose aim is to "invent truly," he is on firm ground. By experience he knows what will do. By observation he knows what will go—like the eminently practical Aristotle of the *Poetics*.

It was once remarked, though not by Aristotle, that the province of esthetics is the true and the beautiful, the province of morality the good. Of Hemingway as a moral writer there will be much to say. It is clear that the strongest conviction in Hemingway the esthetician—the principle underlying his sense of place and fact and scene, the principle supporting his "discipline of double perception"—is the importance of telling truth.

To get at the truth of anything is hard enough. For the young artist the task is complicated by the fact that he must steer his way with the utmost care among a set of fallacies, placed like sand-bunkers around a green, or concealed traps around desirable bait. Three of these fallacies stand out: the pathetic, the apathetic, and what may be called the kinetographic.

Ruskin named the first. It is *pathetic* because it comes about through excess of emotion. It is fallacious because, when we are really dominated by an emotion, it is extremely difficult to see things as they are. The curious may read Hemingway's own half-serious opinions on the subject in a disquisition on "erectile writing," which was written to satirize Waldo Frank's *Virgin Spain* in *Death in the Afternoon*. Fundamentally, as that essay makes plain, the pathetic fallacy is an error in perception. But secondarily and by a logical sequence, it is an error of expression, since what has been wrongly seen cannot be rightly described. The intensity of the emotion felt by the writer, if let go on its own, will determine his choice of words. In Charles Kingsley's *Alton Locke*, Ruskin finds an example in which the writing has been made irrational by the author's failure to control the intensity of his emotion. A girl has died in the surf and the seamen bring her body in.

> They rowed her in across the rolling foam—
> The cruel, crawling foam.

"The foam is not cruel," says Ruskin, "neither does it crawl. The state of mind which attributes to it these characters of a living creature is one in which the reason is unhinged by grief. All violent feelings have the same effect. They produce in us a falseness in all our impressions of external things, which I would generally characterize as the pathetic fallacy."

Ruskin goes on to say that the greatest artists do not often admit this kind of falseness of impression and expression. It is only the second or third rankers who much delight in it. It is a form of self-deception, one of the orders of sentimentality. The good writers are not the creatures of their emotions; theirs is a sanity which helps them to see the world clearly and to see it whole.

Beginning with a standard of performance which rigorously excluded the pathetic fallacy, Hemingway adhered to it with a faith just short of fanatical, all his life. Emotion was of course both permissible and, under proper control, necessary. Excess of emotion, however, was never to be allowed. It would falsify both impression and expression. So many of our habits of seeing and saying take their origin from recollected emotion gone stale. If one could cut loose from these habits, three immediate results might be expected. First, you could see what you really saw rather than what you thought you saw. Second, you could know what you felt rather than "what you were supposed to feel." Third, you could say outright what you really saw and felt instead of setting down a false (and, in the bad sense, a literary) version of it.

Hemingway's earliest plan, therefore, was to start cleanly and all afresh to see what effects could be achieved by straight observation of action, set forth in unadorned prose. The immediate upshot of the effort was the kind of writing presented in the Paris edition of *In Our Time*. This, for example, on part of Act One at a bullfight:

"They whack-whacked the white horse on the legs and he kneed himself up. The picador twisted the stirrups straight and pulled and hauled up into the saddle. The horse's entrails hung down in a blue bunch and swung backward and forward as he began to canter, the monos whacking him on the back of his legs with the rods. He cantered jerkily along the barrera. He stopped stiff and one of the monos held his bridle and walked him forward. The picador kicked in his spurs, leaned forward and shook his lance at the bull. Blood pumped regularly from between the horse's front legs. He was nervously unsteady. The bull could not make up his mind to charge."

This 120-word miniature is a writer's apprentice-exercise, a minute of a Spanish committee meeting. Without ignoring the beginning (a horse has been gored by a bull) or the end (the horse will be gored again and will die), the young writer is concentrating on the middle of an action. He puts down what he sees, exactly as he sees it. He eliminates from his view the panorama, the weather, the crowd, the waiting matadors, the price of the seats, the hardness of the bench on which he sits, the odor of his neighbor, the color of the sky, the degree of the temperature. Instead he watches the horse, and what takes place immediately around the horse, with a tremendous intensity of concentration. He is not guessing, even when he speaks of the horse's nervous unsteadiness or the bull's indecision. These are immediately visible qualities, shown by the animals through their actions. The prose is as clean as the observation. Nothing is ornamental. None but essential modifiers are called, and only a few are chosen. No similes, no metaphors, no literary allusions, no pathetic illusions, no balanced clauses. There is only one trick, and that is a good one: the three-time use of the word *forward*, which adds to the intensity of the account because "forward" is where the bull stands with one wet horn. Otherwise there is nothing in the least fancy. There is only an ancient horse, in very bad shape, waiting for the *coup de grâce*.

Though he never chose similar subjects himself, Ruskin might well have admired Hemingway's "story." He could have placed it alongside Thackeray's account of Amelia in *Vanity Fair:* that time in Chapter 32 in Brussels when she prays quietly for the well-being of her husband George, in ignorance of the fact that he lies dead at Waterloo. Ruskin's term for the literature of straight statement, without moralizing elaboration or rococo interior decorating, is the "Make-What-You-Will-Of-It" school of fiction—a school diametrically opposed to the school of the pathetic fallacy. Scholars at the Spartan school of "What-You-Will" are content to let well enough alone. Like Hemingway at the Spanish committee-meeting, they say the thing the way it was and let the minutes stand as written.

The passage on the horse also steers clear of the apathetic fallacy, where the reason is so cold and tight that the matter of emotion is squeezed out entirely. At first glance, it is true, one might suppose that Hemingway had ignored both his own and the reader's emotions. The account includes no overt allusion to how the observer felt in the presence of Rosinante Agonistes. There is no evident plucking of the heart-strings, no visible pump inserted into the springs of human sympathy.

Yet the close reader can entertain no real doubt. The passage is neither cold, austere, nor cruel. Pity for the horse (if you are a member of that sector of mankind which pities wounded horses) is revealed by the artist's selection of details: the horse's awkward struggle to a standing position, the swinging of the exposed entrails, the jerkiness of the canter, the bite of the spurs, and the awful regularity of the pumping of the blood. A kind of implicit enmity towards the picador and the ring-servants comes out in verbs like *whack-whacked, pulled and hauled,* the second *whacking,* and the *kicking-in* of the spurs. The pity and the enmity are so firmly in check that at first—to use Aristotle's ethical terms—we suppose a *defect* of sympathy. By the same token, the *extreme* of excessive pathos is carefully avoided. What remains is the *mean*, the province of the writer who seeks to avoid both the apathetic and the pathetic fallacies.

Such an esthetic theory of the "emotive mean" leaves the practitioner open to certain criticisms. What about scope, it is asked, and what about depth? Where is the rest of the act? Who were the parents of the horse that we may establish some sort of sympathetic rapport with him? "Hemingway's art," wrote Wyndham Lewis in 1934, "is an art of the surface—and, as I look at it, none the worse for that." Lewis failed, like many of his contemporaries, to look at this particular art long enough. Had he done so, he might have seen what Hemingway was doing with images and with suggestion far below the surfaces of his better stories— though not too far to be overlooked by the close and sympathetic reader. He also ignored Henry James' observation, which applies to all of Hemingway's miniatures: "an exemplary anecdote" may be also "a little rounded drama." Many of our best critics have consistently underrated Hemingway's esthetic intelligence.

If his chosen approach led to pejorative judgments, or even to the suggested kind of limitation on depth and scope, Hemingway as an apprentice craftsman was temporarily prepared to accept them. He began, as he knew he must, by centering attention on action, and on what he felt to be the simpler modes of action. "I was trying to learn to write, commencing with the simplest things," he said in 1932, speaking of his program in 1922. As in the laboratory study of biology, one works up only very gradually to more complex organisms. If he were to begin on the human instead of the frog, the young biologists's ignorance might betray him into the most unscientific (which is to say, untrue) conceptions, and he would have the further hazard of getting lost among the ganglia. Hemingway's writing after 1922 was most certainly none the worse for his rigorous self-imposed apprentice training. He advanced well beyond the early state without losing sight of its importance. He continued to employ what he had learned there at the same time that he continued to learn other things.

The most dangerous pitfall for the young Hemingway was what may be called the kinetographic fallacy. This consists in the supposition that we can get the best art by an absolutely true description of what takes place in observed action. It will be kinetic because it must move by definition. It will be graphic because it is a picture. We write down what we see men doing, what they say, what they look like to us. We hold a mirror and a microphone up to life, and report, with absolute though selective precision, the reflections and the noises.

The dangers of such a program, if it is rigorously followed, are clear. The absolutist desire to see and say the truth and nothing but the truth may keep the best-intentioned writer from doing both. No artist who reports the action of men and animals, merely as such, will record things as they are, or really grasp and project "the way it was." He will record actions from the outside, only as they *look* to be. Facts will be distorted in the very attempt to avoid distortion.

The account of the wounded horse cannot be called distortion. But it does nevertheless consist in a concentration so intense that the miniature itself can be appreciated without remembering the larger context of the bullfight, the arena, the town, and the nation in which the described events took place. The spreading context can, of course, be supplied by the reader's imagination. But one could probably argue that the artist is not justified in overworking his reader's imagination to quite this extent.

Between the "defect" of too little detail and the "excess" of the sand-pile technique (where everything is put in, whether it is relevant or not, until we have a bulk on the horizon too considerable to ignore), there is a mean. By the time Hemingway wrote *The Sun Also Rises*, he was rounding out his writing by allowing the possible to enter his picture of the actual. He was beginning to admit guesses, fictions, motivations, imaginations in far greater profusion than he had done in 1922. He felt justified in doing so because he had so firmly avoided guessing throughout his apprenticeship. Now he had had sufficient experience of the kinetographic reporting of the actual so that he could trust himself to invent, though never to invent except in terms of carefully observed experience. Hemingway, therefore, did not so much avoid as transcend the kinetographic fallacy. His own summary of the "mean position" continued, of course, to stress the importance of truth-telling: "A writer's job is to tell the truth." Then he went on. "His standard of fidelity to the truth must be so high that his invention" which comes always and invariably "out of his experience, should produce a truer account than anything factual can be." This remark, set down in 1942, is the essence of twenty years of experience. It runs very close to a pronouncement by Coleridge, who also based his views on common sense and long experience: "A poet ought not to pick nature's pocket: let him borrow, and so borrow as to repay by the very act of borrowing. Examine nature accurately, but write from recollection; and trust more to your imagination than your memory."

Hemingway's nearly absolute devotion to what is true, coming in an age when absolute devotions are so rare, is not only the dominant drive in his whole esthetic life, but also the firmest guarantee that his works will survive. He continuously entertained a healthy and essentially humble conviction that the truth is difficult to come by, though sometimes it may drop by chance into a writer's lap. The good parts of a book, as he told Fitzgerald in 1929, may be only something a writer is lucky enough to overhear, or they may be the wreck of his "whole damned life." But if both partake of the nature of truth, one is as good as the other, though their scope will naturally differ. Any form of truth, however, if it is put into an art form, will help the writing to survive the erosions of time. For the truth is a sturdy core, impervious to the winds of faddist doctrine and the temporary weather of an age.

THE BEAUTIFUL

From truth it is only a step to beauty and *aisthetes*—"one who perceives"—is ordinarily associated with the perception of the beautiful. Although Hemingway the esthetician has spoken much of truth, he has had little to say about what constitutes for him the nature of the beautiful. In the fiction itself there is scarcely any overt emphasis on beauty for its own sake. Remembering Ruskin, one might call Hemingway's the "make-what-you-will-of-it" approach to the perception of the beautiful. It is as if Hemingway tacitly agreed with the dictum of Herbert Read: "To live according to natural law, this is also the release of the imagination. In discovering truth, we create beauty."

With respect to the beautiful it appears to be a basic assumption in Hemingway's esthetic that what is true, in the sense of being natural and untinkered-with, is also beautiful. Ugliness in Hemingway is almost invariably associated with the abnormal and the unnatural: the unwomanly woman, for example, or the unmanly man. The unclean, the furtive, the cowardly, the enslaved all show an aspect of the sinister. Beauty in Hemingway is the beauty of land, of men and women, of the nobler animals, of the clean, the honest, the well-lighted, the nonconcealing, the brave.

One version of the alliance between the natural and the beautiful was very well summarized by the Emperor Marcus Aurelius.

"The hanging-down of grapes, the brow of the lion, the froth of a foaming wild boar, though by themselves considered they are far from beauty, yet because they happen naturally, they are both comely and beautiful."

The comely is the becoming, the fitting, that which is felt to be naturally right. Whenever in the reading of Hemingway one finds himself arrested by the beauty of a passage, he may discover also that its essential naturalness, in the moral dimension of stoic esthetics, helps to explain its essential beauty.

Following the lead of the Emperor, one might turn to the examples of the rhinoceros and the kudu bull in the *Green Hills of Africa*, one of Hemingway's least appreciated books. About the rhino:

"There he was, long-hulked, heavy-sided, prehistoric-looking, the hide like vulcanized rubber and faintly transparent looking, scarred with a badly healed horn wound that the birds had pecked at, his tail thick, round, and pointed, flat many-legged ticks crawling on him, his ears fringed with hair, tiny pig eyes, moss growing on the base of his horn that grew forward from his nose. M'Cola looked at him and shook his head. I agreed with him. This was the hell of an animal."

Confronted by this passage, the naturalist might well argue that this is the way a dead rhinoceros looks. This is the nature of the beast, and if we follow Marcus Aurelius it would be necessary to conclude that the rhinoceros, since he happens naturally, is a thing of beauty and a joy forever. Yet to argue thus he would have to ignore the very careful accumulation of points in Hemingway's description which suggest the unnatural and the abnormal. The prehistoric look, for example, is not of this present world; the vulcanized-rubber appearance of the skin, though very distinctly of this world, is somehow artificial and ugly on an animal. The horn wound, badly healed and pecked at by the tick birds, has the force of an abnormality. So does the allusion to the verminous ticks, comparable to the horror of flies around a horse's crupper mentioned elsewhere in the same book. The eyes are out of proportion, and the moss at the base of the horn seems an unnatural growth, like festoons of mildew on a neglected book. This is an offensive animal, disproportioned in its long hulk, abnormal in its appurtenances, a kind of mistaken hybrid, not what you would expect an animal to look like—esthetically wrong, in short, and generally objectionable.

Against such disproportion, abnormality, and unnatural natural-ness, one might place the unposed portrait of the kudu bull, killed at long last after many days of unsuccessful hunting.

"It was a huge, beautiful kudu bull, stone-dead, on his side, his horns in great dark spirals, widespread and unbelievable as he lay dead five yards from where we stood. . . . I looked at him, big, long-legged, a smooth gray with the white stripes and the great curling, sweeping horns, brown as walnut meats, and ivory-pointed, at the big ears and the great, lovely, heavy-maned neck, the white chevron between his eyes and the white of his muzzle and I stooped over and touched him to try to believe it. He was lying on the side where the bullet had gone in and there was not a mark on him and he smelled sweet and lovely like the breath of cattle and the odor of thyme after rain."

This is the true hunter's esthetic appreciation. Even the non-hunter, whose conscientious or tempermental objection to killing would not permit him to write in just this way, can share the hunter's admiration for the graceful, strong, handsomely, proportioned animal. The size, the clean natural colors, the wholeness ("there was not a mark on him"), and the sweet natural smell which distinguishes the grazing animals from the meat-eaters, are all factors in the kudu's esthetic attractiveness. "Beautiful . . . lovely . . . lovely." Words like these, in the context of the weary hunt now successfully crowned with antlers, are used without apology. Here is the hunter's and the esthetician's dream of an animal, as the rhinoceros was a kind of tickridden nightmare.

The quality of beauty in Hemingway's work seems to come as naturally as the leaves to a tree. Yet the carefully ordered accounts of natural scenery in his pages reveal, on close examination, a deliberate and intelligent artifice. The description is nearly always directly functional within an action. The beauty—or ugliness—of the land is made to belong to the ugliness—or beauty—of the human events which occur in its midst. Sometimes, as in Frank Norris, natural beauty stands in quiet contrast to whatever it is that men and women are doing in its presence. Hemingway uses this old trick of the naturalistic writers charily and rarely; it is never emphasized in the black-jack manner of, say, Norris in *The Octopus*, or Steinbeck in *The Wayward Bus*. What we tend to get in Hemingway is a subtle interweaving of the natural conditions in the background and the human conditions in the foreground or the middle-distance.

While examining portraits by divers Italian masters, Hemingway always carefully studied the backgrounds, as if to find corroboration in another art for his ideas about the importance of natural settings in prose fiction. As he well knew total effect depends upon placing figures in a context—verbal, schematic, and scenic—and in this respect he is as good a "contextualist" as T.S. Eliot, who adopted if he did not invent this special application of the term. Although Hemingway had rigorously trained himself in the accurate observation of natural objects, his precision of rendering did not prevent these objects from being put to symbolic use. The discipline of double perception requires an ability to penetrate both to the essential qualities of a natural scene and to the essential qualities of a subjective reaction to the scene. These, working together in a dozen ways, produce the total effect.

Hemingway's sense of beauty is stirred, his heart is moved, as much by human beings as by landscapes or the more handsome animals. Here again the normative judgment comes into operation. He scorns perversions of any kind. Whatever is abnormal or unnatural according to his measurement is ugly according to his conclusion. People about their normal business, or people who are able under abnormal circumstances to behave like normal human beings, ordinarily strike him with the impact of the beautiful, though he may not use the word in that connection.

The point may be illustrated by choosing an example of a set of human beings of no extrinsic beauty at all, but modern, unlovely, dirty, urban, and tough. This is a group portrait of the matadors' representatives, the trusted banderilleros who have gathered to appraise the bulls the morning before a *corrida*.

"The representatives, usually short men in caps, not yet shaven for the day, with a great variety of accents, but all with the same hard eyes, argue and discuss."

Goya would have fancied these people; Browning's poet-observer could have met them in Valladolid. Though by themselves considered they are far from beauty, yet because they happen naturally, in the morning chiaroscuro of the plaza corrals, they are both comely and beautiful to the eye of a true esthetician.

Anyone so minded could object to the foregoing position on the grounds that the natural is not by any means always to be equated with the moral. The neohumanists habitually opposed the moral to the natural; they argued that only through the operation of the inner check could the natural be housebroken into conformity with acceptable social standards. Dozens of examples could be assembled to show how anti-social and either amoral or immoral the natural man can be when he really lets himself go.

If such objections were not merely captious, they would be simply irrelevant. The neohumanists, great though their gifts were, could most of them lay no just claim to an understanding of practical esthetics. For the first requirement of esthetics, at least in the area where Hemingway works, is that it shall be based on a moral view of the world. With Anton Chekhov's moral statement that "the aim of fiction is absolute and honest truth," he would agree entirely. He would also agree with Marcus Aurelius that the natural is comely and beautiful, though Hemingway offers evidence throughout his work that the natural must be defined within certain normative and essentially moral limits. Working with the concepts of truth and beauty, it thus becomes possible to see "the way it was" as an idea of empirical truth, taking due account of ugliness and deformity, but warmed and illuminated from within by the strong love of natural beauty.

THE SABIDURÍAN

To complete the portrait of Hemingway as esthetician, it is necessary to look at what may be called the underside of the painting. The upper side is of course that whole face of his effort as artist which has as its purpose the seeing and saying of truth and "natural" beauty. Truth-telling (whether the "objective" portrayal of things and events in the phenomenal world, or the "subjective" representation of mental-emotional responses to these things and events) is one great criterion by which the worth of writing may be judged. For the upper side of Hemingway's esthetic there is perhaps no better general statement than that of Conrad in his celebrated preface to *The Nigger of the Narcissus*.

"The artist . . . like the thinker or the scientist, seeks the truth. . . . And art itself may be defined as a single-minded attempt to render the highest kind of justice to the visible universe. . . . It is an attempt to find in its forms, in its colours, in its light, in its shadows, in the aspects of matter and in the facts of life what of each is fundamental, what is enduring and essential. . . ."

Although Hemingway's admiration for Conrad later became less intense than formerly, his evident agreement with such statements as the one just quoted gave him, in the years 1923–1924, good reason to defend Conrad against his fashionable detractors, and to refuse to share in the disparagement which was at its height about the time of Conrad's death. When Ford issued the Conrad memorial supplement in the *Transatlantic* for September, 1924, Hemingway made his own position clear.

"The second book of Conrad's that I read was *Lord Jim* [said Hemingway]. I was unable to finish it. It is therefore all I have left of him. For I cannot reread them. That may be what my friends mean by saying he is a bad writer. But from nothing else that I have ever read have I gotten what every book of Conrad has given me."

Knowing that he could not reread them, he had saved up four of the novels to be used as a combination anodyne and stimulant whenever his disgust "with writing, writers, and everything written of and to write would be too much." In Toronto the preceding autumn he had used up three, one after the other, borrowing them from a friend who owned a uniform set. When his newspaper sent him to cover the attempt to locate anthracite coal in the Sudbury Basin mining district north of Georgian Bay in Ontario, he bought three back numbers of the *Pictorial Review* and read *The Rover*, "sitting up in bed in the Nickle Range Hotel."

"When morning came [he continued] I had used up all my Conrad like a drunkard. I had hoped it would last me the trip, and felt like a young man who has blown his patrimony. But, I thought, he will write more stories. He has lots of time."

The later reviews had all superciliously agreed that *The Rover* was a bad book. But now Conrad was dead, and "I wish to God," said Hemingway, "they would have taken some great acknowledged technician of a literary figure and left [Conrad] to write his bad stories."

The fashionable derogation of Conrad was often accompanied by the praise of T.S. Eliot as a "good writer." As for Hemingway:

"If I knew that by grinding Mr. Eliot into a fine dry powder and sprinkling that powder over Mr. Conrad's grave, Mr. Conrad would shortly reappear, looking very annoyed at the forced return, and commence writing, I would leave for London early tomorrow morning with a sausage-grinder."

Hemingway neither ground in London nor sprinkled in Canterbury. Had he done so, the topic of conversation between exhumed and exhumer might well have been Conrad's preface. In that very eloquent defence of fiction, Conrad makes three other memorable points besides insisting that the artist must seek truth.

The first is on the language of prose. The phrases "like pebbles fresh from a brook" which Ford Madox Ford admired in the early work of Hemingway were not achieved without the most careful attention to the act of verbal selection. Hemingway told Samuel Putnam in 1926 that "easy writing makes hard reading," and that he wished, if he could, to "strip language clean, to lay it bare down to the bone." In practice this meant the studied deletion of all words and phrases which were in any way false. One of the difficulties with language, as many good writers have felt and as Hemingway said, is that "all our words from loose using have lost their edge." Recognizing this fact, Hemingway always wrote slowly and revised carefully, cutting, eliding, substituting, experimenting with syntax to see what a sentence could most economically carry, and then throwing out all words that could be spared.

Such an artist would be obliged to agree with Conrad: "It is only through an unremitting never-discouraged care for the shape and ring of sentences . . . that the light of magic suggestiveness may be brought to play for an evanescent instant over the commonplace surface of words: of the old, old words, worn thin, defaced by ages of careless usage." Magic suggestiveness is a phrase not to be found anywhere in the published writings of Hemingway; yet everywhere in his language the magic of suggestion is at work among the old, old words. If their surfaces are commonplace, their interiors bear the imaginative supercharging which only the true artist can bring to them. And this positive charge, which on being released plays not over but beneath the verbal surfaces, is one phase of the underside of Hemingway's distinguished achievement in prose.

The second phase is what Conrad calls "communication through temperament." The Spanish word *sabiduría* comes very close to the context of this idea. It may be defined as a kind of natural knowledge, nothing like the "wisdom" of professional philosophers, but a knowledge available under the surface of their lives to all responsive human beings. According to Conrad, "the artist appeals to that part of our being which is not dependent on wisdom: to that in us which is a gift and not an acquisition—and therefore more permanently enduring. . . . Fiction, if it at all aspires to be art, appeals to temperament. And in truth it must be . . . the appeal of one temperament to all the other innumerable temperaments whose subtle and resistless power endows passing events with their true meaning, and creates the moral, the emotional atmosphere of the place and time." One may remark in passing that the closing phrase, "the emotional atmosphere of the place and time," is a very concise description for a part of what Hemingway means by "the way it was." Conrad goes on to say that the artist's appeal must be realized through the senses—provided of course that it is the artist's high desire to reach the secret spring of responsive emotions.

This is also the theory and practice of Hemingway. As one watches the establishment and development of the sabidurian images in his novels or the more ambitious short stories, one comes to see, as Mr. Theodore Bardacke has recently noticed, "this underlying use of associations and emotional suggestion," visible and even audible through the "objectively reported details." It is precisely this power which enabled Mr. Malcolm Cowley to say that "Hemingway's prose at its best gives a sense of depth and of moving forward on different levels that is lacking in even the best of his imitators." Hemingway's own term for it is "the kind of writing that can be done . . . if anyone is serious enough and has luck. There is a fourth and fifth dimension that can be gotten."

In a number of his works, seriously charging and recharging the old, old words and the natural, non-literary temperamental images, Hemingway the sabidurían precisely did such a job. We respond to it as naturally as savages to thunder, or as Dr. Jung's patients to the recurrent opposed symbols of the "Wise Old Man" and "the Shadow." Whether we accept Jung's hypothesis of inherited patterns in the cells of the brain, or try to explain our responses by modern versions of Bentham's psychological hedonism, need not concern us here. However we explain the fact, it operates all through Hemingway's prose.

The total entity we respond to in a work of art is what Conrad's preface calls "the presented vision." It may be a vision of "regret or pity, of terror or mirth." The point is that in its presence no reasonably sensitive human being is an island; he is a part of the mainland. For the presented vision arouses "in the hearts of the beholders that feeling of unavoidable solidarity; of the solidarity in mysterious origin, in toil, in joy, in hope, in uncertain fate, which binds men to each other and all mankind to the visible world."

Hemingway is very clear on this matter of the presented vision. "All good books," he wrote in 1933, "are alike in that they are truer than if they had really happened and after you are finished reading one you will feel that all that happened to you and afterwards it all belongs to you; the good and the bad, the ecstasy, the remorse and sorrow, the people and the places and how the weather was. If you can get so that you can give that to people, then you are a writer."

No two individualist authors will perfectly agree in generals or in particulars. In every author, esthetically and culturally speaking, one finds a muted echo of Blake's "I must create my own system or be enslaved by another man's." Hemingway would never write the matter of Conrad's preface in the manner of Conrad. Yet he would wholly agree with Conrad in saying to all who demand other things of the artist: "My task which I am trying to achieve is, by the power of the written word to make you hear, to make you feel—it is, before all, to make you *see*. That—and no more, and it is everything." It is everything because it encompasses both the upper- and the underside of all we know as human beings. If the artist achieves his task, it will mean that by all the means at his disposal he has transferred to his reader the true essence of "the way it was."

MARK SPILKA

The Death of Love in
"The Sun Also Rises"

She turns and looks a moment in the glass,
Hardly aware of her departed lover;
Her brain allows one half-formed thought to pass:
"Well now that's done: and I'm glad it's over."
When lovely woman stoops to folly and
Paces about her room again, alone,
She smoothes her hair with automatic hand,
And puts a record on the gramophone.

—T.S. ELIOT, *The Waste Land*

One of the most persistent themes of the twenties was the death of love in World War I. All the major writers recorded it, often in piecemeal fashion, as part of the larger postwar scene; but only Hemingway seems to have caught it whole and delivered it in lasting fictional form. His intellectual grasp of the theme might account for this. Where D. H. Lawrence settles for the shock of war on the Phallic Consciousness, or where Eliot presents assorted glimpes of sterility, Hemingway seems to design an extensive parable. Thus, in *The Sun Also Rises*, his protagonists are deliberately shaped as allegorical figures: Jake Barnes and Brett Ashley are two lovers desexed by the war; Robert Cohn is the false knight who challenges their despair; while Romero, the stalwart

From *Twelve Original Essays on Great American Novels*, edited by Charles Shapiro. Copyright © 1958 by Mark Spilka. Wayne State University Press.

bullfighter, personifies the good life which will survive their failure. Of course, these characters are not abstractions in the text; they are realized through the most concrete style in American fiction, and their larger meaning is implied only by their response to immediate situations. But the implications are there, the parable is at work in every scene, and its presence lends unity and depth to the whole novel.

Barnes himself is a fine example of this technique. Cut off from love by a shell wound, he seems to suffer from an undeserved misfortune. But as most readers agree, his condition represents a peculiar form of emotional impotence. It does not involve distaste for the flesh, as with Lawrence's crippled veteran, Clifford Chatterley; instead Barnes lacks the power to control love's strength and durability. His sexual wound, the result of an unpreventable "accident" in the war, points to another realm where accidents can always happen and where Barnes is equally powerless to prevent them. In Book II of the novel he makes this same comparison while describing one of the dinners at Pamplona: "It was like certain dinners I remember from the war. There was much wine, an ignored tension, and a feeling of things coming that you could not prevent happening." This fear of emotional consequences is the key to Barnes's condition. Like so many Hemingway heroes, he has no way to handle subjective complications, and his wound is a token for this kind of impotence.

It serves the same purpose for the expatriate crowd in Paris. In some figurative manner these artists, writers, and derelicts have all been rendered impotent by the war. Thus, as Barnes presents them, they pass before us like a parade of sexual cripples, and we are able to measure them against his own forebearance in the face of a common problem. Whoever bears his sickness well is akin to Barnes; whoever adopts false postures, or willfully hurts others, falls short of his example. This is the organizing principle in Book I, this alignment of characters by their stoic qualities. But, stoic or not, they are all incapable of love, and in their sober moments they seem to know it.

For this reason they feel especially upset whenever Robert Cohn appears. Cohn still upholds a romantic view of life, and since he affirms it with stubborn persistence, he acts like a goad upon his wiser contemporaries. As the narrator, Barnes must account for the challenge he presents them and the decisive turn it takes in later chapters. Accordingly, he begins the book with a review of Cohn's boxing career in Princeton. Though he has no taste for it, college boxing means a lot to Cohn. For one thing, it helps to compensate for anti-Semitic treatment from his classmates. More subtly, it turns him into an armed romantic, a man who can damage others in defense in his own beliefs. He also loves the pose of manhood which it affords him and seems strangely pleased when his nose is flattened in the ring. Soon other tokens of virility delight him, and he often confuses them with actual manliness. He likes the idea of a mistress more than he likes his actual mistress; or he likes the authority of editing and the prestige of writing, though he is a bad editor and a poor novelist. In other words, he always looks for internal strength in outward signs and sources. On leaving Princeton, he marries "on the rebound from the rotten time . . . in college." But in five years the marriage falls through, and he rebounds again to his present mistress, the forceful Frances Clyne. Then, to escape her dominance and his own disquiet, he begins to look for romance in far-off countries. As with most of his views, the source of this idea is an exotic book:

> He had been reading W. H. Hudson. That sounds like an innocent occupation, but Cohn had read and reread "The Purple Land." "The Purple Land" is a very sinister book if read too late in life. It recounts splendid imaginary amorous adventures of a perfect English gentleman in an intensely romantic land, the scenery of which is very well described. For a man to take it at thirty-four as a guidebook to what life holds is about as safe as it would be for a man of the same age to enter Wall Street direct from a French convent, equipped with a complete set of the more practical Alger books. Cohn, I believe, took every word of "The Purple Land" as literally as though it had been an R. G. Dun report.

Cohn's romanticism explains his key position in the parable. He is the last chivalric hero, the last defender of an outworn faith, and his function is to illustrate its present folly—to show us, through the absurdity of his behavior, that romantic love is dead, that one of the great guiding codes of the past no longer operates. "You're getting damned romantic," says Brett to Jake at one point in the novel. "No, bored," he replies, because for this generation boredom has become more plausible than love. As a foil to his contemporaries, Cohn helps to reveal why this is so.

Of course, there is much that is traditional in the satire on Cohn. Like the many victims of romantic literature, from Don Quixote to Tom Sawyer, he lives by what he reads and neglects reality at his own and others' peril. But Barnes and his friends have no alternative to Cohn's beliefs. There is nothing here, for example, like the neat balance between sense and sensibility in Jane Austen's world. Granted that Barnes is sensible enough, that he sees life clearly and that we are meant to contrast his private grief with Cohn's public suffering, his self-restraint with Cohn's deliberate self-exposure. Yet, emasculation aside, Barnes has no way to measure or control the state of love; and though he recognizes this with his mind and tries to act accordingly, he seems no different from Cohn in his deepest feelings. When he is alone with Brett, he wants to live with her in the country, to go with her to San Sebastian, to go up to her room, to keep her in his own room, or to keep on kissing her—though he can never really act upon such sentiments. Nor are they merely the yearnings of a tragically impotent man, for eventually they will lead Barnes to betray his own principles and to abandon self-respect, all for the sake of Lady Ashley. No, at best he is a restrained romantic, a man who carries himself well in the face of love's impossibilities, but who seems to share with Cohn a common (if hidden) weakness.

The sexual parade continues through the early chapters. Besides Cohn and his possessive mistress, there is the prostitute Georgette, whom Barnes picks up one day "because of a vague sentimental idea that it would be nice to eat with someone." Barnes introduces her to his friends as his financée, and as his private joke affirms, the two have much in common. Georgette is sick and sterile, having reduced love to a simple monetary exchange; but, like Barnes, she manages to be frank and forthright and to keep an even keel among the drifters of Paris. Together they form a pair of honest cripples, in contrast with the various pretenders whom they meet along the Left Bank. Among the latter are Cohn and Frances Clyne, the writer Braddocks and his wife, and Robert Prentiss, a rising young novelist who seems to verbalize their phoniness: "Oh, how charmingly you get angry," he tells Barnes. "I wish I had that faculty." Barnes's honest anger has been aroused by the appearance of a band of homosexuals, accompanied by Brett Ashley. When one of the band spies Georgette, he decides to dance with her; then one by one the rest follow suit, in deliberate parody of normal love. Brett herself provides a key to the dizzy sexual medley. With a man's felt hat on her boyish bob, and with her familiar reference to men as fellow "chaps," she completes the distortion of sexual roles which seems to characterize the period. For the war, which has unmanned Barnes and his contemporaries, has turned Brett into the freewheeling equal of any man. It has taken her first sweetheart's life through dysentery and has sent her present husband home in a dangerous state of shock. For Brett these blows are the equivalent of Jake's emasculation; they seem to release her from her womanly nature and expose her to the male prerogatives of drink and promiscuity. Once she claims these rights as her own, she becomes an early but more honest version of Catherine Barkley, the English nurse in Hemingway's next important novel, A Farewell to Arms. Like Catherine, Brett has been a nurse on the Italian front and has lost a sweetheart in the war; but for her there is no saving interlude of love with a wounded patient, no rigged and timely escape through death in childbirth. Instead she survives the colossal violence, the disruption of her personal life, and the exposure to mass promiscuity, to confront a moral and emotional vacuum among her postwar lovers. With this evidence of male default all around her, she steps off the romantic pedestal, moves freely through the bars of Paris, and stands confidently there beside her newfound equals. Ironically, her most recent conquest, Robert Cohn, fails to see the bearing of such changes on romantic love. He still believes that Brett is womanly and therefore deeply serious about intimate matters. After their first meeting, he describes her as "absolutely fine and straight" and nearly strikes Barnes for thinking otherwise; and a bit later, after their brief affair in the country, he remains unconvinced "that it didn't mean anything." But when men no longer command respect, and women replace their natural warmth with masculine freedom and mobility, there can be no serious love.

Brett does have some respect for Barnes, even a little tenderness, though her actions scarcely show abiding love. At best she can affirm his worth and share his standards and perceptions. When in public, she knows how to keep her essential misery to herself; when alone with Barnes, she will express her feelings, admit her faults, and even display good judgment. Thus her friend Count Mippipopolous is introduced to Barnes as "one of us." The count qualifies by virtue of his war wounds, his invariable calmness, and his curious system of values. He appreciates good food, good wine, and a quiet place in which to enjoy them. Love also has a place in his system, but since he is "always in love," the place seems rather shaky. Like Jake and Brett and perhaps Georgette, he simply bears himself well among the postwar ruins.

The count completes the list of cripples who appear in Book I. In a broader sense, they are all disaffiliates, all men and women who have cut themselves off from conventional society and who have made Paris their permanent playground. Jake Barnes has introduced them, and we have been able to test them against his stoic attitudes toward life in a moral wasteland. Yet such life is finally unbearable, as we have also seen whenever Jake and Brett are alone together, or whenever Jake is alone with his thoughts. He needs a healthier code to live by, and for this reason the movement in Book II is away from Paris to the trout stream at Burguete and the bull ring at Pamplona. Here a more vital testing process occurs, and with the appearance of Bill Gorton we get our first inkling of its nature.

Gorton is a successful writer who shares with Barnes a love for boxing and other sports. In Vienna he has helped to rescue a splendid Negro boxer from an angry and intolerant crowd. The incident has spoiled Vienna for him, and, as his reaction suggests, the sports world will provide the terms of moral judgment from this point onward in the novel. Or, more accurately, Jake Barnes's feelings about sports will shape the rest of the novel. For, with Hemingway, the great outdoors is chiefly a state of mind, a projection of moral and emotional attitudes onto physical arenas, so that a clear account of surface action will reproduce these attitudes in the reader. In "Big Two-Hearted River," for example, he describes Nick Adams's fishing and camping activities along a trout stream in Michigan. His descriptions run to considerable length, and they are all carefully detailed, almost as if they were meant for a fishing manual. Yet the details themselves have strong emotional connotations for Nick Adams. He thinks of his camp as "the good place," the place where none of his previous troubles can touch him. He has left society behind him, and, as the story begins, there is even a burnt town at his back, to signify his disaffiliation. He has also walked miles to reach an arbitrary campsite, and this is one of the ways in which he sets his own conditions for happiness and then lives up to them. He finds extraordinary pleasure, moreover, in the techniques of making coffee and pitching camp, or in his responses to fishing and eating. In fact, his sensations have become so valuable that he doesn't want to rush them: they bring health, pleasure, beauty, and a sense of order which is sorely missing in his civilized experience; they are part of a healing process, a private and imaginative means of wiping out the damages of civilized life. When this process is described with elaborate attention to surface detail, the effect on the reader is decidedly subjective.

The same holds true, of course, for the fishing trip in *The Sun Also Rises*. As Barnes and Gorton approach "the good place," each item in the landscape is singled out and given its own importance. Later the techniques of fishing are treated with the same reverence for detail. For, like Nick Adams, these men have left the wasteland for the green plains of health; they have traveled miles, by train and on foot, to reach a particular trout stream. The fishing there is good, the talk free and easy, and even Barnes is able to sleep well after lunch, though he is usually an insomniac. The meal itself is handled like a mock religious ceremony: "Let us rejoice in our blessings," says Gorton. "Let us utilize the fowls of the air. Let us utilize the produce of the vine. Will you utilize a little, brother?" A few days later, when they visit the old monastery at Roncesvalles, this combination of fishing, drinking, and male camaraderie is given an edge over religion itself. With their English friend, Harris, they honor the monastery as a remarkable place, but decide that "it isn't the same as fishing"; then all agree to "utilize" a little pub across the way. At the trout stream, moreover, romantic love is given the same comparative treatment and seems sadly foolish before the immediate joys of fishing:

It was a little past noon and there was not much shade, but I sat against the trunk of two of the trees that grew together, and read. The book was something by A. E. W. Mason, and I was reading a wonderful story about a man who had been frozen in the Alps and then fallen into a glacier and disappeared, and his bride was going to wait twenty-four years exactly for his body to come out on the moraine, while her true love waited too, and they were still waiting when Bill came up [with four trout in his bag]. . . . His face was sweaty and happy.

As these comparisons show, the fishing trip has been invested with unique importance. By sticking closely to the surface action, Barnes has evoked the deeper attitudes which underlie it and which make it a therapeutic process for him. He describes himself now as a "rotten Catholic" and speaks briefly of his thwarted love for Brett; but with religion defunct and love no longer possible, he can at least find happiness through private and imaginative means. Thus he now constructs a more positive code to follow: as with Nick Adams, it brings him health, pleasure, beauty and order, and helps to wipe out the damage of his troubled life in Paris.

Yet somehow the code lacks depth and substance. To gain these advantages, Barnes must move to Pamplona, which stands roughly to Burguete as the swamp in "Big Two-Hearted River" stands to the trout stream. In the latter story, Nick Adams prefers the clear portion of the river to its second and more congested heart:

In the swamp the banks were bare, the big cedars came together overhead, the sun did not come through, except in patches; in the fast deep water, in the half light, the fishing would be tragic. In the swamp fishing was a tragic adventure. Nick did not want it. . . . There were plenty of days coming when he could fish the swamp.

The fishing is tragic here because it involves the risk of death. Nick is not yet ready for that challenge, but plainly it will test his manhood when he comes to face it. In *The Sun Also Rises* Barnes makes no such demands upon himself; but he is strongly attracted to the young bullfighter, Pedro Romero, whose courage before death lends moral weight to the sportsman's code.

So Pamplona is an extension of Burguete for Barnes: gayer and more festive on the surface, but essentially more serious. The spoilers from Paris have arrived, but (Cohn excepted) they are soon swept up by the fiesta: their mood is jubilant, they are surrounded by dancers, and they sing, drink, and shout with the peasant crowd. Barnes himself is among fellow *aficionados*; he gains "real emotion" from the bullfights and feels truly elated afterwards. Even his friends seem like "such nice people," though he begins to feel uneasy when an argument breaks out between them. The tension is created by Brett's fiancé, Mike Campbell, who is aware of her numerous infidelities and who seems to accept them with amoral tolerance. Actually he resents them, so that Cohn (the perennial Jewish scapegoat) provides him with a convenient outlet for his feelings. He begins to bait him for following Brett around like a sick steer.

Mike's description is accurate enough. Cohn is always willing to suffer in public and to absorb insults for the sake of true love. On the other hand, he is also "ready to do battle for his lady," and when the chance finally comes, he knocks his rivals down like a genuine knight-errant. With Jake and Mike he has no trouble, but when he charges into Pedro's room to rescue Brett, the results are disastrous: Brett tells him off, the bullfighter refuses to stay knocked down, and no one will shake hands with him at the end, in accord with prep-school custom. When Brett remains with Pedro, Cohn retires to his room, alone and friendless.

This last encounter is the high point of the parable, for in the Code Hero, the Romantic Hero has finally met his match. As the clash between them shows, there is a difference between physical and moral victory, between chivalric stubbornness and real self-respect. Thus Pedro fights to repair an affront to his dignity; though he is badly beaten, his spirit is untouched by his opponent, whereas Cohn's spirit is completely smashed. From the beginning Cohn has based his manhood on skill at boxing, or upon a woman's love, never upon internal strength; but now, when neither skill nor love supports him, he has bludgeoned his way to his own emptiness. Compare his conduct with Romero's, on the following day, as the younger man performs for Brett in the bull ring:

> Everything of which he could control the locality he did in front of her all that afternoon. Never once did he look up. . . . Because he did not look up to ask if it pleased he did it all for himself inside, and it strengthened him, and yet he did it for her, too. But he did not do it for her at any loss to himself. He gained by it all through the afternoon.

Thus, where Cohn expends and degrades himself for his beloved, Romero pays tribute without self-loss. His manhood is a thing independent of women, and for this reason he holds special attractions for Jake Barnes.

By now it seems apparent that Cohn and Pedro are extremes for which Barnes is the unhappy medium. His resemblance to Pedro is clear enough: they share the same code, they both believe that a man's dignity depends on his own resources. His resemblance to Cohn is more subtle, but at this stage of the book it becomes grossly evident. Appropriately enough, the exposure comes through the knockout blow from Cohn, which dredges up a strange prewar experience:

Walking across the square to the hotel everything looked new and changed. . . . I felt as I felt once coming home from an out-of-town football game. I was carrying a suitcase with my football things in it, and I walked up the street from the station in the town I had lived in all my life and it was all new. They were raking the lawns and burning leaves in the road, and I stopped for a long time and watched. It was all strange. Then I went on, and my feet seemed to be a long way off, and everything seemed to come from a long way off, and I could hear my feet walking a great distance away. I had been kicked in the head early in the game. It was like that crossing the square. It was like that going up the stairs in the hotel. Going up the stairs took a long time, and I had the feeling that I was carrying my suitcase.

Barnes seems to have regressed here to his youthful football days. As he moves on up the stairs to see Cohn, who has been asking for him, he still carries his "phantom suitcase" with him; and when he enters Cohn's room, he even sets it down. Cohn himself has just returned from the fight with Romero: "There he was, face down on the bed, crying. He had on a white polo shirt, the kind he'd worn at Princeton." In other words, Cohn has also regressed to his abject college days: they are both emotional adolescents, about the same age as the nineteen-year-old Romero, who is the only real man among them. Of course, these facts are not spelled out for us, except through the polo shirt and the phantom suitcase, which remind us (inadvertently) of one of those dreamlike fantasies by the Czech genius Franz Kafka, in which trunks and youthful clothes are symbols of arrested development. Yet there has already been some helpful spelling out in Book I, during a curious (and otherwise pointless) exchange between Cohn and another expatriate, the drunkard Harvey Stone. After first calling Cohn a moron, Harvey asks him to say, without thinking about it, what he would rather do if he could do anything he wanted. Cohn is again urged to say what comes into his head first, and soon replies, "I think I'd rather play football again with what I know about handling myself, now." To which Harvey responds: "I misjudged you. . . . You're not a moron. You're only a case of arrested development."

The first thought to enter Cohn's mind here has been suppressed by Barnes for a long time, but in Book II the knockout blow releases it: more than anything else, he too would like to "play football again," to prevent that kick to his head from happening, or that smash to the jaw from Cohn, or that sexual wound which explains either blow. For the truth about Barnes seems obvious now: he has always been an emotional adolescent. Like Nick Adams, he has grown up in a society which has little use for manliness; as an expression of that society, the war has robbed him of his dignity as a man and has thus exposed him to indignities with women. We must understand here that the war, the early football game, and the fight with Cohn have this in common: they all involve ugly, senseless, or impersonal forms of violence, in which a man has little chance to set the terms of his own integrity. Hence for Hemingway they represent the kinds of degradation which can occur at any point in modern society—and the violence at Pamplona is our current sample of such degradation. Indeed, the whole confluence of events now points to the social meaning of Jake's wound, for just as Cohn has reduced him to a dazed adolescent, so has Brett reduced him to a slavish pimp. When she asks for his help in her affair with Pedro, Barnes has no integrity to rely on; he can only serve her as Cohn has served her, like a sick romantic steer. Thus, for love's sake, he will allow her to use him as a go-between, to disgrace him with his friend Montoya, to corrupt Romero, and so strip the whole fiesta of significance. In the next book he will even run to her rescue in Madrid, though by then he can at least recognize his folly and supply his own indictment: "That was it. Send a girl off with one man. Introduce her to another to go off with him. Now go and bring her back. And sign the wire with love. That was it all right." It seems plain, then, that Cohn and Brett have given us a peacetime demonstration, postwar style, of the meaning of Jake's shell wound.

At Pamplona the demonstration continues. Brett strolls through the fiesta with her head high, "as though [it] were being staged in her honor, and she found it pleasant and amusing." When Romero presents her with a bull's ear "cut by popular acclamation," she carries it off to her hotel, stuffs it far back in the drawer of the bed table, and forgets about it. The ear was taken, however, from the same bull which had killed one of the crowd a few days before, during the dangerous bull-run through the streets; later the entire town attended the man's funeral, along with drinking and dancing societies from nearby communities. For the crowd, the death of this bull was a communal triumph and his ear a token of communal strength; for Brett the ear is a private trophy. In effect, she has robbed the community of its triumph, as she will now rob it of its hero. As an *aficionado*, Barnes understands this threat too well. These are decadent times in the bull ring, marred by false esthetics; Romero alone has "the old thing," the old "purity of line through the maximum of exposure": his corruption by Brett will complete the decadence. But mainly the young fighter means something more personal to Barnes. In the bull ring he combines grace, control, and sincerity with manliness; in the fight with Cohn he proves his integrity where skill is lacking. His values are exactly those of the hunter in "Francis Macomber," or of the fisherman in *The*

Old Man and the Sea. As one of these few remaining images of independent manhood, he offers Barnes the comfort of vicarious redemption. Brett seems to smash this as she leaves with Pedro for Madrid. To ward off depression, Barnes can only get drunk and retire to bed; the fiesta goes on outside, but it means nothing now: the "good place" has been ruined.

As Book III begins, Barnes tries to reclaim his dignity and to cleanse himself of the damage at Pamplona. He goes to San Sebastian and sits quietly there in a café, listening to band concerts; or he goes swimming there alone, diving deep in the green waters. Then a telegram from Brett arrives, calling him to Madrid to help her out of trouble. At once he is like Cohn again, ready to serve his lady at the expense of self-respect. Yet in Madrid he learns to accept, emotionally, what he has always faintly understood. As he listens to Brett, he begins to drink heavily, as if her story has driven home a painful lesson. Brett herself feels "rather good" about sending Pedro away: she has at least been able to avoid being "one of these bitches that ruins children." This is a moral triumph for her, as Barnes agrees; but he can scarcely ignore its implications for himself. For when Brett refuses to let her hair grow long for Pedro, it means that her role in life is fixed: she can no longer reclaim her lost womanhood; she can no longer live with a fine man without destroying him. This seems to kill the illusion which is behind Jake's suffering throughout the novel: namely, that if he hadn't been wounded, if he had somehow survived the war with his manhood intact, then he and Brett would have become true lovers. The closing lines confirm his total disillusionment:

> "Oh, Jake," Brett said, "we could have had such a damned good time together."
> Ahead was a mounted policeman in khaki directing traffic. He raised his baton. The car slowed suddenly pressing Brett against me.
> "Yes," I said. "Isn't it pretty to think so?"

"Pretty" is a romantic word which means here "foolish to consider what could *never* have happened," and not "what can't happen now." The signal for this interpretation comes from the policeman who directs traffic between Brett's speech and Barnes's reply. With his khaki clothes and his preventive baton, he stands for the war and the society which made it, for the force which stops the lovers' car, and which robs them of their normal sexual roles. As Barnes now sees, love itself is dead for their generation. Even without his wound, he would still be unmanly, and Brett unable to let her hair grow long.

Yet, according to the opening epigraphs, if one generation is lost and another comes, the earth abides forever; and according to Hemingway himself, the abiding earth is the novel's hero. Perhaps he is wrong on this point, or at least misleading. There are no joyous hymns to the seasons in this novel, no celebrations of fertility and change. The scenic descriptions are accurate enough, but rather flat; there is no deep feeling in them, only fondness, for the author takes less delight in nature than in outdoor sports. He is more concerned, that is, with baiting hooks and catching trout than with the Irati River and more pleased with the grace and skill of the bullfighter than with the bull's magnificence. In fact, it is the bullfighter who seems to abide in the novel, for surely the bulls are dead like the trout before them, having fulfilled their roles as beloved opponents. But Romero is very much alive as the novel ends. When he leaves the hotel in Madrid, he "pays the bill" for his affair with Brett, which means that he has earned all its benefits. He also dominates the final conversation between the lovers, and so dominates the closing section. We learn here that his sexual initiation has been completed and his independence assured. From now on, he can work out his life alone, moving again and again through his passes in the ring, gaining strength, order, and purpose as he meets his own conditions. He provides no literal prescription to follow here, no call to bullfighting as the answer to Barnes's problems; but he does provide an image of integrity, against which Barnes and his generation are weighed and found wanting. In this sense, Pedro is the real hero of the parable, the final moral touchstone, the man whose code gives meaning to a world where love and religion are defunct, where the proofs of manhood are difficult and scarce, and where every man must learn to define his own moral conditions and then live up to them.

GEORGE PLIMPTON

An Interview with Ernest Hemingway

HEMINGWAY: *You go to the races?*
INTERVIEWER: *Yes, occasionally.*
HEMINGWAY: *Then you read the* Racing Form *. . . there you have the true Art of Fiction.*

— Conversation in a Madrid café, May, 1954

Ernest Hemingway writes in the bedroom of his home in the Havana suburb of San Francisco de Paula. He has a special workroom prepared for him in a square tower at the southwest corner of the house, but prefers to work in his bedroom, climbing to the tower room only when "characters" drive him up there.

The bedroom is on the ground floor and connects with the main room of the house. The door between the two is kept ajar by a heavy volume listing and describing "The World's Aircraft Engines." The bedroom is large, sunny, the windows facing east and south letting in the day's light on white walls and a yellow-tinged tile floor.

The room is divided into two alcoves by a pair of chest-high bookcases that stand out into the room at right angles from opposite walls. A large and low double bed dominates one section, oversized slippers and loafers neatly arranged at the foot, the two bedside tables at the head piled seven high with books. In the other alcove stands a massive flattop desk

From *Writers At Work: The Paris Review Interviews*, Second Series, edited by George Plimpton. Copyright © 1963 by The Paris Review, Inc.

with two chairs at either side, its surface an ordered clutter of papers and mementos. Beyond it, at the far end of the room, is an armoire with a leopard skin draped across the top. The other walls are lined with white-painted bookcases from which books overflow to the floor, and are piled on top amongst old newspapers, bullfight journals, and stacks of letters bound together by rubber bands.

It is on the top of one of these cluttered bookcases—the one against the wall by the east window and three feet or so from his bed—that Hemingway has his "work desk"—a square foot of cramped area hemmed in by books on one side and on the other by a newspaper-covered heap of papers, manuscripts, and pamphlets. There is just enough space left on top of the bookcase for a typewriter, surmounted by a wooden reading board, five or six pencils, and a chunk of copper ore to weight down papers when the wind blows in from the east window.

A working habit he has had from the beginning, Hemingway stands when he writes. He stands in a pair of his oversized loafers on the worn skin of a lesser kudu—the typewriter and the reading board chest-high opposite him.

When Hemingway starts on a project he always begins with a pencil, using the reading board to write on onionskin typewriter paper. He keeps a sheaf of the blank paper on a clipboard to the left of the typewriter, extracting the paper a sheet at a time from under a metal clip which reads "These Must Be Paid." He places the paper slantwise on the reading board, leans against the board with his left arm, steadying the paper with his hand, and fills the paper with handwriting which in the years has become larger, more boyish, with a paucity of punctuation, very few capitals, and often the period marked with an x. The page completed, he clips it face down on another clipboard which he places off to the right of the typewriter.

Hemingway shifts to the typewriter, lifting off the reading board, only when the writing is going fast and well, or when the writing is, for him at least, simple: dialogue, for instance.

He keeps track of his daily progress—"so as not to kid myself"—on a large chart made out of the side of a cardboard packing case and set up against the wall under the nose of a mounted gazelle head. The numbers on the chart showing the daily output of words differ from 450, 575, 462, 1250, to 512, the higher figures on days Hemingway puts in extra work so he won't feel guilty spending the following day fishing on the Gulf Stream.

A man of habit, Hemingway does not use the perfectly suitable desk in the other alcove. Though it allows more space for writing, it too has its miscellany: stacks of letters, a stuffed toy lion of the type sold in Broadway nighteries, a small burlap bag full of carnivore teeth, shotgun shells, a shoehorn, wood carvings of lion, rhino, two zebras, and a warthog—these last set in a neat row across the surface of the desk—and, of course, books. You remember books of the room, piled on the desk, bedside tables, jamming the shelves in indiscriminate order—novels, histories, collections of poetry, drama, essays. A look at their titles shows their variety. On the shelf opposite Hemingway's knees as he stands up to his "work desk" are Virginia Woolf's *The Common Reader*, Ben Ames Williams' *House Divided*, *The Partisan Reader*, Charles A. Beard's *The Republic*, Tarlé's *Napoleon's Invasion of Russia*, *How Young You Look* by one Peggy Wood, Alden Brook's *Shakespeare and the Dyer's Hand*, Baldwin's *African Hunting*, T.S. Eliot's *Collected Poems*, and two books on General Custer's fall at the battle of the Little Big Horn.

The room, however, for all the disorder sensed at first sight, indicates on inspection an owner who is basically neat but cannot bear to throw anything away—especially if sentimental value is attached. One bookcase top has an odd assortment of momentos: a giraffe made of wood beads, a little cast-iron turtle, tiny models of a locomotive, two jeeps and a Venetian gondola, a toy bear with a key in its back, a monkey carrying a pair of cymbals, a miniature guitar, and a little tin model of a U.S. Navy biplane (one wheel missing) resting awry on a circular straw place mat— the quality of the collection that of the odds and ends which turn up in a shoebox at the back of a small boy's closet. It is evident, though, that these tokens have their value, just as three buffalo horns Hemingway keeps in his bedroom have a value dependent not on size but because during the acquiring of them things went badly in the bush which ultimately turned out well. "It cheers me up to look at them," Hemingway says.

Hemingway may admit superstitions of this sort, but he prefers not to talk about them, feeling that whatever value they may have can be talked away. He has much the same attitude about writing. Many times during the making of this interview he stressed that the craft of writing should not be tampered with by an excess of scrutiny—"that though there is one part of writing that is solid and you do it no harm by talking about it, the other is fragile, and if you talk about it, the structure cracks and you have nothing."

As a result, though a wonderful raconteur, a man of rich humor, and possessed of an amazing fund of knowledge on subjects which interest him, Hemingway finds it difficult to talk about writing—not because he has few ideas on the subject, but rather that he feels so strongly that such ideas should remain unexpressed, that to be asked questions on them "spooks" him (to use one of his favorite expressions) to the point where he is almost inarticulate. Many of the replies in this interview he preferred to work out on his reading board. The occasional waspish tone of the answers is also part of this strong feeling that writing is a private, lonely occupation with no need for witnesses until the final work is done.

This dedication to his art may suggest a personality at odds with the rambunctious, carefree, world-wheeling Hemingway-at-play of popular conception. The point is, though, that Hemingway, while obviously enjoying life, brings an equivalent dedication to everything he does—an outlook that is essentially serious, with a horror of the inaccurate, the fraudulent, the deceptive, the half-baked.

Nowhere is the dedication he gives his art more evident than in the yellow-tiled bedroom—where early in the morning Hemingway gets up to stand in absolute concentration in front of his reading board, moving only to shift weight from one foot to another, perspiring heavily when the work is going well, excited as a boy, fretful, miserable when the artistic touch momentarily vanishes—slave of a self-imposed discipline which lasts until about noon when he takes a knotted walking stick and leaves the house for the swimming pool where he takes his daily half-mile swim.

Interviewer: Are these hours during the actual process of writing pleasurable?

Hemingway: Very.

Interviewer: Could you say something of this process? When do you work? Do you keep to a strict schedule?

Hemingway: When I am working on a book or a story I write every morning as soon after first light as possible. There is no one to disturb you and it is cool or cold and you come to your work and warm as you write. You read what you have written and, as you always stop when you know what is going to happen next, you go on from there. You write until you come to a place where you still have your juice and know what will happen next and you stop and try to live through until the next day when you hit it again. You have started at six in the morning, say, and may go on until noon or be through before that. When you stop you are as empty, and at the same time never empty but filling, as when you have made love to someone you love. Nothing can hurt you, nothing can happen, nothing means anything until the next day when you do it again. It is the wait until the next day that is hard to get through.

Interviewer: Can you dismiss from your mind whatever project you're on when you're away from the typewriter?

Hemingway: Of course. But it takes discipline to do it and this discipline is acquired. It has to be.

Interviewer: Do you do any rewriting as you read up to the place you left off the day before? Or does that come later, when the whole is finished?

Hemingway: I always rewrite each day up to the point where I stopped. When it is all finished, naturally you go over it. You get another chance to correct and rewrite when someone else types it, and you see it clean in type. The last chance is in the proofs. You're grateful for these different chances.

Interviewer: How much rewriting do you do?

Hemingway: It depends, I rewrote the ending to *Farewell to Arms*, the last page of it, thirty-nine times before I was satisfied.

Interviewer: Was there some technical problem there? What was it that had stumped you?

Hemingway: Getting the words right.

Interviewer: Is it the rereading that gets the "juice" up?

Hemingway: Rereading places you at the point where it *has* to go on, knowing it is as good as you can get it up to there. There is always juice somewhere.

Interviewer: But are there times when the inspiration isn't there at all?

Hemingway: Naturally. But if you stopped when you knew what would happen next, you can go on. As long as you can start, you are all right. The juice will come.

Interviewer: Thornton Wilder speaks of mnemonic devices that get the writer going on his day's work. He says you once told him you sharpened twenty pencils.

Hemingway: I don't think I ever owned twenty pencils at one time. Wearing down seven No. 2 pencils is a good day's work.

Interviewer: Where are some of the places you have found most advantageous to work? The Ambos Mundos hotel must have been one, judging from the number of books you did there. Or do surroundings have little effect on the work?

Hemingway: The Ambos Mundos in Havana was a very good place to work in. This *finca* is a splendid place, or was. But I have worked well everywhere. I mean I have been able to work as well as I can under varied circumstances. The telephone and visitors are the work destroyers.

Interviewer: Is emotional stability necessary to write well? You told me once that you could only write well when you were in love. Could you expound on that a bit more?

Hemingway: What a question. But full marks for trying. You can write any time people will leave you alone and not interrupt you. Or rather you can if you will be ruthless enough about it. But the best writing is certainly when you are in love. If it is all the same to you I would rather not expound on that.

Interviewer: How about financial security? Can that be a detriment to good writing?

Hemingway: If it came early enough and you loved life as much as you loved your work it would take much character to resist the temptations. Once writing has become your major vice and greatest pleasure only death can stop it. Financial security then is a great help as it keeps you from worrying. Worry destroys the ability to write. Ill health is bad in the ratio that it produces worry which attacks your subconscious and destroys your reserves.

Interviewer: Can you recall an exact moment when you decided to become a writer?

Hemingway: No, I always wanted to be a writer.

Interviewer: Philip Young in his book on you suggests that the traumatic shock of your severe 1918 mortar wound had a great influence on you as a writer. I remember in Madrid you talked briefly about his thesis, finding little in it, and going on to say that you thought the artist's equipment was not an acquired characteristic, but inherited, in the Mendelian sense.

Hemingway: Evidently in Madrid that year my mind could not be called very sound. The only thing to recommend it would be that I spoke only briefly about Mr. Young's book and his trauma theory of literature. Perhaps the two concussions and a skull fracture of that year had made me irresponsible in my statements. I do remember telling you that I believed imagination could be the result of inherited racial experience. It sounds all right in good jolly post-concussion talk, but I think that is more or less where it belongs. So until the next liberation trauma, let's leave it there. Do you agree? But thanks for leaving out the names of any relatives I might have implicated. The fun of talk is to explore, but much of it and all that is irresponsible should not be written, Once written you have to stand by it. You may have said it to see whether you believed it or not. On the question you raised, the effects of wounds vary greatly. Simple wounds which do not break bone are of little account. They sometimes give confidence. Wounds which do extensive bone and nerve damage are not good for writers, nor anybody else.

Interviewer: What would you consider the best intellectual training for the would-be writer?

Hemingway: Let's say that he should go out and hang himself because he finds that writing well is impossibly difficult. Then he should be cut down without mercy and forced by his own self to write as well as he can for the rest of his life. At least he will have the story of the hanging to commence with.

Interviewer: How about people who've gone into the academic career? Do you think the large numbers of writers who hold teaching positions have compromised their literary careers?

Hemingway: It depends on what you call compromise. Is the usage that of a woman who has been compromised? Or is it the compromise of the statesman? Or the compromise made with your grocer or your tailor that you will pay a little more but will pay it later? A writer who can both write and teach should be able to do both. Many competent writers have proved it could be done. I could not do it, I know, and I admire those who have been able to. I would think though that the academic life could put a period to outside experience which might possibly limit growth of knowledge of the world. Knowledge, however, demands more responsibility of a writer and makes writing more difficult. Trying to write something of permanent value is a full-time job even though only a few hours a day are spent on the actual writing. A writer can be compared to a well. There are as many kinds of wells as there are writers. The important thing is to have good water in the well and it is better to take a regular amount out than to pump the well dry and wait for it to refill. I see I am getting away from the question, but the question was not very interesting.

Interviewer: Would you suggest newspaper work for the young writer? How helpful was the training you had with the *Kansas City Star*?

Hemingway: On the *Star* you were forced to learn to write a simple declarative sentence. This is useful to anyone. Newspaper work will not harm a young writer and could help him if he gets out of it in time. This is one of the dustiest clichés there is and I apologize for it. But when you ask someone old tired questions you are apt to receive old tired answers.

Interviewer: You once wrote in the *transatlantic review* that the only reason for writing journalism was to be well paid. You said: "And when you destroy the valuable things you have by writing about them, you want to get big money for it." Do you think of writing as a type of self-destruction?

Hemingway: I do not remember ever writing that. But it sounds silly and violent enough for me to have said it to avoid having to bite on the nail and make a sensible statement. I certainly do not think of writing as a type of self-destruction though journalism, after a point has been reached, can be a daily self-destruction for a serious creative writer.

Interviewer: Do you think the intellectual stimulus of the company of other writers is of any value to an author?

Hemingway: Certainly.

Interviewer: In the Paris of the twenties did you have any sense of "group feeling" with other writers and artists?

Hemingway: No. There was no group feeling. We had respect for each other. I respected a lot of painters, some of my own age, others older—Gris, Picasso, Braque, Monet, who was still alive then—and a few writers: Joyce, Ezra, the good of Stein. . . .

Interviewer: When you are writing, do you ever find yourself influenced by what you're reading at the time?

Hemingway: Not since Joyce was writing *Ulysses.* His was not a direct influence. But in those days when words we knew were barred to us, and we had to fight for a single word, the influence of his work was what changed everything, and made it possible for us to break away from the restrictions.

Interviewer: Could you learn anything about writing from the writers? You were telling me yesterday that Joyce, for example, couldn't bear to talk about writing.

Hemingway: In company with people of your own trade you ordinarily speak of other writers' books. The better the writers the less they will speak about what they have written themselves. Joyce was a very great writer and he would only explain what he was doing to jerks. Other writers that he respected were supposed to be able to know what he was doing by reading it.

Interviewer: You seem to have avoided the company of writers in late years. Why?

Hemingway: That is more complicated. The further you go in writing the more alone you are. Most of your best and oldest friends die. Others move away. You do not see them except rarely, but you write and have much the same contact with them as though you were together at the café in the old days. You exchange comic, sometimes cheerfully obscene and irresponsible letters, and it is almost as good as talking. But you are more alone because that is how you must work and the time to work is shorter all the time and if you waste it you feel you have committed a sin for which there is no forgiveness.

Interviewer: What about the influence of some of these people— your contemporaries—on your work? What was Gertrude Stein's contribution, if any? Or Ezra Pound's? Or Max Perkins'?

Hemingway: I'm sorry but I am no good at these post-mortems. There are coroners literary and nonliterary provided to deal with such matters. Miss Stein wrote at some length and with considerable inaccuracy about her influence on my work. It was necessary for her to do this after she had learned to write dialogue from a book called *The Sun Also Rises*. I was very fond of her and thought it was splendid she had learned to write conversation. It was no new thing to me to learn from everyone I could, living or dead, and I had no idea it would affect Gertrude so violently. She already wrote very well in other ways. Ezra was extremely intelligent on the subjects he really knew. Doesn't this sort of talk bore you? This backyard literary gossip while washing out the dirty clothes of thirty-five years ago is disgusting to me. It would be different if one had tried to tell the whole truth. That would have some value. Here it is simpler and better to thank Gertrude for everything I learned from her about the abstract relationship of words, say how fond I was of her, reaffirm my loyalty to Ezra as a great poet and a loyal friend, and say that I cared so much for Max Perkins that I have never been able to accept that he is dead. He never asked me to change anything I wrote except to remove certain words which were not then publishable. Blanks were left, and anyone who knew the words would know what they were. For me he was not an editor. He was a wise friend and a wonderful companion. I liked the way he wore his hat and the strange way his lips moved.

Interviewer: Who would you say are your literary forebears—those you have learned the most from?

Hemingway: Mark Twain, Flaubert, Stendhal, Bach, Turgenev, Tolstoi, Dostoevski, Chekhov, Andrew Marvell, John Donne, Maupassant, the good Kipling, Thoreau, Captain Marryat, Shakespeare, Mozart. Quevedo, Dante, Vergil, Tintoretto, Hieronymus Bosch, Breughel, Patinier, Goya, Giotto, Cézanne, Van Gogh, Gauguin, San Juan de la Cruz, Góngora—it would take a day to remember everyone. Then it would sound as though I were claiming an erudition I did not possess instead of trying to remember all the people who have been an influence on my life and work. This isn't an old dull question. It is a very good but a solemn question and requires an examination of conscience. I put in painters, or started to, because I learn as much from painters about how to write as from writers. You ask how this is done? It would take another day of explaining. I should think what one learns from composers and from the study of harmony and counterpoint would be obvious.

Interviewer: Did you ever play a musical instrument?

Hemingway: I used to play cello. My mother kept me out of school a whole year to study music and counterpoint. She thought I had ability, but I was absolutely without talent. We played chamber music—someone came in to play the violin; my sister played the viola, and mother the piano. That cello—I played it worse than anyone on earth. Of course, that year I was out doing other things too.

Interviewer: Do you reread the authors of your list—Twain, for instance?

Hemingway: You have to wait two or three years with Twain. You remember too well. I read some Shakespeare every year, *Lear* always. Cheers you up if you read that.

Interviewer: Reading, then, is a constant occupation and pleasure.

Hemingway: I'm always reading books—as many as there are. I ration myself on them so that I'll always be in supply.

Interviewer: Do you ever read manuscripts?

Hemingway: You can get into trouble doing that unless you know the author personally. Some years ago I was sued for plagiarism by a man who claimed that I'd lifted *For Whom the Bell Tolls* from an unpublished screen scenario he'd written. He'd read this scenario at some Hollywood party. I was there, he said, at least there was a fellow called "Ernie" there listening to the reading, and that was enough for him to sue for a million dollars. At the same time he sued the producers of the motion pictures *Northwest Mounted Police* and the *Cisco Kid*, claiming that these, as well, had been stolen from that same unpublished scenario. We went to court and, of course, won the case. The man turned out to be insolvent.

Interviewer: Well, could we go back to that list and take one of the painters—Hieronymus Bosch, for instance? The nightmare symbolic quality of his work seems so far removed from your own.

Hemingway: I have the nightmares and know about the ones other people have. But you do not have to write them down. Anything you can omit that you know you still have in the writing and its quality will show. When a writer omits things he does not know, they show like holes in his writing.

Interviewer: Does that mean that a close knowledge of the works of the people on your list helps fill the "well" you were speaking of a while back? Or were they consciously a help in developing the techniques of writing?

Hemingway: They were a part of learning to see, to hear, to think, to feel and not feel, and to write. The well is where your "juice" is. Nobody knows what it is made of, least of all yourself. What you know is if you have it, or you have to wait for it to come back.

Interviewer: Would you admit to there being symbolism in your novels?

Hemingway: I suppose there are symbols since critics keep finding them. If you do not mind I dislike talking about them and being questioned about them. It is hard enough to write books and stories without being asked to explain them as well. Also it deprives the explainers of work. If five or six or more good explainers can keep going why should I interfere with them? Read anything I write for the pleasure of reading it. Whatever else you find will be the measure of what you brought to the reading.

Interviewer: Continuing with just one question on this line: One of the advisory staff editors wonders about a parallel he feels he's found in *The Sun Also Rises* between the dramatis personae of the bull ring and the characters of the novel itself. He points out that the first sentence of the book tells us Robert Cohn is a boxer; later, during the *descencajonada*, the bull is described as using his horns like a boxer, hooking and jabbing. And just as the bull is attracted and pacified by the presence of a steer, Robert Cohn defers to Jake who is emasculated precisely as is a steer. He sees Mike as the picador, baiting Cohn repeatedly. The editor's thesis goes on, but he wondered if it was your conscious intention to inform the novel with the tragic structure of the bullfight ritual.

Hemingway: It sounds as though the advisory staff editor was a little bit screwy. Who ever said Jake was "emasculated precisely as is a steer"? Actually he had been wounded in quite a different way and his testicles were intact and not damaged. Thus he was capable of all normal feelings as a *man* but incapable of consummating them. The important distinction is that his wound was physical and not psychological and that he was not emasculated.

Interviewer: These questions which inquire into craftsmanship really are an annoyance.

Hemingway: A sensible question is neither a delight nor an annoyance. I still believe though that it is very bad for a writer to talk about how he writes. He writes to be read by the eye and no explanations nor dissertations should be necessary. You can be sure that there is much more there than will be read at any first reading and having made this it is not the writer's province to explain it or to run guided tours through the more difficult country of his work.

Interviewer: In connection with this, I remember you have also warned that it is dangerous for a writer to talk about a work in progress, that he can "talk it out" so to speak. Why should this be so? I only ask because there are so many writers—Twain, Wilde, Thurber, Steffens, come to mind—who would seem to have polished their material by testing it on listeners.

Hemingway: I cannot believe Twain ever "tested out" *Huckleberry Finn* on listeners. If he did they probably had him cut out good things and put in the bad parts. Wilde was said by people who knew him to have been a better talker than a writer. Steffens talked better than he wrote. Both his writing and his talking were sometimes hard to believe, and I heard many stories change as he grew older. If Thurber can talk as well as he writes he must be one of the greatest and least boring talkers. The man I know who talks best about his own trade and has the pleasantest and most wicked tongue is Juan Belmonte, the matador.

Interviewer: Could you say how much thought-out effort went into the evolvement of your distinctive style?

Hemingway: That is a long-term tiring question and if you spent a couple of days answering it you would be so self-conscious that you could not write. I might say that what amateurs call a style is usually only the unavoidable awkwardness in first trying to make something that has not heretofore been made. Almost no new classics resemble other previous classics. At first people can see only the awkwardness. Then they are not so perceptible. When they show so very awkwardly people think these awkwardnesses are the style and many copy them. This is regrettable.

Interviewer: You once wrote me that the simple circumstances under which various pieces of fiction were written could be instructive. Could you apply this to "The Killers"—you said that you had written it, "Ten Indians" and "Today Is Friday" in one day—and perhaps to your first novel *The Sun Also Rises?*

Hemingway: Let's see. *The Sun Also Rises* I started in Valencia on my birthday, July 21st. Hadley, my wife, and I had gone to Valencia early to get good tickets for the *feria* there which started the 24th of July. Everybody my age had written a novel and I was still having a difficult time writing a paragraph. So I started the book on my birthday, wrote all through the *feria,* in bed in the morning, went on to Madrid and wrote there. There was no *feria* there, so we had a room with a table and I wrote in great luxury on the table and around the corner from the hotel in a beer place in the Pasaje Alvarez where it was cool. It finally got too hot to write and we went to Hendaye. There was a small cheap hotel there on the big long lovely beach and I worked very well there and then went up to Paris and finished the first draft in the apartment over the sawmill at 113 rue Notre Dame des Champs six weeks from the day I started it. I showed the first draft to Nathan Asch, the novelist, who then had quite a strong accent and he said, "Hem, vaht do you mean saying you wrote a novel? A novel huh. Hem, you are riding a trahvel buch." I was not too discouraged by Nathan and rewrote the book, keeping in the travel (that was the part about the fishing trip and Pamplona) at Schruns in the Vorarlberg at the Hotel Taube.

The stories you mention I wrote in one day in Madrid on May 16 when it snowed out the San Isidro bullfights. First I wrote "The Killers," which I'd tried to write before and failed. Then after lunch I got in bed to keep warm and wrote "Today Is Friday." I had so much juice I thought maybe I was going crazy and I had about six other stories to write. So I got dressed and walked to Fornos, the old bullfighters' café, and drank coffee and then came back and wrote "Ten Indians." This made me very sad and I drank some brandy and went to sleep. I'd forgotten to eat and one of the waiters brought me up some bacalao and a small steak and fried potatoes and a bottle of Valdepeñas.

The woman who ran the pension was always worried that I did not eat enough and she had sent the waiter. I remember sitting up in bed and eating, and drinking the Valdepeñas. The waiter said he would bring up another bottle. He said the señora wanted to know if I was going to write all night. I said no, I thought I would lay off for a while. Why don't you try to write just one more, the waiter asked. I'm only supposed to write one, I said. Nonsense, he said. You could write six. I'll try tomorrow, I said. Try it tonight, he said. What do you think the old woman sent the food up for?

I'm tired, I told him. Nonsense, he said (the word was not nonsense). You tired after three miserable little stories. Translate me one.

Leave me alone, I said. How am I going to write it if you don't leave me alone. So I sat up in bed and drank the Valdepeñas and thought what a hell of a writer I was if the first story was as good as I'd hoped.

Interviewer: How complete in your own mind is the conception of a short story? Does the theme, or the plot, or a character change as you go along?

Hemingway: Sometimes you know the story. Sometimes you make it up as you go along and have no idea how it will come out. Everything changes as it moves. That is what makes the movement which makes the story. Sometimes the movement is so slow it does not seem to be moving. But there is always change and always movement.

Interviewer: Is it the same with the novel, or do you work out the whole plan before you start and adhere to it rigorously?

Hemingway: For Whom the Bell Tolls was a problem which I carried on each day. I knew what was going to happen in principle. But I invented what happened each day I wrote.

Interviewer: Were the *Green Hills of Africa, To Have and Have Not,* and *Across the River and into the Trees* all started as short stories and developed into novels? If so, are the two forms so similar that the writer can pass from one to the other without completely revamping his approach?

Hemingway: No, that is not true. The *Green Hills of Africa* is not a novel but was written in an attempt to write an absolutely true book to see whether the shape of a country and the pattern of a month's action could, if truly presented, compete with a work of the imagination. After I had written it I wrote two short stories, "The Snows of Kilimanjaro" and "The Short Happy Life of Francis Macomber." These were stories which I invented from the knowledge and experience acquired on the same long hunting trip one month of which I had tried to write a truthful account of in the *Green Hills*. *To Have and Have Not* and *Across the River and into the Trees* were both started as short stories.

Interviewer: Do you find it easy to shift from one literary project to another or do you continue through to finish what you start?

Hemingway: The fact that I am interrupting serious work to answer these questions proves that I am so stupid that I should be penalized severely. I will be. Don't worry.

Interviewer: Do you think of yourself in competition with other writers?

Hemingway: Never. I used to try to write better than certain dead writers of whose value I was certain. For a long time now I have tried simply to write the best I can. Sometimes I have good luck and write better than I can.

Interviewer: Do you think a writer's power diminishes as he grows older? In the *Green Hills of Africa* you mention that American writers at a certain age change into Old Mother Hubbards.

Hemingway: I don't know about that. People who know what they are doing should last as long as their heads last. In that book you mention, if you look it up, you'll see I was sounding off about American literature with a humorless Austrian character who was forcing me to talk when I wanted to do something else. I wrote an accurate account of the conversation. Not to make deathless pronouncements. A fair per cent of the pronouncements are good enough.

Interviewer: We've not discussed character. Are the characters of your work taken without exception from real life?

Hemingway: Of course they are not. *Some* come from real life. Mostly you invent people from a knowledge and understanding and experience of people.

Interviewer: Could you say something about the process of turning a real-life character into a fictional one?

Hemingway: If I explained how that is sometimes done, it would be a handbook for libel lawyers.

Interviewer: Do you make a distinction—as E.M. Forster does—between "flat" and "round" characters?

Hemingway: If you describe someone, it is flat, as a photograph is, and from my standpoint a failure. If you make him up from what you know, there should be all the dimensions.

Interviewer: Which of your characters do you look back on with particular affection?

Hemingway: That would make too long a list.

Interviewer: Then you enjoy reading over your own books—without feeling there are changes you would like to make?

Hemingway: I read them sometimes to cheer me up when it is hard to write and then I remember that it was always difficult and how nearly impossible it was sometimes.

Interviewer: How do you name your characters?

Hemingway: The best I can.

Interviewer: Do the titles come to you while you're in the process of doing the story?

Hemingway: No. I make a list of titles *after* I've finished the story or the book—sometimes as many as 100. Then I start eliminating them, sometimes all of them.

Interviewer: And you do this even with a story whose title is supplied from the text—"Hills Like White Elephants," for example?

Hemingway: Yes. The title comes afterwards. I met a girl in Prunier where I'd gone to eat oysters before lunch. I knew she'd had an abortion. I went over and we talked, not about that, but on the way home I thought of the story, skipped lunch, and spent that afternoon writing it.

Interviewer: So when you're not writing, you remain constantly the observer, looking for something which can be of use.

Hemingway: Surely. If a writer stops observing he is finished. But he does not have to observe consciously nor think how it will be useful. Perhaps that would be true at the beginning. But later everything he sees goes into the great reserve of things he knows or has seen. If it is any use to know it, I always try to write on the principle of the iceberg. There is seven eighths of it under water for every part that shows. Anything you know you can eliminate and it only strengthens your iceberg. It is the part that doesn't show. If a writer omits something because he does not know it then there is a hole in the story.

The Old Man and the Sea could have been over a thousand pages long and had every character in the village in it and all the processes of how they made their living, were born, educated, bore children, etc. That is done excellently and well by other writers. In writing you are limited by what has already been done satisfactorily. So I have tried to learn to do something else. First I have tried to eliminate everything unnecessary to conveying experience to the reader so that after he or she has read something it will become a part of his or her experience and seem actually to have happened. This is very hard to do and I've worked at it very hard.

Anyway, to skip how it is done, I had unbelievable luck this time and could convey the experience completely and have it be one that no one had ever conveyed. The luck was that I had a good man and a good boy and lately writers have forgotten there still are such things. Then the ocean is worth writing about just as man is. So I was lucky there. I've seen the marlin mate and know about that. So I leave that out. I've seen a school (or pod) of more than fifty sperm whales in that same stretch of water and once harpooned one nearly sixty feet in length and lost him. So I left that out. All the stories I know from the fishing village I leave out. But the knowledge is what makes the underwater part of the iceberg.

Interviewer: Archibald MacLeish has spoken of a method of conveying experience to a reader which he said you developed while covering baseball games back in those *Kansas City Star* days. It was simply that experience is communicated by small details, intimately preserved, which have the effect of indicating the whole by making the reader conscious of what he had been aware of only subconsciously. . . .

Hemingway: The anecdote is apocryphal. I never wrote baseball for the *Star.* What Archie was trying to remember was how I was trying to learn in Chicago in around 1920 and was searching for the unnoticed things that made emotions such as the way an outfielder tossed his glove without looking back to where it fell, the squeak of resin on canvas under a fighter's flat-soled gym shoes, the gray color of Jack Blackburn's skin when he had just come out of stir and other things I noted as a painter sketches. You saw Blackburn's strange color and the old razor cuts and the way he spun a man before you knew his history. These were the things which moved you before you knew the story.

Interviewer: Have you ever described any type of situation of which you had no personal knowledge?

Hemingway: That is a strange question. By personal knowledge do you mean carnal knowledge? In that case the answer is positive. A writer, if he is any good, does not describe. He invents or *makes* out of knowledge personal and impersonal and sometimes he seems to have unexplained knowledge which could come from forgotten racial or family experience. Who teaches the homing pigeon to fly as he does; where does a fighting bull get his bravery, or a hunting dog his nose? This is an elaboration or a condensation on that stuff we were talking in Madrid that time when my head was not to be trusted.

Interviewer: How detached must you be from an experience before you can write about it in fictional terms? The African air crashes, for instance?

Hemingway: It depends on the experience. One part of you sees it with complete detachment from the start. Another part is very involved. I think there is no rule about how soon one should write about it. It would depend on how well adjusted the individual was and on his or her recuperative powers. Certainly it is valuable to a trained writer to crash in an aircraft which burns. He learns several important things very quickly. Whether they will be of use to him is conditioned by survival. Survival, with honor, that outmoded and all-important word, is as difficult as ever and as all-important to a writer. Those who do not last are always more beloved since no one has to see them in their long, dull, unrelenting, no quarter given and no quarter received, fights that they make to do something as they believe it should be done before they die. Those who die or quit early and easy and with very good reason are preferred because they are understandable and human. Failure and well-disguised cowardice are more human and more beloved.

Interviewer: Could I ask you to what extent you think the writer should concern himself with the sociopolitical problems of his times?

Hemingway: Everyone has his own conscience and there should be no rules about how a conscience should function. All you can be sure about in a political-minded writer is that if his work should last you will have to skip the politics when you read it. Many of the so-called politically enlisted writers change their politics frequently. This is very exciting to them and to their political-literary reviews. Sometimes they even have to rewrite their vewpoints . . . and in a hurry. Perhaps it can be respected as a form of the pursuit of happiness.

Interviewer: Has the political influence of Ezra Pound on the segregationalist Kasper had any effect on your belief that the poet ought to be released from St. Elizabeth's Hospital?

Hemingway: No. None at all. I believe Ezra should be released and allowed to write poetry in Italy on an undertaking by him to abstain from any politics. I would be happy to see Kasper jailed as soon as possible. Great poets are not necessarily girl guides nor scoutmasters nor splendid influences on youth. To name a few: Verlaine, Rimbaud, Shelley, Byron, Baudelaire, Proust, Gide, should not have been confined to prevent them from being aped in their thinking, their manners or their morals by local

Kaspers. I am sure that it will take a footnote to this paragraph in ten years to explain who Kasper was.

Interviewer: Would you say, ever, that there is any didactic intention in your work?

Hemingway: Didactic is a word that has been misused and has spoiled. *Death in the Afternoon* is an instructive book.

Interviewer: It has been said that a writer only deals with one or two ideas throughout his work. Would you say your work reflects one or two ideas?

Hemingway: Who said that? It sounds much too simple. The man who said it possibly *had* only one or two ideas.

Interviewer: Well, perhaps it would be better put this way: Graham Greene said in one of these interviews that a ruling passion gives to a shelf of novels the unity of a system. You yourself have said, I believe, that great writing comes out of a sense of injustice. Do you consider it important that a novelist be dominated in this way—by some such compelling sense?

Hemingway: Mr. Greene has a facility for making statements that I do not possess. It would be impossible for me to make generalizations about a shelf of novels or a wisp of snipe or a gaggle of geese. I'll try a generalization though. A writer without a sense of justice and of injustice would be better off editing the year book of a school for exceptional children than writing novels. Another generalization. You see; they are not so difficult when they are sufficiently obvious. The most essential gift for a good writer is a built-in, shockproof, shit detector. This is the writer's radar and all great writers have had it.

Interviewer: Finally, a fundamental question: namely, as a creative writer what do you think is the function of your art? Why a representation of fact, rather than fact itself?

Hemingway: Why be puzzled by that? From things that have happened and from things as they exist and from all things that you know and all those you cannot know, you make something through your invention that is not a representation but a whole new thing truer than anything true and alive, and you make it alive, and if you make it well enough, you give it immortality. That is why you write and for no other reason that you know of. But what about all the reasons that no one knows?

REYNOLDS PRICE

For Ernest Hemingway

If I had been conscious of caring enough, as late as the spring of 1970, to check the state of my own feelings about the work of Hemingway (nine years after his death and at least five since I'd read more of him than an occasional story for teaching purposes), I'd probably have come up with a reading close to the postmortem consensus—that once one has abandoned illusions of his being a novelist and has set aside, as thoroughly as any spectator can, the decades of increasingly public descent into artistic senility (dosing those memories with the sad and sterile revelations of Carlos Baker's biography), then one can honor him as "a minor romantic poet" who wrote a lovely early novel, *The Sun Also Rises*, and a handful of early stories of the north woods, the first war, postwar Americans in Europe, which are likely to remain readable and, despite their truculent preciosity, leanly but steadily rewarding. But I don't remember caring enough to come up with even that grudging an estimate.

Why? Partly a participation in the understandable, if unlikable, international sigh of relief at the flattening of one more Sitting Bull, expecially one who had made strenuous attempts to publicize his own worst nature; partly an attenuation of my lines to the work itself; partly a response to the discovery that in my first three years of teaching, *A Farewell to Arms* had dissolved with alarming ease, under the corrosive of prolonged scrutiny, into its soft components (narcissism and blindness) when a superficially softer-looking book like *The Great Gatsby* proved diamond; but mostly the two common responses to any family death: forgetfulness and ingratitude.

Then two reminding signals. In the summer of '70, I visited Key West and wandered with a friend one morning down Whitehead to the Hemingway house, tall, square, and iron-galleried, with high airy rooms on ample grounds thick with tropic green, still privately owned (though not by his heirs) and casually open, once you've paid your dollar, for the sort of slow unattended poking around all but universally forbidden in other American shrines. His bed, his tile bath, his war souvenirs (all distinctly small-town Southern, human-sized; middle-class careless well-to-do—the surroundings of, say, a taciturn literate doctor and his tanned leggy wife just gone for two weeks with their kin in Charleston or to Asheville, cool and golfy; and you inexplicably permitted to hang spectral in their momentarily cast shell). But more—the large room over the yard house in which Hemingway wrote a good part of his work between 1931 and 1939 (six books) at a small round table, dark brown and unsteady; the small swimming pool beneath, prowled by the dozens of deformed multi-toed cats descended from a Hemingway pair of the thirties. Green shade, hustling surly old Key West silent behind walls, a rising scent of sadness— that Eden survived, not destroyed at all but here and reachable, though not by its intended inhabitants, who are barred by the simple choices of their lives and, now, by death (Hemingway lost the house in 1939 at his second divorce). The rising sense that I am surrounded, accompanied by more than my friend—

> I am moved by fancies that are curled
> Around these images, and cling:
> The notion of some infinitely gentle
> Infinitely suffering thing.

The center of my strong and unexpected response began to clarify when I discovered, at home, that I had recalled Eliot's first adjective as *delicate*— "some infinitely delicate/Infinitely suffering thing." What thing?

In October, the second signal. *Islands in the Stream* was published and received, with one or two enthusiastic notices, a few sane ones (Irving Howe, John Aldridge), and a number of tantrums of the beat-it-to-death, scatter-the-ashes sort. In fact, the kinds of notices calculated to rush serious readers to a bookstore (such response being a fairly sure sign that a book is alive and scary, capable of harm); and no doubt I'd have read the book eventually, but a combination of my fresh memories of Key West and a natural surge of sympathy after such a press sent me out to buy it, a ten-dollar vote of—what? *Thanks*, I suddenly knew, to Hemingway.

For what? For being a strong force in both my own early awareness of a need to write and my early sense of how to write. Maybe the strongest. A fact I'd handily forgot but was firmly returned to now, by *Islands in the Stream*.

A long novel—466 pages—it threatens for nearly half its length to be his best. And the first of its three parts—"Bimini," two hundred pages—is his finest sustained fiction, itself an independent novella. Finest, I think, for a number of reasons that will be self-evident to anyone who can bury his conditioned responses to the Hemingway of post-1940, but chiefly because in it Hemingway deals for the first time substantially, masterfully, and to crushing effect with the only one of the four possible human relations which he had previously avoided—parental devotion, filial return. (The other three relations—with God, with the earth, with a female or male lover or friend—he had worked from the start, failing almost always with the first, puzzlingly often with the third, succeeding as richly as anyone with the second.)

It would violate the apparent loose-handedness of those two hundred pages to pick in them for exhibits. Hemingway, unlike Faulkner, is always badly served by spot quotation, as anyone will know who turns from critical discussions of him (with their repertoire of a dozen Great Paragraphs) back to the works themselves. Faulkner, so often short-winded, can be flattered by brief citation, shown at the stunning moment of triumph. But Hemingway's power, despite his continued fame for "style," is always built upon *breath*, long breath, even in the shortest piece—upon a sustained legato of quiet pleading which acts on a willing reader in almost exactly the same way as the opening phrase of Handel's *"Care selve"* or *"Ombra mai fù."* What the words are ostensibly saying in both Hemingway and Handel is less true, less complete, than the slow arc of their total movement throughout their length. Therefore any excerpt is likely to emphasize momentary weakness—artificiality of pose, frailty of emotion—which may well dissolve in the context of their intended whole. The words of *"Ombra mai fù"* translate literally as "Never was the shade of my dear and lovable vegetable so soothing"; and any three lines from say, the beautifully built trout-fishing pages of *The Sun Also Rises* are likely to read as equally simple-minded, dangerously vapid—

> He was a good trout, and I banged his head against the timber so that he quivered out straight, and then slipped him into my bag.

So may this from Part I of *Islands in the Stream*—

> The boys slept on cots on the screened porch and it is much less lonely sleeping when you can hear children breathing when you wake in the night.

But in the last novel, the love among Thomas Hudson, a good marine painter, and his three sons is created—compelled in the reader—by a slow lateral and spiral movement of episodes (lateral and spiral because no episode reaches a clear climax or peaks the others in revelation). All the episodes are built not on "style" or charged moments, though there are lovely moments, or on the ground-bass hum of a cerebral dynamo like Conrad's or Mann's, but on simple *threat*—potentially serious physical or psychic damage avoided: the middle son's encounter with a shark while spear fishing, the same boy's six-hour battle to bloody near-collapse with a giant marlin who escapes at the last moment (the only passage outside *The Old Man and the Sea* where I'm seduced into brief comprehension of his love of hunting), the boys' joint participation in a funny but sinister practical joke at a local bar (they convincingly pretend to be juvenile alcoholics, to the alarm of tourists). Threats which delay their action for the short interim of the visit with their father but prove at the end of the section to have been dire warnings or prophecies (warnings imply a chance of escape)—the two younger boys are killed with their mother in a car wreck, shortly after their return to France. Only when we—and Thomas Hudson—are possessed of that news can the helix of episodes deliver, decode, its appalling message, to us and to him. The lovely-seeming lazy days were white with the effort to speak their knowledge. *Avoid dependence, contingency.* The rest of the novel (a little more than half) tries to face those injunctions (restated in further calamities) and seems to me to fail, for reasons I'll guess at later; but the first part stands, firm and independent, simultaneously a populated accurate picture and an elaborate unanswerable statement about that picture. Or scenes with music.

For in that first two hundred pages, the junction of love and threat, encountered for the first time in Hemingway within a family of blood kin, exact from him a prose which, despite my claims of its unexcerptibility, is as patient and attentive to the forms of life which pass before it (shark, marlin, men) and as richly elliptical as any he wrote, requiring our rendezvous with him in the job—and all that as late as the early 1950s, just after the debacle of *Across the River and into the Trees.* Take these lines of the son David after his ordeal with the marlin—

"Thank you very much, Mr. Davis, for what you said when I first lost him," David said with his eyes still shut.
Thomas Hudson never knew what it was that Roger had said to him.

Or this between Hudson and young Tom, his eldest—

"Can you remember Christmas there?"

"No. Just you and snow and our dog Schnautz and my nurse. She was beautiful. And I remember mother on skis and how beautiful she was. I can remember seeing you and mother coming down skiing through an orchard. I don't know where it was. But I can remember the Jardin du Luxembourg well. I can remember afternoons with the boats on the lake by the fountain in the big garden with trees."

(That last sentence, incidentally, reestablishes Hemingway's mastery of one of the most treacherous but potentially revealing components of narrative—the preposition, a genuine cadenza of prepositions set naturally in the mouth of a boy, not for exhibit but as a function of a vision based as profoundly as Cézanne's on the *stance* of objects in relation to one another: a child, late light, boats on water near shore, flowers, shade.)

Such prose, recognizable yet renewed within the old forms by the fertility of its new impetus—family love—is only the first indication, coming as late as it does, of how terribly Hemingway maimed himself as an artist by generally banishing such passionate tenderness and emotional reciprocity from the previous thirty years of his work (it is clear enough from A *Moveable Feast*, the Baker biography, and private anecdotes from some of his more credible friends that such responses and returns were an important component of his daily life). The remaining 260 pages suggest—in their attempt to chart Hudson's strategies for dealing with external and internal calamity, his final almost glad acceptance of solitude and bareness—an even more melancholy possibility: that the years of avoiding permanent emotional relations in his work left him at the end unable to define his profoundest subject, prevented his even seeing that after the initial energy of his north-woods-and-war youth had spent itself (by 1933), he began to fail as artist and man not because of exhaustion of limited resource but because he could not or would not proceed from that first worked vein on into a richer, maybe endless vein, darker, heavier, more inaccessible but of proportionately greater value to him and his readers; a vein that might have fueled him through a long yielding life with his truest subject (because his truest need).

Wasn't his lifelong subject *saintliness*? Wasn't it generally as secret from him (a lapsing but never quite lost Christian) as from his readers? And doesn't that refusal, or inability, to identify and then attempt understanding of his central concern constitute the forced end of his work—and our failure as his readers, collusive in blindness? Hasn't the enormous and repetitive critical literature devoted to dissecting his obsession with codes and rituals, which may permit brief happiness in a meaningless world, discovered only a small (and unrealistic, intellectually jejune) portion of his long search? But doesn't he discover at last—and tell us in *Islands in the Stream*—that his search was not for survival and the techniques of survival but for goodness, thus victory?

What kind of goodness? Granted that a depressing amount of the work till 1940 (till *For Whom the Bell Tolls*) is so obsessed with codes of behavior as to come perilously close to comprising another of those deadest of all ducks—etiquettes: Castiglione, Elyot, Post (and anyone reared in middle-class America in the past forty years has known at least one Youth, generally aging, who was using Hemingway thus—a use which his own public person and need for disciples persistently encouraged). Yet beneath the thirty years of posturing, his serious readers detected, and honored, great pain and the groping for unspecific, often brutal anodynes— pain whose precise nature and origin he did not begin to face until the last pages of *For Whom the Bell Tolls* and which, though he can diagnose in *Islands in the Stream*, he could not adequately dramatize: the polar agonies of love, need, contingency, and of solitude, hate, freedom.

What seems to me strange and sad now is that few of his admirers and none of his abusers appear to have sighted what surfaces so often in his last three novels and in *A Moveable Feast*—the signs that the old quest for manly skills (of necessity, temporary skills) became a quest for virtue. The quest for skills was clearly related to *danger*—danger of damage to the self by Nada, Chance or Frederic Henry's "They": "They threw you in and told you the rules and the first time they caught you off base they killed you." But the quest of Col. Cantwell in *Across the River* (which metamorphoses from obsession with narcotic rituals for living well to the study of how to die), the unconscious quest of Santiago in *The Old Man and the Sea* (too heavily and obscurely underscored by crucifixion imagery), the clear fact that the subject of *A Moveable Feast* is Hemingway's own early failure as a man (husband, father, friend), and the fully altered quest of Thomas Hudson in *Islands in the Stream* (from good father and comrade in life to good solitary animal in death)—all are related not so much to danger as to mystery. No longer the easy late-Victorian "They" or the sophomore's Nada (both no more adequate responses to human experience than the tub-thumping of Henley's "Invictus") but something that might approximately be described as God, Order, the Source of Vaguely Discernible Law. The attempt not so much to "understand" apparent Order and Law as to detect its outlines (as by Braille in darkness), to strain to hear and obey some of its demands.

What demands did he hear? Most clearly, I think, the demand to survive the end of pleasure (and to end bad, useless pleasures). That is obviously a demand most often heard by the aged or middle-aged, droning through the deaths of friends, lovers, family, their own fading faculties. But Hemingway's characters from the first have heard it, and early in their lives—Nick Adams faced on all sides with disintegrated hopes, Jake Barnes deprived of genitals, Frederic Henry of Catherine and their son, the Italian major of his family in "In Another Country," Marie Morgan of her Harry, and on and on. Those early characters generally face deprivation with a common answer—activity. And it is surprising how often the activity is artistic. Nick Adams becomes a writer after the war (the author of his own stories); Jake Barnes is a journalist with ambitions (and, not at all incidentally, a good Catholic); Frederic Henry, without love, becomes the man who dictates to us A *Farewell to Arms*; Robert Jordan hopes to return, once the Spanish Civil War is over, to his university teaching in Missoula, Montana, and to write a good book. But whatever its nature, activity remains their aim and their only hope of survival intact—activity as waiting tactic (waiting for the end, total death), as gyrostabilizer, narcotic. In the last novels, however—most explicitly in *Islands in the Stream*—deprivation is met by *duty*, what the last heroes see as the performance of duty (there are earlier heroes with notions of duty—Nick, Jack—but their duty is more nearly chivalry, a self-consciously graceful *noblesse oblige*).

The duty is not to survive or to grace the lives of their waiting companions but to do their work—lonely fishing, lonely soldiering, lonely painting and submarine hunting. For whom? Not for family (wives, sons) or lovers (there are none; Cantwell knows his teenage contessa is a moment's dream). Well, for one's human witnesses then. Why? Cantwell goes on apparently, and a little incredibly, because any form of stop would diminish the vitality of his men, his friend the headwaiter, his girl—their grip upon the rims of their own abysses. Santiago endures his ordeal largely for the boy Manolin, that he not be ashamed of his aging friend and withdraw love and care. Thomas Hudson asks himself in a crucial passage in Part III (when he has, disastrously for his soul, stopped painting after the deaths of his three sons and gone to chasing Nazi subs off Cuba)—

> Well, it keeps your mind off things. What things? There aren't any things any more. Oh yes, there are. There is this ship and the people on her and the sea and the bastards you are hunting. Afterwards you will see your animals and go into town and get drunk as you can and your ashes dragged and then get ready to go out and do it again.

Hudson deals a few lines later with the fact that his present work is literally murder, that he does it "Because we are all murderers"; and he never really faces up to the tragedy of having permitted family sorrow to derail his true work—his rudder, his *use* to God and men as maker of ordered reflection—but those few lines, which out of context sound like a dozen Stoic monologues in the earlier work, actually bring Hudson nearer than any other Hemingway hero toward an explicit statement of that yearning for goodness which I suspect in all the work, from the very start—the generally suppressed intimation that *happiness* for all the young sufferers, or at least *rest*, would lie at the pole opposite their present position, the pole of pure solitude, detachment from the love of other created beings (in the words of John of the Cross), and only then in work for the two remaining witnesses: one's self and the inhuman universe. "There is this ship and the people on her and the sea and the bastards you are hunting"—brothers, the Mother, enemies: all the categories of created things. Hudson, and Hemingway, halt one step short of defining the traditional goal of virtue—the heart of God. And two pages before the end, when Hudson has taken fatal wounds from a wrecked sub crew, he struggles to stay alive by thinking—

> Think about the war and when you will paint again. . . . You can paint the sea better than anyone now if you will do it and not get mixed up in other things. Hang on good now to how you truly want to do it. You must hold hard to life to do it. But life is a cheap thing beside a man's work. The only thing is that you need it. Hold it tight. Now is the true time you make your play. Make it now without hope of anything. You always coagulated well and you can make one more real play. We are not the lumpenproletariat. We are the best and we do it for free.

But again, do it for whom? Most of Hudson's prewar pictures have been described as intended for this or that person—he paints for his middle son the lost giant marlin, Caribbean waterspouts for his bartender, a portrait of his loved-and-lost first wife (which he later gives her). Intended then as gifts, *from* love and *for* love, like most gifts. But now, in death, the reverberations threaten to deepen—Thomas Hudson's paintings (and by intimation, the clenched dignity of Nick Adams and Jake Barnes, Robert Jordan's inconsistent but passionate hunger for justice, Cantwell's tidy death, Santiago's mad endurance—most of Hemingway's work) seem intended to enhance, even to create if necessary, the love of creation in its witnesses and thereby to confirm an approach by the worker toward goodness, literal virtue, the manly performance of the will of God. *Saintliness*, I've called it (*goodness* if you'd rather, though *saintliness* suggests at least the fierce need, its desperation)—a saint being, by one definition, a life which shows God lovable.

Any God is seldom mentioned (never seriously by Hudson, though

Jake Barnes is a quiet Catholic, Santiago a rainy-day one—and though Hemingway himself nursed an intense if sporadic relation with the Church, from his mid-twenties on, saying in 1955, "I like to think I am [a Catholic] insofar as I can be" and in 1958 that he "believed in belief"). Isn't that the most damaging lack of all, in the life and the work?—from the beginning but most desperate toward the end, as the body and its satellites dissolved in age and the abuse of decades? I mean the simple fact that neither Hemingway nor any of his heroes (except maybe Santiago and, long before, the young priest from the Abruzzi who lingers in the mind, with Count Greffi, as one of the two polar heroes of A *Farewell to Arms*) could make the leap from an enduring love of creatures to a usable love of a Creator, a leap which (barring prevenient grace, some personal experience of the supernal) would have been the wildest, most dangerous act of all. Maybe, though, the *saving* one—leap into a still, or stiller, harbor from which (with the strengths of his life's vision about him, none canceled or denied but their natural arcs now permitted completion) he could have made further and final works, good for him and us. That he didn't (not necessarily *couldn't*, though of modern novelists maybe only Tolstoy, Dostoevsky, and Bernanos have given us sustained great work from such a choice) has become the single most famous fact of his life—its end: blind, baffled.

But he wrote a good deal, not one of the Monster Oeuvres yet much more than one might guess who followed the news reports of his leisure; and there remain apparently hundreds of pages of unpublished manuscript. What does it come to?—what does it tell us; do to us, for us, against us?

I've mentioned the low present standing of his stock, among critics and reviewers and older readers. Young people don't seem to read him. My university students—the youngest of whom were nine when he died— seem to have no special relations with him. What seemed to us cool grace seems to many of them huffery-puffery. But then, as is famous, a depressing majority of students have special relations with only the feyest available books. (Will Hemingway prove to be the last Classic Author upon whom a generation modeled its lives?—for *classic* read *good*.) Even his two earliest, most enthusiastic, and most careful academic critics have lately beat sad retreat. Carlos Baker's long love visibly disintegrates as he tallies each breath of the sixty-two years; and Philip Young nears the end of the revised edition of his influential "trauma" study (which caused Hemingway such pain) with this—

> Hemingway wrote two very good early novels, several very good stories and a few great ones . . . and an excellent if quite small book of

reminiscence. That's all it takes. This is such stuff as immortalities are made on.

The hope is that the good books will survive a depression inevitable after so many years of inflation (Eliot is presently suffering as badly; Faulkner, after decades of neglect, has swollen and will probably assuage until we see him again as a very deep but narrow trench, not the Great Meteor Crater he now seems to many)—and that we may even, as Young wagers gingerly, come to see some of the repugnant late work in the light of Hemingway's own puzzling claim that in it he had gone beyond mathematics into the calculus (differential calculus is defined, for instance, as "the branch of higher mathematics that deals with the relations of differentials to the constant on which they depend"—isn't his constant clarifying now, whatever his reluctance to search it out, his failures to dramatize its demands?).

But since no reader can wait for the verdict of years, what can one feel now? What do I feel?—an American novelist, age thirty-eight (the age at which Hemingway published his eighth book, *To Have and Have Not;* his collected stories appeared a year later), whose work would appear to have slim relations, in matter or manner, with the work of Hemingway and whose life might well have had his scorn? (he was healthily inconsistent with his scorn).

I have to return to my intense responses of a year ago—to the powerful presence of a profoundly attractive and needy man still residing in the Key West house and to the reception of his final novel. I've hinted that these responses were in the nature of neglected long-due debts, payment offered too late to be of any likely use to the lender. All the same—what debts?

To go back some years short of the start—in the summer of 1961, I was twenty-eight years old and had been writing seriously for six years. I had completed a novel but had only published stories, and those in England. Still, the novel was in proof at Atheneum—*A Long and Happy Life*—and was scheduled for publication in the fall. I had taken a year's leave from teaching and was heading to England for steady writing—and to be out of reach on publication day. On my way in mid-July I stopped in New York and met my publishers. They had asked me to list the names of literary people who might be interested enough in my book to help it; and I had listed the writers who had previously been helpful. But as we speculated that July (no one on the list had then replied)—and as we brushed over the death of Hemingway ten days before—Michael Bessie startled me by saying that he had seen Hemingway in April, had given him a copy of the proofs of A Long and Happy Life, and had (on the basis of past kindnesses Hemingway had done for young writers) half hoped for a comment. None had come. But I boarded my ship with three feelings. One was a response to Bessie's reply to my asking "How did you feel about Hemingway when you saw him?"—"That he was a wounded animal who should be allowed to go off and die as he chose." The second was my own obvious curiosity—had Hemingway read my novel? what had he thought? was there a sentence about it, somewhere, in his hand or had he, as seemed likely, been far beyond reading and responding? The third was more than a little self-protective and was an index to the degree to which I'd suppressed my debts to Hemingway—what had possessed Bessie in thinking that Hemingway might conceivably have liked my novel, the story of a twenty-year-old North Carolina farm girl with elaborate emotional hesitations and scruples? My feelings, close on a death as they were, were so near to baffled revulsion that I can only attribute them to two sources. First, the success of Hemingway's public relations in the forties and fifties. He had managed to displace the unassailable core of the work itself from my memory and replace it with the coarse useless icon of Self which he planted, or permitted, in dozens of issues of Life and Look, gossip columns, Photoplay—an icon which the apparent sclerosis of the later work had till then, for me at least, not made human. Second, emotions of which I was unconscious—filial envy, the need of most young writers to believe in their own utter newness, the suppression of my own early bonds with Hemingway. In short, and awfully, I had come close to accepting his last verdict on himself—forgetting that he laid the death sentence on his life, not the work.

Yet, a month later, I received a statement which Stephen Spender had written, knowing nothing of the recent distant pass with Hemingway. It said, in part, that I was a "kinetic" writer of a kind that recalled certain pages of Hemingway, and Joyce. I was pleased, of course, especially by Joyce's name ("The Dead" having long seemed to me about as great as narrative prose gets—certain pages of the Bible excepted); but again I was surprised by the presence of Hemingway. Spender had known my work since 1957. He was the first editor to publish a story of mine, in Encounter; and in his own World Within World, he had written briefly but with great freshness of his own acquaintance with Hemingway in Spain during the civil war (one of the first memoirs to counter the received image of Loud Fist). So I might well have paused in my elation to think out whatever resemblance Spender saw. But I was deep in a second book— and in the heady impetus toward publication of the first—and a sober rereading of Hemingway (or a reading; I'd read by no means half his work) was low on my list of priorities.

It should have been high; for if I had attempted to trace and understand Hemingway's help in my own work, I'd have been much better equipped for dealing with (in my own head at least) a comment that greeted A Long and Happy Life from almost all quarters, even the most sympathetic—that it sprang from the side of Faulkner. It didn't; but in my resentment at being looped into the long and crowded cow chain that stretched behind a writer for whom I felt admiration but no attraction, I expended a fair amount of energy in denials and in the offering of alternative masters—the Bible, Milton, Tolstoy, Eudora Welty. If I had been able to follow the lead offered by Bessie and Spender, I could have offered a still more accurate, more revealing name.

So it was ten years before my morning in the house in Key West and my admiration for Islands in the Stream reminded me that, for me as a high school student in Raleigh in the early fifties and as an undergraduate at Duke, the most visible model of Novelist was Hemingway (artist of any sort, except maybe Picasso, with whom Hemingway shared many external attributes but whose central faculty—continuous intellectual imagination, a mind like a frightening infallible engine endowed with the power of growth—he lacked). For how many writers born in the twenties and thirties can Hemingway not have been a breathing Mount Rushmore?— though his presence and pressure seem to have taken a far heavier toll on the older generation, who not only read Hemingway but took him to war as well. Not only most visible but, oddly, most universally certified. Even our public school teachers admired him, when they had been so clearly pained by Faulkner's Nobel—the author of Sanctuary and other sex books. In fact, when I reconstruct the chronology of my introduction to Hemingway, I discover that I must have encountered the work first, at a distant remove, in movies of the forties—The Short Happy Life of Francis Macomber, For Whom the Bell Tolls. It was apparently not until the tenth or eleventh grade—age fifteen or sixteen—that I read any of him. As the first thing, I remember "Old Man at the Bridge" in the textbook. And then, for an "oral book report" in the eleventh grade, A Farewell to Arms. (I remember standing on my feet before forty healthy adolescents—it was only 1949—and saying that Hemingway had shown me that illicit love could be pure and worth having. I don't remember remarking that, like water, it could also kill you—or your Juliet—but I must have acquired, subliminally at least, the welcome news that it made Frederic Henry, a would-be architect, into a highly skilled novelist.)

It was not till my freshman year in college, however, that the effect began to show (in high school, like everyone else, I'd been a poet). My first serious pieces of prose narrative have a kind of grave faith in the eyes, the gaze of the narrator at the moving objects who are his study—a narrowed gaze, through lashes that screen eighty percent of "detail" from the language and the helpless reader, which seems now surely helped onward by, if not grounded in, early Hemingway. Here, for example, is the end of the first "theme" I remember writing in freshman English, a five-hundred-word memory of the death of my aunt's dog Mick—

> It was still hot for late afternoon, but I kept walking. Mick must have been getting tired; but she bounced along, doing her best to look about as pert as a race horse. My head was down, and I was thinking that I would turn around and head home as soon as I could tear that auction sale sign off the telephone pole down the road. A car passed. It sounded as if it threw a rock up under the fender. I looked up at the highway. Mick was lying there. The car did not stop. I went over and picked her up. I carried her to the shoulder of the road and laid her down in the dry, gray dust. She was hardly bleeding, but her side was split open like a ripe grape, and the skin underneath was as white and waxy as soap. I was really sorry that it had happened to Mick. I really was. I sat down in the dust, and Mick was in front of me. I just sat there for a long time thinking, and then I got up and went home. It was almost supper time.

The fact that I'd read *The Catcher in the Rye* a couple of months earlier may account for the *about* in the second sentence and the *I really was*, though they are normal in the context; but it would be hard to maintain now, in the face of the elaborate syntax required by my later work, that this early sketch wasn't actually a piece of ventriloquism—the lips of my memory worked by Hemingway, or by my notion of Hemingway. This was remarked on, and mildly lamented, by my instructor, an otherwise helpful man who would probably have been better advised to wonder: Why is this boy, visibly so polar to Hemingway or Hemingway's apparent heroes, nonetheless needful of lessons from him, and lessons in vision not behavior? (Strangely, the man shot himself three years later.) Maybe it's as well that he didn't. I suspect now that I was responding, at the butt end of an adolescence perceived as monstrously lonely and rejected, to the siren song in the little Hemingway I'd read and that I heard it this way—"If you can tell what you know about pain and loss (physical and spiritual damage, incomprehension, bad love) and tell it in language so magically bare in its bones, so lean and irresistible in its threnody, as to be instantly audible to any passerby, then by your clarity and skill, the depth and validity of your own precarious experience, you will compel large amounts of good love from those same passers, who'll restore your losses or repair them." And if I'd been conscious of the degree of self-pity involved in that first exchange, I might have been revolted and turned from narrative (as I'd turned, two years before, from drawing and painting). But I was only warned that I "sounded like Hemingway"; and since I knew perfectly well that everyone in America sounded like Hemingway, that was no obstacle. So I had written several sketches and my first real story, "Michael Egerton"—all under the tutelage of Hemingway's voice and stance—before I had read more than one or two of his stories and A Farewell to Arms. An "influence" can be exerted by the blinking of an eye, the literal movement of a hand from here to there, five words spoken in a memorable voice; and the almost universal sterility of academic-journalistic influence-hunting has followed from a refusal to go beyond merely symptomatic surface likenesses toward causes and the necessary question "Why was this writer hungry for this; what lack or taste was nourished by this?"

I did go on. One of the exciting nights of my life was spent in early September 1952, reading The Old Man and the Sea in Life magazine, straight through by a naked light bulb, in the bed in which I was born (reread now, after years of accepting secondhand opinions on its weakness, it again seems fresh and dangerous, and though a little rigid, one of the great long stories). I remember reading, admiring, and—better—feeling affection for The Sun Also Rises during a course at Harvard in the summer of 1954; and I still have my old Modern Library edition of the first forty-nine stories, with neat stern notes to less than half the stories in my college senior's hand—the notes of a technician, and as knowing and disapproving as only a young technician can be, but so unnaturally attentive as to signal clearly that some sort of unspoken love was involved, exchanged in fact—the exchange I began to define above, and to which I'll return. But oddly, that was it—after 1955, I don't recall reading any more Hemingway till 1963, A Moveable Feast, well after I'd written two books of my own—and then not again till 1971, when I reread all I'd covered and the two-thirds I hadn't.

Why? Not why was I rereading? but why had I read him in the first place, more than twenty years ago; and why had he helped so powerfully that I felt last summer—and still—this strong rush of gratitude? And why did I put him down so soon? Maybe another piece of Spender's comment will crack the door. He suggested that A Long and Happy Life advanced the chief discovery of Joyce and Hemingway, "which was to involve the reader, as with his blood and muscles, in the texture of the intensely observed and vividly imagistic writing." Assuming what I hope is true—that I needn't drown in self-contemplation if I think that out a little, and that I'm not pressing to death a comment made in kindness—what can

Spender have meant? I remember, at the time, being especially pleased by his calling the prose "kinetic," which I took to mean concerned with and productive of movement. I don't recall telling Spender, but it had been my premise or faith before beginning A Long and Happy Life that by describing fully and accurately every physical gesture of three widely separated days in the lives of two people, I could convey the people—literally deliver them—to you, your room, your senses (I considered *thought* a physical gesture, which it is, though often invisible to the ordinary spectator). That faith, consciously held, guided the book through two years of writing and seems to me still the motive force of its claim on readers.

Isn't it also Hemingway's faith, in every line he wrote? Isn't it Tolstoy's, Flaubert's? Doesn't it provide the terrible force of the greatest narratives of the Bible?—Genesis 22, John 21. I'd read those as well, long before my discovery of Hemingway; and from the ninth grade, after *Anna Karenina*, I'd had my answer to the question "Who's best?" But as a tyro, I clearly took light from Hemingway. He was there, alive in Cuba, nine hundred miles from the desk in my bedroom, still writing—ergo, *writing was possible*. The texture of his work, his method, was apparently more lucid than Tolstoy's, unquestionably more human than Flaubert's (at least as I knew them in translation); and everything was briefer and thus more readily usable. But far more important—again I don't remember thinking about it—was what lay beneath that apparent lucidity. He said more than once that a good writer could omit anything from a story—knowingly, purposely—and the reader would respond to its presence with an intensity beyond mere understanding. There are striking examples—the famous one of "Big Two-Hearted River," which is utterly silent about its subject, and now *Islands in the Stream*, which has a huge secret embedded in its heart, its claim against love, against life (as terrible as Tolstoy's in *The Kreutzer Sonata* or Céline's, though entirely personal and, like theirs, not dramatized). But what I discovered, detected with the sensing devices no one possesses after, say, sixteen, was both more general and more nourishingly specific—the knowledge that Hemingway had begun to write, and continued, for the reasons that were rapidly gathering behind me as my nearly terminal case of adolescence was beginning to relent: write or choke in self-loathing; write to comprehend and control fear. Loathing and fear of what? Anyone who has read my early fiction will probably know (they are not rare fears), and in the only way that might conceivably matter to anyone but me; nor is it wise-guy reductive to say that any sympathetic reader of Hemingway has possessed that knowledge of him since *In Our Time*—and that such knowledge is precisely what Hemingway intended, knowledge acquired from the work, not directly from the life. But the magnetic fields of fear in both cases—or so I felt, and feel—are located in simultaneous desperate love and dread of parents, imagined and actual abandonment by one's earliest peers, the early discovery that the certified emotions (affection, love, loyalty) are as likely to produce waste, pain, and damage to the animal self as are hate, solitude, freedom—perhaps more likely.

But Hemingway's work, at least, is complete and no damage can be done him or it by one more consideration of his technical procedures and their engines, their impetus (harm to a dead writer could only be the destruction of all copies of his work). And oddly, in all that I know of the vast body of Hemingway criticism, there is almost no close attention to the bones of language, of the illuminating sort which Proust, for instance, gave to Flaubert. This despite the fact that most of his readers have always acknowledged that he gave as passionate a care to word and rhythm as Mallarmé. The most interesting discussion of his method is in fact by a writer—Frank O'Connor in his study of the short story, The Lonely Voice— and though it is finally destructive in its wrongheadedness and envy, it is near enough to insight to be worth a look. O'Connor feels that Hemingway studied and understood Joyce's early method and then proceeded to set up shop with Joyce's tools—"and a handsome little business he made of it." And regardless of the justice of that (it's at least a refreshing alternative to the usual references to Gertrude Stein and Sherwood Anderson), it is in O'Connor's description of the Joyce of Dubliners that he casts indirect light on Hemingway—

> It is a style that originated with Walter Pater but was then modeled very closely on that of Flaubert. It is a highly pictorial style; one intended to exclude the reader from the action and instead to present him with a series of images of the events described, which he may accept or reject but cannot modify to suit his own mood or environment.

The following, however, is as far as he goes toward an attempt at understanding the motive for such procedure, in either Joyce or Hemingway—

> By the repetition of key words and key phrases . . . it slows down the whole conversational movement of prose, the casual, sinuous, evocative quality that distinguishes it from poetry and is intended to link author and reader in a common perception of the object, and replaces it by a series of verbal rituals which are intended to evoke the object as it may be supposed to be. At an extreme point it attempts to substitute the image for the reality. It is a rhetorician's dream.

And finally—

> in neither of these passages [from Joyce and Hemingway] is there what
> you could call a human voice speaking, nobody resembling yourself who
> is trying to persuade you to share in an experience of his own, and whom
> you can imagine yourself questioning about its nature—nothing but an
> old magician sitting over his crystal ball, or a hypnotist waving his hands
> gently before your eyes and muttering, "You are falling asleep; you are
> falling asleep; slowly, slowly your eyes are beginning to close; your eyelids
> are growing heavy; you are—falling—asleep."

Despite the fact that *I* feel strong bonds with the voice in early
Hemingway at least, the core of that seems roughly true of both writers—
Joyce in the cold dexterity of A *Portrait of the Artist* and Hemingway all his
life, though in an entirely different way. Why true? Surely the motives are
different and infinitely complex in each case (though one might suspect,
especially after Ellman's biography, that Joyce's production of such a
distancing method was only one more cast skin of an essentially reptilian
nature). If I attempt my own description of Hemingway's procedure (a
description largely coincident with what I *felt* as a student and what drew
me to him as I began to write), then I can guess more legitimately at
motives.

Hemingway's attempt, in all his fiction, is *not* to work magic spells
on a reader, locking him into a rigid instrument of vision (in fact, into a
movie) which controls not only what he sees but what he feels. The
always remarked absence of qualifiers (adjectives, adverbs) is the simplest
and surest sign here. Such an attempt—and one does feel and resent it
often, in Flaubert and Joyce—is essentially the dream of achieving perfect
empathic response, of making the reader become the story, or the story's
emotional center at any given moment: Emma Bovary, Gabriel Conroy.
And it is the dream not only of a few geniuses but of a large percentage of
readers of fiction—the hunger for literally substitute life. Doomed of
course, for the sane at least. But while Hemingway attempts as unremit-
tingly as anyone to control his reader—to station him precisely in relation
to both the visible and the invisible actions of the story and to the author
himself, and finally to trigger in him the desired response (again, to both
story and author)—his strategy is entirely his own, and is in fact his great
invention (the pure language itself being older than literature). Look at
the famous opening of A *Farewell to Arms*—

> In the late summer of that year we lived in a house in a village that
> looked across the river and the plain to the mountains. In the bed of the
> river there were pebbles and boulders, dry and white in the sun, and the
> water was clear and swiftly moving and blue in the channels.

As classical as Horace—in the sense of generalized, delocalized, deprived of native texture. What size house and what color, built how and of what? What village, arranged how around what brand of inhabitants, who do what to live? What river, how wide and deep? What kind of plain, growing what; and what mountains? Later—considerably later—he will tell you a little more, but very little. If you have never traveled in northern Italy in late summer—or seen the film of the book—you'll have no certainty of knowing how the earth looks above and beneath the action, in this or any other of his works. Or in fact, how anything or anyone else *looks*. But by the audacity of its filterings, it demands that you lean forward toward the voice which is quietly offering the story—only then will it begin to yield, to give you what it intends. And the gift will be what you *hear*—the voices of imagined characters speaking a dialect which purports to be your own (and has now convinced two generations of its accuracy). His early strategy is always, at its most calculated, an oral strategy. If we hear it read, it seems the convincing speaking voice of this sensibility. Only on the silent page do we discover that it is as unidiomatic, as ruthlessly intentional, as any *tirade* of Racine's. For behind and beneath all the voices of actors (themselves as few in number as in Sophocles) rides the one real voice—the maker's. And what it says, early and late, is always this—"This is what I see with my clean keen equipment. Work to see it after me." What it does not say but implies is more important—"For you I have narrowed and filtered my gaze. I am screening my vision so you will not see all. Why? Because you must enact this story for yourself; cast it, dress it, set it. Notice the chances I've left for you: no noun or verb is colored by me. I require your senses." What is most important of all—and what I think is the central motive—is this, which is concealed and of which the voice itself may be unconscious: "I tell you this, in this voice, because you must share—*must* because I require your presence, your company in my vision. I beg you to certify my knowledge and experience, my goodness and worthiness. I mostly speak as *I*. What I need from you is not empathy, identity, but patient approving witness—loving. License my life. Believe me." (If that many-staged plea is heard only intermittently in Hemingway's work after 1940—broken then by stretches of "confidence"—I'd guess that the cause would be the sclerosis consequent upon his success, the success of the voice which *won* him love, worship, a *carte blanche* he lacked the power to use well. Goethe said, "Beware of what you want when young; you'll get it when old." And the memory of the famished face of the deathbound Hemingway, quilted with adoration and money, is among the saddest and most instructive memories of Americans over twenty-five; his last gift to us.)

I've suggested that a final intention of Hemingway's method is the production of belief in the reader, belief in his total being and vision. Remember that he always spoke of the heavy role of the Bible in his literary education. The role has been generally misunderstood; seen as a superficial matter of King James rhythms, the frequent use of *and*, narrative "simplicity." But look at a brief though complete story from Genesis 32—

> In the night Jacob rose, took his two wives, the two slave girls, and his eleven sons, and crossed the ford of Jabbok. When he had carried them all across, he sent his belongings. Then Jacob was alone, and some man wrestled with him there till daybreak. When he saw that he could not pin Jacob, he struck him in the pit of his thigh so that Jacob's hip unsocketed as they wrestled. Then he said, "Let me go; it is daybreak."
> Jacob said, "I will not let go till you bless me."
> The man said, "What is your name?"
> He said, "Jacob."
> The man said, "You are Jacob no more but Israel—you have fought gods and men and lasted."
> Jacob said, "Tell me your name, please."
> He said "Why ask my name?" and departed.
> So Jacob called the place *Penuel*, face of God, "For I have seen God's face and endured"; and the sun struck him as he passed Penuel, limping.

—and then at Erich Auerbach's description of Old Testament narrative:

> the externalization of only so much of the phenomena as is necessary for the purpose of the narrative, all else left in obscurity; the decisive points of the narrative alone are emphasized, what lies between is nonexistent; time and place are undefined and call for interpretation; thoughts and feelings remain unexpressed, are only suggested by the silence and the fragmentary speeches; the whole, permeated with the most unrelieved suspense and directed toward a single goal . . . remains mysterious and "fraught with background."

There is, give or take an idiom, a profound likeness between the account of Jacob's struggle and any scene in Hemingway; and Auerbach might well be describing Hemingway, not the Bible. I have already implied the nature of the likeness, the specific hunger in Hemingway which was met by biblical method. Both require our strenuous participation, in the hope of compelling our allegiance, our belief. Here are three passages chosen at random from a continuous supply—the opening of "A Very Short Story":

> One hot evening in Padua they carried him up onto the roof and he could look out over the top of the town. There were chimney swifts in the sky.

After a while it got dark and the searchlights came out. The others went down and took the bottles with them. He and Luz could hear them below on the balcony. Luz sat on the bed. She was cool and fresh in the hot night.

a moment from Thomas Hudson's Nazi hunt in the Cuban keys:

They called to the shack and a woman came out. She was dark as a sea Indian and was barefooted and her long hair hung down almost to her waist. While she talked, another woman came out. She was dark, too, and long-haired and she carried a baby. As soon as she finished speaking, Ara and Antonio shook hands with the two women and came back to the dinghy. They shoved off and started the motor and came out.

and—curiously analogous to Jacob's ordeal with "some man"—the almost intolerably charged and delicate exchange between Frederic Henry and his friend the young Italian priest who has visited him in hospital with a gift of vermouth:

"You were very good to come, father. Will you drink a glass of vermouth?"
"Thank you. You keep it. It's for you."
"No, drink a glass."
"All right. I will bring you more then."
The orderly brought the glasses and opened the bottle. He broke off the cork and the end had to be shoved down into the bottle. I could see the priest was disappointed but he said, "That's all right. It's no matter."
"Here's to your health, father."
"To your better health."

Given the basic narrative strategies of the Old Testament and Hemingway, only the tone of the motives is different—and in the third-person Old Testament the voice is plain command; in Hemingway, a dignified pleading: *Believe!* and *Please believe.* Believe what? *The thing I know.* What do you know? In one case, the presence of the hidden hand of God; in the other, that his life is good and deserving of your witness, will even help your life. Then why believe? In one case, simply and awfully, so that God be served; in the other, so that the voice—and the man behind it—may proceed through his life. That is the sense in which both styles are almost irresistibly kinetic. And the reason why they have been two of the most successful styles in the history of literature.

Why did it fail him then?—his work, the literal words in their order on the page. In one sense, it succeeded too brilliantly—won him millions of readers willing to exert the energy and certify the life, some of them willing even to alter their own lives in obedience to what they, understandably though ludicrously, took to be injunctions of the work (there are certainly injunctions, though not to noise and bluster). But for nothing—or too little. In the only sense that can have mattered to him, his vision and its language failed him appallingly. It won him neither the relatively serene middle working years of a Conrad or a Mann nor the transcendent old age of a Tolstoy, a James, Proust's precocious mastery of a silly life. Nor did it, with all its success in the world, allay even half his daily weight of fear. Immense time and energy were thrown elsewhere in flagging hope—sport, love, companions, drink, all of which took dreadful cuts of their own. Maybe it's permissible to *ask* why the words failed him; but to dabble in answers if one did not at least share a long stretch of his daily life and witness the desperate efforts in their long mysterious complexity is only a game, though a solemn game which can be played more or less responsibly and one which can no longer harm him or the work.

I've indulged already in the early pages of this with a guess, from the gathering evidence of his last four books, about his submerged subject which he found and attempted to float too late, when the search itself—or flight from the search—had dangerously depleted his senses and, worse, prevented the intellectual growth which might have compensated. But the words themselves? and the vision and needs which literally pressed words from him? Were they doomed from the start to kill him? A language fatally obsessed with defending the self and the few natural objects which the self both loves and trusts? A vision narrowed, crouched in apprehension of the world's design to maul, humiliate? Insufficiently surrendered to that design? Whatever the answers (and I'd guess that each is a mysterious Yes), it's clear that he was never capable of the calm firm-footed gaze of the godlike Tolstoy, who at twenty-six was producing from his own military experience, in a story called "The Wood-Felling," narrative so sure of its power as to be a near-lethal radiation—

> The wounded man lay at the bottom of the cart holding on to the sides with both hands. His broad healthy face had completely changed during those few moments; he seemed to have grown thinner and years older, his lips were thin and pale and pressed together with an evident strain. The hasty and dull expression of his glance was replaced by a kind of bright clear radiance, and on the bloody forehead and nose already lay the impress of death. Though the least movement caused him excruciating pain, he nevertheless asked to have a small *chérez* with money taken from his left leg.
> The sight of his bare, white, healthy leg, when his jack-boot had been taken off and the purse untied, produced on me a terribly sad feeling.

Or even of the constitutionally hectic D. H. Lawrence, who in fragments from an unfinished novel could see and speak in a language of open trust in man and nature which promises the stamina of his death—

> Quickly the light was withdrawn. Down where the water was, all grew shadow. The girl came tramping back into the open space, and stood before the holly tree. She was a slim, light thing of about eighteen. Her dress was of weathered blue, her kerchief crimson. She went up to the little tree, reached up, fingering the twigs. The shadow was creeping uphill. It went over her unnoticed. She was still pulling down the twigs to see which had the thickest bunch of berries. All the clearing died and went cold. Suddenly the whistling stopped. She stood to listen. Then she snapped off the twig she had chosen and stood a moment admiring it.
>
> A man's voice, strong and cheerful, shouted: "Bill—Bill—Bi-ill!"
>
> The donkey lifted its head, listened, then went on eating.
>
> "Go on!" said the girl, waving her twig of holly at it. The donkey walked stolidly two paces from her, then took no notice.
>
> All the hillside was dark. There was a tender flush in the east. Away among the darkening blue and green over the west, a faint star appeared. There came from far off a small jangling of bells—one two three—one two three four five! The valley was all twilight, yet near at hand things seemed to stand in day.
>
> "Bill—Bill!" came the man's voice from a distance.
>
> "He's here!" shrilled the girl.
>
> "Wheer?" came the man's shout, nearer, after a moment.
>
> "Here!" shrilled the girl.
>
> She looked at the donkey that was bundled in its cloth.
>
> "Why don't ye go, dummy!" she said.
>
> "Wheer is 'e?" said the man's voice, near at hand.
>
> "Here!"
>
> In a moment a youth strode through the bushes.
>
> "Bill, tha chump!" he said.
>
> The donkey walked serenely towards him. He was a big boned, limber youth of twenty. His trousers were belted very low, so that his loins remained flexible under the shirt. He wore a black felt hat, from under which his brown eyes gazed at the girl.
>
> "Was it you as shouted?" he said.
>
> "I knowed it was you," she replied, tapping her skirt with the richly berried holly sprig.

Yet Hemingway's work—its damaged tentative voice, for all its large failures, its small ignorances and meannesses—did a great deal, for him and us. Beyond carrying him through an after all long life and conveying an extraordinary, apparently usable portion of that life's texture of pleasure and pain to millions of contemporary strangers, it has left live remains—a body of fourteen volumes which, in my guess, will winnow to eight and then stand as an achievement so far unexcelled in American letters, certainly by no one in his own century. For what? For the intensity of their gaze, however screening, at a range of men and dangers which, with the inevitable allowances for private obsession, are as broadly and deeply representative as any but the great masters' (we don't yet possess one); for the stamina of their search, however veiled, through four decades for the demands and conditions and duties of human goodness in relation to other men, beasts and objects, and finally God; and then (strongest but most unprovable, most primitive and mysterious) for the language in which the search externalized itself, his optics and shield, weapon and gift. Gift to whom?

Me, as I've said, who have responded over twenty-five years to what I took to be an asking voice with what I now see was apprenticeship, neither exclusive nor conscious and quickly renegade, but clearly the gravest homage I can offer. Useless to him but profound nonetheless. The profoundest—for I also see that I loved his voice and studied its shapes, not for its often balked and raging message but because I, balked and enraged, shared the motives at which I've guessed and, stranger, its two subjects: freedom and virtue. Polar heights, inaccessible maybe to climbers more intent on self-protection (footholds, handholds) than on the climb itself, the route and destination.

Gift also to all other living American writers as obsessed as he with defense of what the self is and what it knows, any one of whom seems to me more nearly brother to him—in need and diet, dream and fulfillment, vision and blindness—than to any other artist in our history, or anyone else's (and, oddly, our avatar of Byron, the proto-American artist). Like it or not, our emblem and master whose lessons wait, patient and terrible.

Gift especially to the young. For it is almost certainly with them that his life now lies. It is easy enough to patronize Children's Classics—Omar, Mrs. Browning, Wolfe, lately Hesse—but any writer's useful survival is in heavy danger when the young abandon him entirely; it is only on them that he stands a chance of inflicting permanent damage (are Milton and Dante effectively alive? can they yet be saved in some form they'd have agreed to?—not by schools, apparently). In all Hemingway's work, until *The Old Man and the Sea* and *Islands in the Stream*, the warnings, if not the pleas, are for them; the lessons of one master, diffidently but desperately offered—*Prepare, strip, divest for life that awaits you; learn solitude and work; see how little is lovely but love that.*

Half the lesson of the desert fathers, and given in language of the desert, bleached, leached to essence. The other half—an answer to *Why?*—is withheld until the last, and then only muttered. Surely there are young people now, readers and writers—children when he died—to whom he is speaking his dark secret language of caution and love, help and beggary, in the lean voice of an infinitely delicate, infinitely suffering thing. No shield, no help at all, of course, to him or us (he never said it would be); yet more—a diamond point that drills through time and pain, a single voice which moves through pain toward rest and presses forward shyly with its greeting and offer, its crushing plea, like that of the hermit Paul when St. Anthony had tracked him through beasts and desert and begged for instruction:

> Behold, thou lookest on a man that is soon to be dust. Yet because love endureth all things, tell me, I pray thee, how fares the human race: if new roofs be risen in the ancient cities, whose empire is it that now sways the world; and if any still survive, snared in the error of the demons.

MALCOLM COWLEY

Mr. Papa and the Parricides

"G reat men die twice," Paul Valéry
said, "once as men and once as great." Their second death, in the public
mind, may be no more than a forgetting, but in other cases it becomes a
noisy spectacle that makes one think of a very old tree assaulted by a band
of savages. The tree is the great man's reputation, which has hidden the
sky and prevented lesser reputations from growing in its shade. Now it
must be destroyed, by tribal necessity, but the tribesmen have only stone
axes that shatter against the enormous trunk. So they start by hacking off
roots and branches one by one, then wait for the weakened tree to crash
in the first gale.

That process of severing roots and lopping off branches is known in
the critical world as "reassessment." If the critic is also a teacher, he is
likely to speak of "establishing a canon," which means choosing the works
that his students will be required to read and more or less abolishing the
others. For many years I have been taking notes on a classical example of
that operation, as performed by critics of a younger age group on the
works of Ernest Hemingway.

The earlier notes became an article published in the June 1967
number of Esquire and here reprinted without substantial revision. I have
followed the critical record of the Hemingway case in later years, and it
shows an effort by some critics, notably Alfred Kazin and Scott Donaldson,
to reach a fairer estimate of his work. It also provides fresh evidence as
regards the conflict of age groups, but it does not seem to affect my earlier
conclusions.

I

"At the time of his death in 1961," says one critic, John Thompson, who teaches English at the State University of New York at Stony Brook, Hemingway "was probably the best-known writer in the world, and one of the most popular. But his writing no longer exerted an influence on literature, and serious critics usually disposed of his work as being of minor interest compared to that of writers like Fitzgerald and Faulkner, whom he had once completely overshadowed.

"Such questions as may arise about his writing today," Mr. Thompson continues in the tone of a Supreme Court justice reading an almost unanimous opinion, "are only manifestations of the slow and uneven filtering down of accepted opinion, or of the uneven rates at which the glamour of his settings evaporates in different minds. Nearly everyone agrees now on the order of quality in the canon of his work. *The Sun Also Rises* and many of his short stories are absolutely first-rate, surpassed in scope by other novelists of his time but unsurpassed by anyone in their perfection." Nothing else that Hemingway wrote is really worth the trouble of rereading. "Thus, while he is still recognized clearly enough as an artist of occasional success," the critic concludes in *The New York Review*, "his work no longer seems to contain promises for others, and his books are not much regarded by writers anymore."

I envy the assurance with which Mr. Thompson, never speaking in the first person, repeats what he thinks that other people think who he thinks are serious critics. He might not regard Vance Bourjaily as one of them, since Bourjaily makes the critical *gaffe* of speaking for himself and in any case is not a critic primarily. His profession is writing novels, and he owes a substantial debt to Hemingway, as do other writers of talent in his World War II generation. In an article contributed to *The New York Times Book Review*, Bourjaily acknowledges the debt, but he also engages in what seems to be the inevitable business of drawing up a canon. "As a reader," he says, "and claiming to speak for other readers, I suppose I rank the works quite simply according to the frequency with which it seems to me that I would now enjoy rereading a given one. By this test, *The Sun Also Rises* is incomparably the best novel; I reread it every fourth or fifth year. There are between fifteen and twenty short stories, mostly early but including 'Macomber' and 'Kilimanjaro,' which I read as often and feel to be of the same extraordinary merit. *A Farewell to Arms* is somewhat below these, but not far—perhaps on a seven-year or eight-year cycle. I suspect that *Green Hills of Africa*, which I discovered quite recently, will come in next."

From other books Mr. Bourjaily recalls "a few moving things," but he does not propose to reread them. Thus, even in his favorable report, the Hemingway canon is reduced to fifteen or twenty short stories, most of them early, the first two novels, and a travel book. But all the Hemingway critics are engaged in critical canoneering, and most of them carry it to a greater extreme—as does, for example, Stanley Edgar Hyman, who says in *The New Leader*, ". . . at his best Hemingway left us, in *The Sun Also Rises* and a handful of short stories, authentic masterpieces, small-scale but immortal." How many stories make a handful? Certainly fewer than the fifteen or twenty that Vance Bourjaily delights in rereading. Robert Emmet Long, writing in *The North American Review*, wants to shorten the list of canonical works to a few of those produced in the early or vintage years. "Almost all of his best work," Mr. Long says, "was done while he was still in his twenties. . . . *The Sun Also Rises, A Farewell to Arms* and half a dozen short stories present Hemingway at his best." Having added a novel to Mr. Hyman's version of the canon, Mr. Long subtracts from it three or four stories—unless "half a dozen" and "a handful" are synonyms.

Leslie Fiedler places the same emphasis on the early work, which he admires for a curious reason, as Hemingway's celebration of "the bleak truth it had been given him to know." That truth was "death and the void," or so we learn from Fiedler's *Waiting for the End* (1964), where we are also told that "after the first two novels and the early stories, he was able only to echo, in the end parody, himself." Other critics want to reject even those first two novels. "The fact is Hemingway is a short-story writer and not a novelist," Dwight Macdonald says in *Against the American Grain* (1963). "He has little understanding of the subject matter of the novel: character, social setting, politics, money matters, human relations, all the prose of life. . . . In a novel he gets lost, wandering aimlessly in a circle as lost people are said to do, and the alive parts are really short stories, such as the lynching of the Fascists and the blowing up of the bridge in *For Whom the Bell Tolls*."

I shall resist the temptation to argue with Mr. Macdonald, though it would be easy to cite passages from Hemingway's novels that reveal his understanding of character, social setting, politics, money matters, human relations, and—if only by implication, since he does not burden the story with extraneous material—all the prose of life. It would be still easier to show that instead of getting lost in a novel he marches ahead in a straight-line narrative that appears to be simple, but is actually a difficult type of writing, since it avoids the tricks by which novelists are enabled to impart or withhold information at their own convenience. Those citations and proofs, however, can wait for another occasion. At present what interests me is that Mr. Macdonald's judgment, however debatable, seems to have been accepted by segments of the academic world. I remember the comment made by a professor of American literature on an anthology I was helping to revise. "Why not include Hemingway's two or three best stories," he said, "and omit any reference to his novels? Hemingway is beginning to be taught chiefly as a short-story writer." "Pretty soon," I said to myself, "they will have him chipped down to 'Big Two-Hearted River.' " The next step would be to chip that story down to a single paragraph, presented by critics as the only true essence of his work, from which they could infer the rest of it much in the fashion that paleontologists reconstruct the skeleton of an extinct animal from a single bone. Perhaps it would be the paragraph that reads:

> He watched them holding themselves with their noses into the current, many trout in deep, fast moving water, slightly distorted as he watched far down through the glassy convex surface of the pool, its surface pushing and swelling smooth against the resistance of the log-driven piles of the bridge. At the bottom of the pool were the big trout. Nick did not see them at first. Then he saw them at the bottom of the pool, big trout looking to hold themselves on the gravel bottom in a varying mist of gravel and sand, raised in spurts by the current.

The echo of that paragraph has sounded first loudly, then faintly but still discernibly, through fifty years of American prose. But would the critics choose another paragraph for fear of having to confess that they had never seen the big trout? I respect most of those whose judgments I have quoted and some of them are my friends, but in the present connection they evoke a mental picture I should like to forget. This time the picture is not of a tree being felled, but of a dead lion surrounded by a pack of jackals. At first they gather round him cautiously, ready to take flight at any sign of life, and then, gaining courage from one another, they rush in to tear the flesh from the bones. I suppose the bones are the critical canon, but they will not remain undisturbed; soon the hyenas will come to crack them for their marrow. There will be nothing left but a white skull on the wide African plain, and hunters will say as they look at it, "Why, it wasn't such a big lion after all."

But Hemingway for much of his life was our biggest lion. In the midst of those posthumous assaults on his reputation, I should like to interject a few remarks about the lasting values in his work and about the whole business of setting up a critical canon.

II

It seems to me a snobbish business essentially. Each critic is tempted to display his superior discrimination by excluding a little more than other critics excluded. The process is exactly similar to the one by which drinkers some years ago used to display their superior taste by insisting on less and less vermouth in their martinis: the man who ordered eight parts of gin to one of vermouth was obviously twice as high in the social-drinking scale as the man who was satisfied with four parts to one. Just so in the critical scale: Vance Bourjaily, who admits to liking two Hemingway novels and fifteen or twenty stories, is only half as discriminating as Stanley Hyman, who praises only one novel and "a handful" of stories—would it be a single or a double handful?—while Hyman in turn must bow to Dwight Macdonald, who retains a few stories but completely excludes the novels. They can each be assigned a rank, but it has nothing to do with their sense of literary values.

There are other reasons for distrusting the process of critical canoneering when it is applied to an author of any standing. Of course it has the practical justification that students can't be expected to read everything; the instructor has to make choices. But when he chooses a book for them to read, he shouldn't imply, except in special cases, that nothing else by the same author is worth their attention. The special cases are those of one-book authors, a genus that has some famous members; Hemingway isn't one of them. Some of his books are immensely better than others. Some I should surrender without regret, as notably *Across the River and into the Trees*; perhaps that is the only one. *Green Hills of Africa* and *To Have and Have Not* fall short of their mark, each for a different reason, but both contain passages I should hate to relinquish.

For Whom the Bell Tolls does not belong among those partial failures. It seems to me the most complex and powerful of Hemingway's works, as it is certainly the longest. Often it is dismissed by critics as if they had reached a tacit agreement, but that appears to be the result of circumstances quite apart from its literary value. One circumstance is its popular success; critics always distrust a novel that has had an enormous sale—in this case eight hundred thousand hardbound copies in the first few years—after being announced as a masterpiece by the daily reviewers. *For Whom the Bell Tolls* has suffered from the additional handicaps of dealing with the Spanish Civil War, a subject that many critics wanted to forget, and of dealing with it in a fashion that offended most of the political factions: Fascists, Stalinists, Trotskyites, pacifists, Spanish patriots on both sides, almost the whole spectrum. As time passed the book was so bitterly condemned on political grounds that critics did not feel they had to read it with close attention. Nothing they said against it was likely to be challenged, even if their judgments were based on obvious misinterpretations.

Take for example Dwight Macdonald's judgment, already quoted, that "the alive parts are really short stories, such as the lynching of the Fascists and the blowing up of the bridge in *For Whom the Bell Tolls*." His notion that the parts would be better if separated from the whole is not supported by the text. Conceivably the lynching of the Fascists might stand alone, but it is an essential shadow in the picture that Hemingway has been presenting all through the novel. The blowing up of the bridge, with Robert Jordan's death as recounted in the last forty pages of the novel, clearly depends for its power on the tensions that have been created in the preceding four hundred pages. It is no more a short story than the fifth act of *Hamlet* is a one-act play.

There is more to be said about Jordan's fight at the bridge. In addition to being the end of a novel, it is also last in a series of events that had continued through several books. Most of Hemingway's early heroes are aspects of the same person, whether we call him Nick Adams or Frederic Henry or Jake Barnes, and of course he reappears in Robert Jordan. The hero's adventures began in Michigan, but they reached their first climax in *A Farewell to Arms*, when, falsely charged with being a spy, he deserted from the Italian army (and also, in a sense, from organized society). The fight at the bridge might be read as a sequel to that earlier climax, which had taken place at another bridge; this time the hero accepts the fate from which, in *A Farewell to Arms*, he had escaped by plunging into a flooded river. Hemingway's books are interconnected in several fashions; the connections are what many critics miss by their canoneering. Though a story in itself may be an authentic masterpiece, small-scale but immortal—to quote Stanley Hyman—the scale is magnified when we read it with other stories, which in turn are enhanced in value by the novels. Almost everything is part of the same pattern.

In the background of the pattern are death, loneliness, and the void, but these are not Hemingway's subject—Leslie Fiedler to the contrary—except in two or three of the early vignettes and in a few stories written during the thirties. In "A Clean, Well-Lighted Place," for example, the old waiter says, "What did he fear? It was not fear or dread. It was a nothing that he knew too well." But although the old waiter seems to speak from the depths of nihilism, he suggests a remedy against that feeling of nothingness: it is for the lonely man to sit all night in a bright, pleasant café where he will be surrounded with order and decorum. That appears to be an essential statement, and we can see more clearly in other stories that Hemingway's real subject is the barriers that can be erected against fear and loneliness and the void.

Decorum in the broadest sense, in which it becomes the discipline of one's calling and the further discipline required of every human being if he is to live as a man, not collapse into a jelly of emotions, is the strongest of those barriers. "Be a man, my son," a priest in one of the early vignettes says to Sam Cardinella when he loses control of his sphincter muscle as he is being strapped for the gallows. Sam is the specter of fear that seems more repulsive to Hemingway than death itself. To maintain discipline in the face of death requires a strict control of the imagination, lest it get to racing "like a flywheel with the weight gone," as Robert Jordan says in *For Whom the Bell Tolls*. It also requires complete attention to every action in its proper sequence, as if that single action, at the moment, were the whole of life. Meanwhile the sequence of actions is being reported in a disciplined style that is in harmony with the subject matter and that also becomes a means of suggesting—while at the same time warding off—fears that are not directly expressed.

Besides imposing a discipline, the implied or actual presence of death in Hemingway's fiction has compensations that are also part of his subject. This feature of his work, not often discussed, is one that I found easy to recognize from a memory of youth; there must be many others with a similar memory. In my case it goes back to Paris in the early summer of 1917. I was on leave from driving a munitions truck for the French army, not a proud occupation in those days when one's friends were enlisting in various flying corps and getting killed with astonishing dispatch. In the Lafayette Escadrille, for example, the average expectancy of life was something less than three months. I decided on that June morning to enlist in American aviation, knowing that I should make an incompetent pilot and should certainly be killed with greater dispatch than the others; nevertheless the decision was made. Suddenly everything changed for me. The chestnut trees in the Champs-Elysées seemed greener, their blossoms pinker, the girls on the sidewalk more beautiful, and the sky an unprecedented shade of blue, as if my senses had been sharpened and my capacity for enjoyment vastly increased by the imminence of death. Humming a silly wartime song, stumbling at the curb, smiling to passersby, I went to a restaurant and ordered what seemed to me the best meal I had ever eaten, washed down with a bottle of miraculous wine.

The experience had no sequel in life, since I was rejected by the army doctors, but much later it helped me to recognize a lasting quality in Hemingway's prose. It is life-conscious and death-conscious at the same time; one feeling is linked with the other. Because, at moments in his writing, death seems to hover in the air like an obscene bird—or moves silently in pairs, on bicycles, like French policemen, or has a hyena's wide snout and prowls outside his tent as in "The Snows of Kilimanjaro"— because of this wordless presence, the author himself seems doubly alive, with all his senses more acute than those of ordinary persons. He sniffs the morning air like a hunting dog. He feels and transmits to the reader a special cleanness and freshness in the physical world in a way that has not been equaled by any other novelist of our time. It is a quality one finds in many poems of the Middle Ages, also written by men whose enjoyment of nature was sharpened by their feeling that death lay in ambush at the turn of the road.

Landscapes, the sea, the weather, fishing for trout or marlin, the taste of food, drinking round a campfire (or almost anywhere), killing big animals, and making love: those are the magical things in Hemingway. The ideas are interesting too, even though merely implied, for he was always more of an intellectual than he pretended to be; but he was most at ease in describing natural scenes and activities. He made everything palpable, so that a landscape was suggested by hills to be climbed with aching muscles or by the feel of hemlock needles under bare feet, all remembered with a sense of precarious joy. His readers envied the joy while disregarding the nightmares that lurked in the shadows. Young men of three or four successive age groups were eager to go where he went and have a share in his pleasures, with the result that, in his favored localities, he became an economic force of measurable importance. As I wrote of him in *A Second Flowering*, "Yes, he brought the fishermen to Key West and Bimini, and bands of hunters to the high African plains, and American college students by hundreds, then by thousands, to the yearly festival at Pamplona. Ski resorts in Tyrol and Idaho, bullfights all over Spain, restaurants in Venice, Milan, Paris, Havana: he had good times at all of them, he told with gusto what they had to offer, and the crowds came streaming after."

That side of his career is not what interests me. Many writers were inclined to resent it, on the ground that there was no place in it for books and bookmen. Not sharing that resentment, I still find that Hemingway the writer paid a high price for his activities as a sportsman and war correspondent. His real excuse for engaging in them, implicit in everything he wrote, was that he liked them. That was not the same as his public excuse, which was that they furnished him with material. "In going where you have to go, and doing what you have to do, and seeing what you have to see," he said in his preface to *The Fifth Column and the First Forty-nine Stories*, "you dull and blunt the instrument you write with.

But I would rather have it bent and dulled and know I had to put it on the grindstone again and hammer it into shape and put a whetstone to it, and know that I had something to write about, than to have it bright and shining and nothing to say, or smooth and well-oiled in the closet, but unused."

It is the old doctrine of experience at any cost that held an important place in the mind of the 1920s. Hemingway carried it farther than others. Long before the end, and in fact before World War II, he had gathered more material than he could ever put into his writing. In "The Snows of Kilimanjaro" (1936), he deliberately threw away material for a dozen stories, each of which was reduced to one or two paragraphs of the dying hero's recollections, as if both hero and author were trying to get rid of compulsive memories. As for "the instrument you write with"—if Hemingway meant his head—it was scarred and battered like a punch-drunk boxer's head in a dozen serious accidents, from one of which, the second airplane crash in Africa, he never recovered. That was our loss, but we should remember that in all those costly adventures there was something on the other side of the ledger too, not for literature, but for the world. The public career was in itself an artistic creation. By the enormous zest with which he studied the rules of every game, including those of love and war and the chase, he made our world more dramatic than it would have been without him.

III

But the work is what interests me, not the career, and that is why I am disturbed by the later sapping and pruning of his literary reputation. Does nothing survive of the work but a few short stories? Why not toss them out with the novels and finally reduce the Hemingway canon to a blank page? As yet that gesture of total rejection has not been made by any reputable critic. Even Dwight Macdonald, who comes nearest to making it, still finds a few things he would like to save. There were, however, premonitory hints of the gesture in a few newspaper reviews of A Moveable Feast, in 1964, mixed in with favorable comments by others. ". . . aging boy that he became," Glendy Culligan said in The Washington Post, "Hemingway was finally surpassed by his own imitators." I wonder what books by which imitators she had in mind. The anonymous reviewer for The Harrisburg Patriot News wanted to dismiss Hemingway's readers along with the books and their author (again that conflict of age groups). "The reputation he built up studiously," the reviewer said, "will linger among the middle-aged generation that naturally clings to the illusions of youth."

What this cry from Harrisburg, Pennsylvania, suggests—when taken with other evidence—is the broader scope of the operation that had seemed to be directed against Hemingway and no one else. He isn't the only victim; he isn't even the first. Thomas Wolfe has already gone down under repeated assaults—for which there was more excuse in his case—and Dos Passos, though not stoned to death, has been loaded with the sins of the literary community and driven into the desert. Of course the ultimate goal of the operation is the whole age group of which Hemingway was a member. A few of his coevals have escaped the attacks, notably Faulkner and Fitzgerald and Edmund Wilson, but it is not hard to foresee that their turn is coming. What we are witnessing is a crucial stage in an event that has been delayed beyond expectations, that is, the ritual murder of the literary fathers.

To cast some light on that ceremony revived from prehistoric times, I might quote a famous passage from the last chapter of *Totem and Taboo*. Freud introduces the passage by recalling Darwin's notion that the first form of human society may have been a primal horde in which a violent, jealous father kept all the females for himself and drove away his growing sons. The notion has never been confirmed by anthropologists, but Freud accepts it as the basis for a more dramatic picture of his own:

> One day [he says] the expelled brothers joined forces, slew and ate the father, and thus put an end to the father horde. Together they dared and accomplished what would have remained impossible for them singly. . . . Of course these cannibalistic savages ate their victim. The violent primal father had surely been the envied and feared model for each of the brothers. Now they accomplished their identification with him by devouring him and each acquired a part of his strength.

Freud goes on to explain that the original parricide, or *Vatermord*, was the original sin and hence was the beginning of religion. I shall not follow him into those further conjectures. All I wanted to suggest is that a ritual murder of the fathers has become a custom in the literary world. Each new generation or age group provides admired, then feared and envied models for the generation that follows. The new men and women, however, have their own sense of life, which they are bent on expressing in their own fashion, and therefore they have to break free from the models. Often they do so by denying that the models have any virtues, by rejecting their works one after another, and, in effect, by killing them as men of letters. Of course they eat them too, in the sense of absorbing what they can from the slaughtered parents.

For a new generation of parricides, Hemingway becomes an especially tempting victim, partly because he had been so abundantly paternal. All the hard-boiled novelists of the 1930s, with most of the proletarian novelists, were his sons in one way or another, and so too were almost all the war novelists of the 1940s. He had been extremely kind to them in the beginning, so long as they did not threaten his pre-eminence, but later, when they promised to become rivals, he expelled them one by one from the primal horde. No wonder that many of the sons joined forces against him. Hemingway, in fact, had offered them a model of filial ingratitude in his early career, since his third book, *The Torrents of Spring*, was a ritual murder of Sherwood Anderson, from whom he had learned valuable lessons. The young men might argue that they were paying him back a death for a death.

If I deplore the continued attacks on Hemingway's reputation, it is not because I think that the critics are guilty of more than the customary measure of ingratitude. It is not for personal reasons, because I want to defend my own generation or the man who for thirty years and more embodied many of its perceptions (notwithstanding his defects of character), and it is not because I think the attacks will be successful in the end. With the necessary subtractions made, Hemingway's work as a whole is so clearly permanent that, even if his reputation were destroyed for the moment, and the work buried, it would be exhumed after a hundred years, as Melville's was. My protest is simply in defense of American literature. This is vastly richer now than it was when Hemingway started writing, but it is not yet so rich that it can afford to disown and devalue one of its lasting treasures.

STEVEN K. HOFFMAN

"Nada" and the Clean, Well-Lighted Place: The Unity of Hemingway's Short Fiction

One of his most frequently discussed tales, "A Clean, Well-Lighted Place" is justly regarded as one of the stylistic masterpieces of Ernest Hemingway's distinguished career in short fiction. Not only does it represent Hemingway at his understated, laconic best, but, according to Carlos Baker, "It shows once again that remarkable union of the naturalistic and the symbolic which is possibly his central triumph in the realm of practical aesthetics." In a mere five pages, almost entirely in dialogue and interior monologue, the tale renders a complex series of interactions between three characters in a Spanish café just prior to and immediately after closing: a stoic old waiter, a brash young waiter, and a wealthy but suicidal old man given to excessive drink.

Aside from its well-documented stylistic achievement, what has drawn the most critical attention is Hemingway's detailed consideration of the concept of *nada*. Although the old waiter is the only one to articulate the fact, all three figures actually confront nothingness in the course of the tale. This is no minor absence in their lives. Especially "for the old waiter," Carlos Baker notes, "the word *nothing* (or *nada*) contains huge actuality. The great skill in the story is the development, through the most carefully controlled understatement, of the young waiter's mere *nothing*

From *Essays in Literature* 6, no. 1 (Spring 1979). Copyright © 1979 by Steven K. Hoffman.

into the old waiter's Something—a Something called Nothing which is so huge, terrible, overbearing, inevitable and omnipresent that once experienced, it can never be forgotten." Because the terrifying "Something called Nothing" looms so very large, and since "A Clean, Well-Lighted Place" appeared in a 1933 collection in which even "winners" take "nothing," critics have generally come to see the piece as a nihilistic low point in Hemingway's career, a moment of profound despair both for the characters and the author.

If this standard position does have a certain validity, it also tends to overlook two crucial points about the story. First is its relation to the rest of Hemingway's highly unified short story canon. In the same way that two of the three characters in "A Clean, Well-Lighted Place" meet *nada* without voicing the fact, all of the major short story characters also experience it in one of its multiple guises. Thus "A Clean, Well-Lighted Place," a rather late story written in 1933, is something of a summary statement on this recurrent theme; the tale brings to direct expression the central crisis of those that precede it—including the most celebrated of the Nick Adams stories—and looks forward to its resolution in the masterpieces that come later, "The Short Happy Life of Francis Macomber" (1936) and "The Snows of Kilimanjaro" (1936).

Second, because *nada* appears to dominate "A Clean, Well-Lighted Place," it has been easy to miss the fact that the story is not about *nada per se* but the various available human responses to it. As a literary artist, Hemingway was generally less concerned with speculative metaphysics than with modes of practical conduct within certain *a priori* conditions. The ways in which the character triad in "A Clean, Well-Lighted Place" respond to *nada* summarize character responses throughout the canon. The fact that only one, the old waiter, directly voices his experience and manages to deal successfully with nothingness is also indicative of a general trend. Those few Hemingway characters who continue to function even at the razor's edge do so in the manner of this heroic figure—by establishing for themselves a clean, well-lighted place from which to withstand the enveloping darkness. For these reasons, "A Clean, Well-Lighted Place" must be termed the thematic as well as the stylistic climax of Hemingway's career in short fiction.

Although the difficulty of attributing certain individual statements in the tale creates some ambiguity on the subject, it is clear that the young waiter's use of the term *nada* to convey a personal lack of a definable commodity (*no thing*) is much too narrowly conceived. In his crucial meditation at the end, the old waiter makes it quite clear that *nada* is not an individual state but one with grave universal implications: "It was a nothing that he knew too well. It was *all* a nothing and a man was nothing too" [my italics]. According to William Barrett, the *nada*-shadowed realm of "A Clean, Well-Lighted Place" is no less than a microcosm of the existential universe as defined by Martin Heidegger and the existentialist philosophers who came before and after him, principally Kierkegaard and Sartre. Barrett's position finds internal support in the old waiter's celebrated parody prayer: "Our nada who art in nada, nada be thy name thy kingdom nada thy will be nada in nada as it is in nada. Give us this nada our daily nada and nada us our nada as we nada our nadas and nada us not into nada but deliver us from nada; pues nada." The character's deft substitution of the word *nada* for all the key nouns (entities) and verbs (actions) in the Paternoster suggests the concept's truly metaphysical stature. Obviously, *nada* is to connote a series of significant absences: the lack of a viable transcendent source of power and authority; a correlative lack of external physical or spiritual sustenance; the total lack of moral justification for action (in the broadest perspective, the essential meaninglessness of *any* action); and finally, the impossibility of deliverance from this situation.

The impact of *nada*, however, extends beyond its theological implications. Rather, in the Heideggerian sense ("das Nicht"), it is an umbrella term that subsumes all of the irrational, unforseeable, existential forces that tend to infringe upon the human self, to make a "nothing." It is the absolute power of chance and circumstance to negate individual free will and the entropic tendency toward ontological disorder that perpetually looms over man's tenuous personal sense of order. But the most fearsome face of *nada*, and clear proof of man's radical contingency, is death—present here in the old man's wife's death and his own attempted suicide. Understandably, the old waiter's emotional response to this composite threat is mixed. It "was not fear or dread," which would imply a specific object to be feared, but a pervasive uneasiness, an existential anxiety that, according to Heidegger, arises when one becomes fully aware of the precarious status of his very being.

That the shadow of *nada* looms behind much of Hemingway's fiction has not gone entirely unnoticed. Nathan Scott's conclusions on this issue serve as a useful summary of critical opinion: "Now it is blackness beyond a clean, well-lighted place—this 'nothing full of nothing' that betrays 'confidence'; that murders sleep, that makes the having of plenty of money a fact of no consequence at all—it is this blackness, ten times black, that constitutes the basic metaphysical situation in Hemingway's fiction and that makes the human enterprise something very much like a huddling about a campfire beyond which looms the unchartable wilderness, the great Nada." The problem with this position is that it tends to locate *nada* somewhere outside of the action, never directly operative within it. It is, to William Barrett, "the presence that had circulated, *unnamed* and *unconfronted*, throughout much of [Hemingway's] earlier writing" [my italics].

The clearest indication of *nada*'s direct presence in the short stories is to be found in the characters' frequent brushes with death, notably the characteristic modern forms of unexpected, unmerited, and very often mechanical death that both Frederick J. Hoffman and R. P. Warren consider so crucial in Hemingway. Naturally, these instances are the climactic moments in some of the best known tales: the interchapters from *In Our Time*, "Indian Camp," "The Killers," "The Capital of the World," and "The Snows of Kilimanjaro." But the death or the imminent threat of death need not be literally present to signal an encounter with *nada*. What Philip Young and others have called Nick Adams's "initiation" to life's trials is actually his initiation to *nada*. In "The End of Something" and "The Three Day Blow," Nick must cope with the precariousness of love in a precarious universe; in "The Battler," with the world's underlying irrationality and potential for violence; in "Cross-Country Snow," with the power of external circumstance to circumscribe individual initiative. In several important stories involving the period in Nick's chronology after the critical "wound," *nada*, as the ultimate unmanageability of life, appears as a concrete image. In "Big Two-Hearted River," it is both the burnt-out countryside and the forbidding swamp; in "Now I Lay Me," the night; in "A Way You'll Never Be," a "long yellow house" (evidently the site of the wound).

Other imagistic references to *nada* appear in the non-Nick Adams tales. In "The Undefeated," it is the bull, a particularly apt concrete manifestation of active malevolence in the universe, also suggested by the lion and buffalo in "The Short Happy Life of Francis Macomber." These particular images, however, are potentially misleading because *nada* does not usually appear so actively and personally combative. An example to the contrary may be found in "The Gambler, the Nun, and the Radio" where *nada* is the distinctly impersonal and paralyzing banality of life in an isolated hospital, as well as the constant "risk" of a gambler's uncertain profession. Regardless of its specific incarnation, *nada* is always a dark presence which upsets individual equilibrium and threatens to overwhelm the self. And, as Jackson Benson has pointed out, "A threat to selfhood is the ultimate horror that the irrational forces of the world can accomplish." In that each story in the canon turns on the way in which particular characters respond to the inevitable confrontation with *nada*, the nature of that response is particularly important. The only effective way to approach the Void is to develop a very special mode of being, the concrete manifestation of which is the clean, well-lighted place.

Again, it is the old waiter who speaks most directly of the need for a physical bastion against the all-encompassing night: "It is the light of course but it is necessary that the place be clean and pleasant. You do not want music. Certainly you do not want music. Nor can you stand before a bar with dignity." In direct contrast to the dirty, noisy *bodega* to which he repairs after closing and all the "bad" places that appear in Hemingway's fiction, the pleasant café at which the old waiter works possesses all of these essential attributes: light, cleanness, and the opportunity for some form of dignity. Perhaps the most direct antithesis of this legitimate clean, well-lighted place is not even in this particular story but in one of its companion pieces in *Winner Take Nothing*, the infernal bar in "The Light of the World" (1933). Here, light does little more than illuminate the absence of the other qualities, the lack of which moves one of the characters to ask pointedly, " 'What the hell kind of place is this?' " Thus, in an inversion of the typical procedure in Hemingway, Nick and his companion are impelled outside where it is "good and dark."

Evidently, well-lighted places in Hemingway do not always meet the other requirements of the clean, well-lighted place. Moreover, since the café in "A Clean, Well-Lighted Place" must eventually close, even the legitimate haven has distinct limitations. These facts should be enough to alert us to the possibility that tangible physical location is not sufficient to combat the darkness. The clean, well-lighted place that is, is not actually a "place" at all; rather, it is metaphor for an attitude toward the self and its existential context, a psychological perspective which, like the café itself with its fabricated conveniences and electric light, is man-made, artificial. The "cleanliness" of the metaphor connotes a personal sense of order, however artificial and temporary, carved out within the larger chaos of the universe, a firm hold on the self with which one can meet any contingency. By "light" Hemingway refers to a special kind of vision, the clear-sightedness and absolute lack of illusion necessary to look into the darkness and thereby come to grips with the *nada* which is everywhere. At the same time, vision must also be directed at the self so as to assure *its* cleanness. With cleanness and light, then, physical locale is irrelevant. Whoever manages to internalize these qualities carries the clean, well-lighted place with him, even into the very teeth of the darkness. The degree to which the Hemingway character can develop and maintain this perspective determines his success (or lack thereof) in dealing with the Void.

The man who does achieve the clean, well-lighted place is truly an existential hero, both in the Kierkegaardian and Heideggerian senses of the term. In the former, he is content to live with his *angst*, and, because there is no other choice, content to be in doubt about ultimate causes. Nevertheless, he is able to meet the varied and often threatening circumstances of day-to-day living, secure in the knowledge that he will always "become" and never "be." In the latter, he can face the unpleasant realities of his own being and the situation into which he has been "thrown," and can accept with composure the inevitability of his death. In both instances, he is an "authentic" man.

Two of the main characters in "A Clean, Well-Lighted Place," as well as a host of analogous figures in other tales, fail to develop this attitude either for lack of "light" (the young waiter) or for lack of "cleanness" (the old man). As is evidenced by his inability to grasp the full impact of his partner's use of the word *nothing*, the egotistic young waiter has not even grasped the fact of *nada*—has not *seen* clearly—and therefore can hardly deal with it. "To him," comments Joseph Gabriel, "*nada* can only signify a personal physical privation. *Nothing* refers simply to the absence of those objects capable of providing material satisfaction. And by extension he applies the term to all behavior which does not grant the sufficiency of things." Unable to see that the old man's wealth is a woefully inadequate bulwark against the Void, he is, in his ignorance, contemptuous both of the man and his predicament. Perhaps as a direct outgrowth of this lack of light, the young waiter also violates the principle of cleanness by sloppily pouring his customer's desperately needed brandy over the sides of the glass. Thus, he easily loses himself in a fool's paradise of blindness and illusion. Still young, secure in his job, and, as he boasts, " 'I'm not lonely. I have a wife waiting in bed for me,' " he is "all confidence": as such, a particularly patent example to the old waiter of those who "lived in it [*nada*] and never felt it."

Yet, in the course of the story, even this naif has an unsettling glimpse of the fundamental uncertainty of existence and its direct impact on his own situation. What else can account for his sharply defensive reaction to the old waiter's joke? [Old Waiter]: " 'And you? You have no fear of going home before your usual hour?' " [Young Waiter]: " 'Are you trying to insult me?' " [Old Waiter]: " 'No, hombre, only to make a joke.' " The youth's subsequent grandiose claims to security notwithstanding, the force with which he objects to the merest possibility of marital infidelity clearly underscores the shaky foundations of his "confidence." This bogus self-assurance does not emanate from a mature awareness of himself and his world, but is based on the most transitory of conditions: youth, present employment, sexual prowess, and the assumed loyalty of his wife. The young waiter depends for his very being on factors over which he has no control, leaving him particularly vulnerable, in the case of marital uncertainty, to what Warren Bennett calls the "love wound," a common form of deprivation in Hemingway. But because he is essentially devoid of light or insight, he is not cognizant of the significance of his testy reply; his vision is so clouded by putative "confidence" that he fails to see through the ephemeral to the underlying darkness in his own life. Consequently, he cannot even begin to reconstruct his existence upon a more substantial basis.

Hemingway must have reveled in such naifs, aflame with so obviously compromised bravado, for he created many of them. Perhaps the most notable is Paco, the would-be bullfigher of "The Capital of the World" (1936), who even in the face of his own death, is "full of illusions." For many of these characters, moreover, blindness is not a natural state but a willed escape from *nada*. Conscious flight from reality is particularly prevalent in the early stages of the "education" of Nick Adams. In "Indian Camp" (1924), for instance, one of the first segments in the Adams chronology, Nick has a youthful encounter with *nada* both as the incontrovertible fact of death (the Indian husband's suicide) and as human frailty, the intrinsic vulnerability of mankind to various species of physical and psychic suffering (the Indian woman's protracted and painful labor). The pattern of avoidance set when he refuses to witness the Caesarean section climaxes in his more significant refusal to recognize the inevitability of death itself at the end. Lulled by the deceptive calm of his present circumstances—a purely fortuitous and temporary clean, well-lighted place—he maintains an internal darkness by retreating into willed ignorance:

> They were seated in the boat, Nick in the stern, his father rowing. The sun was coming up over the hills. A bass jumped, making a circle in the water. Nick trailed his hand in the water. It felt warm in the sharp chill of the morning.
>
> In the early morning on the lake sitting in the stern of the boat with his father rowing, he felt quite sure that he would never die.

In another early story, "The Killers" (1927), the somewhat older Nick is again faced with harsh reality, but his reaction to it has not appreciably altered. Again, death (the Swede's) is the primary manifestation of the Void. But here the manner of its coming is also particularly important as a signature of *nada*. As represented by the black-clad henchmen who invade the café—another inadequate place of refuge—*nada* is totally impersonal; in the words of one of the killers, " 'He [the Swede] never had a chance to do anything to us. He never even seen us.' " Moreover, *nada* displays its tendency to disrupt without warning any established external order, and, ironically, is visited upon its victims not without a certain macabre humor. Naturally, as Nick learns from the intended victim, its effects are totally irremediable. Thus, in spite of their suggestive black clothing, the killers do not represent forces of evil unleashed in an otherwise good world, as so many critics have claimed: rather, they stand for the wholly amoral, wholly irrational, wholly random operation of the universe, which, because it so clearly works to the detriment of the individual, is *perceived* to be malevolent and evil.

In spite of the clearly educational nature of his experience, Nick once again refuses initiation. Only now his unreasoned compulsion to escape is more pronounced than that of his younger counterpart. Deluded into thinking that this is the kind of localized danger that can be avoided by a mere change in venue, Nick vows not only physical flight (" 'I'm going to get out of this town' ") but psychological flight as well: " 'I can't stand to think about him waiting in the room and knowing he's going to get it. It's too damned awful.' " Both versions of Nick Adams, then, are "young waiter" figures because they neither will allow themselves to look directly at the fearsome face of *nada* nor recognize its direct applicability to their own insecure lives.

That such an attitude is ultimately insupportable is exemplified by a third early tale, "Cross-Country Snow" (1925). Here, yet another Nick employs a physically demanding activity, skiing, as an escape from yet another incarnation of *nada*, entrapping circumstance. This appearance of the Void is also ironic in that the specific circumstance involved is the life-enhancing pregnancy of Nick's wife. Nevertheless, its impact on the character is much the same as before in that it serves to severely circumscribe independent initiative, even to the point of substituting an externally imposed identity—in this case, fatherhood—on the true self. Once again misled by the temporary security of the "good place," this Nick also attempts to escape the inescapable, and, at the height of his self-delusion, is moved to raise his pursuit of physical release to the level of absolute value: " 'We've got to [ski again] . . . It [life] isn't worth while if you can't.' "

The ski slope, however, offers only apparent protection from *nada*, for even in his joyous adventure, Nick encounters its own form of hidden danger: "Then a patch of soft snow, left in a hollow by the wind, spilled him and he went over and over in a clashing of skis, feeling like a shot rabbit." Unlike the others, this story ends with clarified vision, and Nick does come to terms with the inevitable external demands upon him.

Finally, he is no longer able to pretend that the pleasures of the ski slopes—themselves, not always unmixed—are anything more than temporary, in no way definitive of human existence or even a long-lived accommodation to it. Thus, in response to his companion's suggested pact to repeat their present idyll, Nick must realistically counter, " 'There isn't any good in promising.' "

In his relationship to *nada*, the old man of "A Clean, Well-Lighted Place" is cast as the polar opposite of the young waiter. Said to be eighty years old, virtually deaf, and recently widowed, he is "in despair" in spite of his reputed wealth, and has attempted suicide shortly before the story begins. Unlike the young waiter, he has the light of unclouded vision because he has clearly seen the destructive effects of time and circumstance on love and the self and directly witnessed *nada* in its death mask. But unlike the old waiter, he has not been able to sustain a satisfactory mode of being in the face of these discoveries. He therefore seeks escape from his knowledge either through the bottle or the total denial of life in suicide. Undoubtedly, the old man senses the importance of the clean, well-lighted place, but to him it is very literally a "place" and thereby no more helpful in combatting *nada* than Nick's ski slope. That it is inadequate is suggested imagistically at the outset; darkness has indeed invaded this character's "place," for he sits "in the shadows the leaves of the trees made against the electric light."

What seems to offer the old man the little balance he possesses, and thus helps keep him alive, is a modicum of internal cleanness and self-possession, his dignity or style. Of course, this is an issue of great import in Hemingway in that an ordered personal style is one of the few sources of value in an otherwise meaningless universe. The old waiter draws attention to this pitiful figure's style when he rebukes the young waiter for callously characterizing the old man as " 'a nasty old thing' ": " 'This old man is clean. He drinks without spilling. Even now, drunk.' " But even this vestige of grace has been compromised over time. While the old man leaves the café "with dignity," he is "walking unsteadily."

The product of a series of encounters with *nada*, the old man's despair is mirrored in two Nick Adams stories on the period immediately following the critical war wound. In "Now I Lay Me" (1927), the emotional dislocation stemming from his brush with death is continued in an almost psychotic dread of the night and sleep. *Nada* is imaged both as the night itself and, as Carlos Baker has suggested, by the disturbing and seemingly ceaseless munching of silkworms, just out of sight but most assuredly not out of Nick's disturbed mind. Paradoxically, the protagonist's abject terror in the face of potential selflessness—permanent in death; temporary in sleep—has resulted in a severe dissociation of the self. Using Paul Tillich's descriptive terminology from *The Courage To Be*, one can say that he is burdened by "pathological" anxiety: a condition of drastically reduced self-affirmation, a flight from nonbeing that entails a corresponding flight from being itself: "I myself did not want to sleep because I had been living for a long time with the knowledge that if I ever shut my eyes in the dark and let myself go, my soul would go out of my body. I had been that way for a long time, ever since I had been blown up at night and felt it go out of me and go off and then come back."

Awakened to the fact of his own death, Nick experiences *angst* so strongly that he is virtually paralyzed. Unwilling to sleep in the dark and not yet able to develop an internal light and cleanness to cope with his trauma, he depends entirely on external sources of illumination: "If I could have a light I was not afraid to sleep." In the absence of this light, however, he attempts to pull back from the awareness of *nada* by reliving the happier times of his youth, a period of cleanness and assured order. But the search for a good "place" in the past is ultimately fruitless; his memories of favorite trout streams tend to blur in his mind and inevitably lead him to unpleasant reminiscences of his father's ruined collection of arrowheads and zoological specimens, a chaotic heap of fragments that merely mirrors his present internal maelstrom.

In "A Way You'll Never Be" (1933), Nick's dissociation has not been remedied and is suggested initially by the post-battle debris with which the story opens. Plagued by a recurring dream of "a low house painted yellow with willows all around it and a low stable and there was a canal, and he had been there a thousand times and never seen it, but there it was every night as plain as the hill, only it frightened him," he is close to an old man's despair. He now intuits something of the significance of the vision: "That house meant more than anything and every night he had it [the dream]. That was what he needed." But he is still too traumatized by the experience there to examine it more closely, and can only ramble on in self-defense about the "American locust," another familiar item from his childhood. In his present condition, Nick is an oddly appropriate choice for the absurd mission on which he has been sent, to display his American uniform in order to build morale among the Italian troops. At the moment, his "self," like the entire American presence in the region, is solely the uniform; the clothes are as dimly suggestive of a more substantial identity as they are of the substantial military support they are designed to promise. For the present, though, this barely adequate package for his violently disturbed inner terrain is Nick's only semblance of the clean, well-lighted place. Still insufficiently initiated into the dangerous world in which he is doomed to live, he desperately clutches at any buffer that will hold *nada* in abeyance.

The other side of Hemingway's "old man" figure is epitomized by Manuel Garcia, the aging bullfighter of "The Undefeated" (1925). After numerous brushes with death in the bullring, he too depends for his very being on style. Garcia's style has also eroded, leaving him defenseless against the bull, Harold Kaplan's "beast of *nada*." Banished from the brightly lit afternoon bouts, he now performs in the shadowy nocturnals for a "second string critic" and with bulls that "the veterinaries won't pass in the daytime." The performance itself is merely "acceptable" if not "vulgar." Largely as a result of his diminished capabilities, he is seriously (and perhaps mortally) wounded, and, at the conclusion, is left with only his *coletta*, as is the old man his shred of dignity. With these all-important manifestations of internal cleanness sullied, the fates of both are equally uncertain: Manuel's on the operating table, and the old man's in the enveloping night.

Of all Hemingway's short story characters, however, the one who most fully recapitulates the "old man" typology is Mr. Frazer of "The Gambler, the Nun, and the Radio" (1933). Confined to a backcountry hospital as a result of a riding accident, Frazer too experiences *nada*, "the Nothingness that underlies pain, failure, and disillusionment alike," in the form of his own incapacity and that of the broken men who share his predicament. He also experiences banality, one of the less overtly disturbing but nonetheless ominous visages of *nada*, in the form of the numbing routine of this claustrophobic, but clean and well-lighted place. If Frazer has an old man's clear perspective on nothingness, he is no better able to achieve the cleanness of character necessary to cope with it. As is suggested by Hemingway's first title for the story, "Give Us a Prescription, Doctor," Frazer too seeks external anodynes for his *nada*-induced pain. His compulsion to monitor random radio broadcasts and so imaginatively transport himself from his present circumstances is analogous to the old man's drinking because each involves a flight from, rather than a confrontation with reality. His very choice of songs—"Little White Lies" and "Sing Something Simple"—serves to underscore the escapism of this pastime.

In the end, however, neither escape succeeds. The old man remains in despair, and Frazer is given to periodic fits of uncontrollable weeping. In the same way that the former cannot entirely banish the specter of loneliness and death from his consciousness, neither can Frazer, nor any man, completely cloud his view of *nada* with the various "opiums" at his disposal. The very consideration of the question of release leads Frazer through the opium haze to the terrible truth that lies beneath:

> Religion is the opium of the people. . . . Yes, and music is the opium of the people. . . . And now economics is the opium of the people; along with patriotism the opium of the people in Italy and Germany. . . . But drink was a sovereign opium of the people, oh, an excellent opium. Although some prefer the radio, another opium of the people, a cheap one he had just been using. . . . What was the real, the actual opium of the people? . . . What was it? Of course; bread was the opium of the people. . . . [Only] Revolution, Mr. Frazer thought, is no opium. Revolution is a catharsis; an ecstasy which can only be prolonged by tyranny. The opiums are for before and for after. He was thinking well, a little too well.

The old waiter definitely stands apart from the other two characters in "A Clean, Well-Lighted Place." If the running controversy over dialogue attribution has thrown some doubt on whether he or his young partner first learns of the old man's attempted suicide, it has done nothing to contradict earlier assumptions on which of the two is more sensitive to the reasons for it. It is evident throughout that the old waiter's insight into the word *nothing* he so frequently uses is much broader. He recognizes from the first that the old man's despair is not a reaction to a material lack but to a basic metaphysical principle. Thus, he is unable to delude himself into a bogus "confidence." When he responds to the youth's boasting with " 'You have everything,' " he is clearly being ironic; the latter indeed has "everything," *except* a firm hold on the "nothing" which underlies "everything." They are "of two different kinds" because the old waiter knows the ability to withstand the dark "is not only a question of youth and confidence although those things are very beautiful." In spite of their superficial beauty, both the transitory condition of youth and the illusory confidence that so often goes with it are clearly inadequate tools with which to combat the darkness.

There is a closer connection with the old man, however, initially because the news of his attempted suicide begins the old waiter's formal consideration of the reasons for it. In this sense, at the beginning of the tale, the old waiter is a representation of Earl Rovit's "tyro" and Philip Young's "Hemingway hero" (as opposed to the "tutor" and "code hero") in that he is in the process of learning about the dark underside of life. But while the old man's plight is a necessary goad for the old waiter's musings on his own situation, the latter certainly outstrips his "mentor" in the lengths to which he pushes his speculations on *nada*: "What did [the old waiter] fear? It was not fear or dread. It was a nothing that he knew too well. It was all a nothing and a man was nothing too. It was only that and light was all it needed and a certain cleanness and order. Some lived in it and never felt it but he knew it all was nada y pues nada y nada y pues nada."

Like the old man, then, the old waiter sees clearly, in fact more clearly, the fearsome nothing, but he reacts far differently to his discovery. Instead of lapsing into despair or escaping into drunkenness, this character displays true metaphysical courage in raising the concept of *nada* to a central article in his overtly existentialist creed, climaxing with his mock prayer of adoration, "Hail nothing full of nothing, nothing is with thee." Perhaps even more importantly, he refuses to limit himself to abstract speculation but willingly embraces the impact of universal nothingness on his own person. Thus, in response to the barman's question, " 'What's yours?' " he demonstrates the ironic sense of humor that typifies him throughout by unflinchingly answering, " 'Nada.' " No other statement in the tale so clearly designates the old waiter as the central figure of Hemingway's 1933 collection: he is the "winner" who truly takes "nothing" as his only possible reward.

If this stoic courage in the shadow of the Void differentiates the old waiter from the old man, so does his method for dealing with it. Again, the old waiter provides some grounds for confusing the two modes of existence when he insists upon the importance of a purely physical haven: " 'I am one of those who like to stay late at the café. . . . With all those who do not want to go to bed. With all those who need a light for the night.' " Yet, he does more than merely accept the dubious protection of an already established "place"; he is, in fact, the keeper of the "clean, well-lighted place," the one who maintains both its cleanness and its light. To cite Cleanth Brooks on this subject, "The order and light are supplied by *him*. They do *not* reflect an inherent, though concealed, order in the universe. What little meaning there is in the world is imposed upon that world by man." Given the stark contrast between his café and the distinctly unclean and ill-lighted bar he frequents after work, his almost ritualistic efforts to furnish and consistently maintain these essential qualities are definitely not representative of those around him. Finally, the old waiter's clean, well-lighted place is distinctly portable—transcending "place" altogether—because it is so thoroughly internalized. He carries it in the form of equanimity and dignity to the shabby *bodega*, and he carries it home as well.

Thus, it is the old waiter, a man who can see clearly the darkness surrounding him yet so order his life that he can endure this awareness, who most fully attains the attitude symbolized by the clean, well-lighted place. In the society presented by this tale, and in the Hemingway canon as a whole, he is indeed "*otro loco mas*" when set against a standard of sanity epitomized by an egotistical partner, unfeeling barmen, lustful soldiers, and suicidal old men. Both realist and survivor, epitome of "grace under pressure," he is by the end of the tale an exceptional man and very much a representation of the highest level of heroism in Hemingway's fictional world, whether it be denoted by Young's "code hero" or Rovit's "tutor." Even his insomnia, which he regards as a common trait ("Many must have it"), is a mark of his extraordinary character: his vision is too clear, his sense of self too firm, to allow him the ease of insensate slumber. One need only compare this insomnia with Nick Adams' pathological fear of sleep in "Now I Lay Me" to appreciate the qualitative difference between the old waiter and other men.

Some of Hemingway's most important tales also contain characters who either presage an achievement of or actually attain the old waiter's clean, well-lighted place. A notable early example is the Nick Adams of "Big Two-Hearted River" (1925). Again, the confrontation with *nada* is critical here, but the appearance of *nada* is more artfully veiled than in other tales. There are hints of the Void in the description of the burned-over countryside at the beginning, in Nick's vision of the trout "tightened facing up into the current" shortly thereafter, and in the methodical series of tasks that comprise the central action of the story. As Malcolm Cowley first suggested and Sheridan Baker has since amplified, the ritualistic series connotes a desperate attempt to hold off something "he had left behind"; in Philip Young's reading, the "something" is the memory of the traumatic war wound that so discomfits other versions of Nick in "Now I Lay Me" and "A Way You'll Never Be." But *nada* is most overtly suggested by the forbidding swamp: "Nick did not want to go in there now. . . . In the swamp the banks were bare, the big cedars came together overhead, the sun did not come through, except in patches; in the fast deep water, in the half light, the fishing would be tragic." Aside from the old waiter's prayer, this is Hemingway's most detailed characterization of *nada*; it too is dark; its depth is ungauged but considerable; and, with its swiftly moving current and bare banks, it is most assuredly inhospitable to man.

As the "patches" of sunlight suggest, though, the *nada*/swamp can be discerned and therefore analyzed by human vision. And, by the end of the story, Nick seems to have gained the light necessary to see into the Void—at the very least, to realize that he can never truly leave it behind him. Yet Nick still lacks the inner cleanness to delve further into *nada*; he is still too dependent on a distinct physical locale as a buffer zone. As he says early on, "He was there, in the good place." But the very ritualistic behavior that alerted Cowley to the possibility of a mind not right also suggests progress toward an internalized order. Like the trout's in the potentially destructive current, this discipline could hold Nick steady in the dangerous eddies of life and so enable him eventually to enter the swamp. Thus, while the tale ends with a temporary withdrawal from direct confrontation, Nick strikes a positive note when he says, "There were plenty of days coming when he could fish the swamp."

Two characters in the late short stories actually do "fish" the swamp of *nada*, the sportsman Macomber in "The Short Happy Life of Francis Macomber" (1936) and the writer Harry of "The Snows of Kilimanjaro" (1936). The two men approach the clean, well-lighted place from different directions, however: Macomber, from an old man's despair; and Harry, from a young waiter's naive faith in transitory material security. For Macomber, the master of "court games" and darling of drawing rooms, it is necessary to leave the protective enclosures of the rich to meet his *nada* in the African tall grass in the figure of the wounded lion, an epitome of pure destructive force: "All of him [the lion], pain, sickness, hatred and all of his remaining strength, was tightening into an absolute concentration for a rush." The brush with externally conceived *nada* triggers Macomber's cowardly flight, but more importantly leads him to an appreciation of his own inner emptiness, a Sartrian version of nothingness, as well as a Sartrian *nausea* at his inauthenticity. Granted, Macomber responds to the threat with fear, but it is also more than fear, "a cold slimy hollow in all the emptiness where once his confidence had been and it made him feel sick." Thus Macomber comes face to face with the fact that *nada* need not destroy the physical being to make man a "nothing"; man *is* a nothing unless and until he makes himself "something."

The black despair that follows his initiation to *nada* without and within is not Macomber's final stage. Through the ministrations of the hunter Wilson and the familiar, secure place (the jeep), he undergoes a significant and almost miraculous change at the buffalo hunt. As Wilson describes it, "Beggar had probably been afraid all his life. Don't know what started it. But over now. Hadn't had time to be afraid with the buff. That and being angry too. Motor car too. Motor cars made it familiar. Be a damn fire eater now." The jeep is indeed useful as a means for facing *nada* analogous to the old waiter's café and Nick Adams' peaceful campsite, but Macomber's real "place" is distinctly internal. Again, Wilson furnishes the analysis: "Fear gone like an operation. *Something else grew in its place.* Main thing a man had. Made him into a man [italics mine]." Macomber's real achievement, then, is the creation of an ordered "something" to fill the inner void. It not only prepares him for the buffalo hunt but enables him to see clearly, as if for the first time, his inauthentic condition, not the least important facet of which has been his sacrifice of personal identity to an unfulfilling marriage and social expectation. With his "place" securely inside him, he can face with dignity and courage another brush with *nada* in the "island of bushy trees," a hostile testing ground certainly reminiscent of Nick's swamp.

In "Snows of Kilimanjaro," Harry too has multiple confrontations with *nada*, the first of which is with the ultimate manifestation of the Void, death: "It came with a rush; not as a rush of water nor of wind; but of a sudden evil-smelling emptiness." As we learn later, this appearance certainly fits Carlos Baker's oxymoronic designation for *nada* as the "nothing that is something," for "It had no shape, any more. It simply occupied space." The immediate effect of the experience is to lead Harry to an appreciation of the underlying absurdity of an existence that could be doomed by such a trivial injury—a small scratch which becomes gangrenous for lack of proper medication. With this awareness of his radical contingency, the protagonist can defuse death of its terror: "Since the gangrene started in his right leg he had no pain and with the pain the horror had gone and all he felt now was a great tiredness and anger that this was the end of it. . . . For years it had obsessed him; but now it meant nothing in itself."

Like Macomber's, Harry's brush with imminent death also awakens him to a second face of *nada*, the inner nothing caused by his failure to preserve artistic integrity, his very self, against the lures of the inconsequential: material comfort, financial security, hedonistic pleasure. Every bit as much as Macomber, this most autobiographical of Hemingway's short story characters suffers a hollowness at the very core. Therefore, the basic thrust of the tale is Harry's effort to cleanse and reorder his life through a pointed self criticism. Gradually he manages to "work the fat off his soul" by jettisoning the excess baggage of a young waiter's facile confidence in the material and replaces it with something more substantial, a pledge to take up his writing once more. Again, the process is facilitated by his being situated in a tangible clean, well-lighted place: "This was a pleasant camp under big trees against a hill, with good water, and close by, a nearly dry water hole where sand grouse flighted in the mornings." But again, the important "place" is actually within. According to Gloria Dussinger, Harry's difficult rite of purification leads, as it should, to a reclamation of his own identity: "Harry is left with his naked self, the irreducible *I am* that defies chaos." Though the climactic dream flight from the plain is decidedly ambiguous, it does seem to vouchsafe Harry's success at this endeavor, for the author allows him imaginative entry into the cleanest and best lighted of all the places in the short story canon: "great, high, and unbelievably white in the sun, was the square top of Kilimanjaro. And then he knew that there was where he was going."

Although Harry and Macomber both achieve the clean, well-lighted place, their premature deaths deprive them of the opportunity to bring additional value to their lives, as the old waiter most assuredly does. Having controlled his own life through the implementation of a clean, well-lighted place, he fulfills the remaining provisions of Eliot's "Waste Land" credo by sympathizing with the plight of others and aiding them in their own pursuits of this all important attitude. In so doing, he becomes an existential hero in Martin Buber's particular sense of the term, a champion of the "I-Thou" relationship. His "style" is essentially compassion, the willingness to treat others as valid, subjective "Thous" rather than depersonalized "Its." This facet of his personality is implicit as early as his expression of sympathy for the pleasure-seeking soldier who risks curfew violation. As he himself comments on the risks involved, " 'What does it matter if he gets what he's after?' " But his capacity for true compassion is made most explicit near the end, particularly in his admission, " 'Each night I am reluctant to close up because there may be some one who needs the café.' "

The ability to extend outward to others from a firmly established self is once again in direct contrast to the narrow, selfish pride of the young waiter, who is unmoved by the needs of the old man and sees love as a matter of blind loyalty (verging on bondage) and physical gratification. This inclination is made all too clear by his insensitive comment on the old widower's plight: " 'A wife would be no good to him now.' " The old waiter's attitude is also contrasted to that of the old man, who is so absorbed by his own misery that he is barely cognizant of others. This admirable figure passes beyond Rovit's "tyro" stage to that of "tutor" when he humorously, but pointedly, attempts to instruct the youth on the evanescence of "confidence" and the latter's serious misuse of love (e.g., by the joke). Moreover, he tries to provide the morose old man with some basis upon which to reconstruct his shattered life by rendering to this wretched figure the respect and sympathy he so desperately needs. Thus, in Buber's sense as in Heidegger's, Kierkegaard's, and Sartre's, the old waiter "authenticates" his life by fulfilling his responsibilities both to himself and to others.

The picador Zurito in "The Undefeated," the dignified major in "Another Country" (1927), and the guide Wilson of "The Short Happy Life of Francis Macomber" all transcend the limits of self-sufficiency by sympathizing with and proferring aid to those who most need it. But the character who most closely approximates the old waiter's multi-faceted heroism is Cayetano Ruiz, the luckless gambler of "The Gambler, the Nun, and the Radio," a story whose three main characters (Ruiz, Frazer, Sister Cecilia) form a triadic grouping analogous to the hero, victim, and naif of "A Clean, Well-Lighted Place."

That the gambler does attain the exemplary attitude is implicit in William Barrett's summary characterization of him: "Cayetano is the absurd hero who carries on his code, even if it is only the code of a cheap gambler, defiantly and gracefully against the Void." Cayetano, of course, earns his heroism in that he too encounters the death mask of *nada*. Like Harry's, his wound comes totally without warning, and, given the rather unreliable aim of his assailant, almost totally by accident. Yet even before this crisis, the perspicacious gambler with eyes "alive as a hawk's" has undoubtedly sensed its presence in the form of chance and the ever-present risk of his chosen profession. In spite of the fact that his work takes him into places that are anything but clean and well-lighted, he has so internalized the "place" that he can calmly face external hostility and internal suffering, and face them with honor and exemplary courage. Consequently, he refuses to inform on his assailant and also refuses opiates to dull the physical pain that serves as metaphor for the metaphysical pain *nada* induces.

But Ruiz is far more than Barrett's "cheap," albeit heroic, gambler because he strives to communicate his insights on life to others. Indirect proof of his compassion is to be found both in his embarrassment over the offensive odor of his peritonitis and in his considerate silence even in periods of terrible pain. Direct evidence is available in the conversations with Frazer. Here Ruiz incisively analyses the untreatable ills of the human condition—the absurd irony, the prevalence of accident and risk, and, most of all, the difficulty of maintaining a self amidst the vagaries of fortune that have driven his auditor to tears. Like the old waiter, he is quite capable of humbling himself, denigrating his own considerable courage, in order to provide comfort to one less able to withstand *nada*. Surely he consciously misstates fact when, in an attempt to assuage Frazer's shame at lapsing into tears, he declares, " 'If I had a private room and a radio I would be crying and yelling all night long.' " Evidently this self-described "victim of illusions" also possesses the old waiter's ironic consciousness, for it is at the very heart of his dispassionate self-analysis, also delivered principally for Frazer's benefit: " 'If I live long enough the luck will change. I have bad luck now for fifteen years. If I ever get any good luck I will be rich.' " Although he fully realizes that "bad luck" will continue to predominate, like the other residents of the *metaphoric* clean, well-lighted place, the gambler is content to "continue, slowly, and wait for luck to change." In the interim, he will continue to try to instill in others some of the light and cleanness essential to the authentication of the self.

In their dealings with the various faces of *nada*, then, the old waiter figures represent the highest form of heroism in the Hemingway short story canon, a heroism matched in the novels perhaps only by the fisherman Santiago. Those who manage to adjust to life on the edge of the abyss do so because they see clearly the darkness that surrounds them yet create a personal sense of order, an identity, with which to maintain balance on this precarious perch. The failure either to see the significance of the encounter with *nada* or, if seen, to constitute an inner cleanness vitiates the lives not only of the young waiter and old man of "A Clean, Well-Lighted Place" but also of a host of similarly flawed figures throughout the canon.

Because of the frequency with which *nada* appears in the short fiction, we can only assume that the Void also played a major role in Hemingway's own life, whether as the shattering war wound or the countless subsequent experiences, both real and imagined, that threatened to make him a "nothing." Carlos Baker concluded as much in his biography: " 'A Clean, Well-Lighted Place' was autobiographical . . . in the sense that it offered a brief look into the underside of Ernest's spiritual world, the nightmare of nothingness by which he was still occasionally haunted." But if we are justified in seeing Hemingway's life in terms of his encounters with *nada*, are we not equally justified in following Earl Rovit's lead and thereby treating his fiction as one of the by-products of these encounters—in fact, as a primary strategy for dealing with *nada*?

Both the fiction itself and the author's comments on it seem to support us in this regard, for Hemingway's basic aesthetic suggests precisely the sort of perspective symbolized by the clean, well-lighted place. The need for clearsightedness, for instance, is the essence of the writer's celebrated remark on art in *Death in the Afternoon* (1932), a personal testament published just a year before "A Clean, Well-Lighted Place": "Let those who want to save the world if you can get to see it clear and as a whole. Then any part you make will represent the whole if it is made truly." But unclouded vision alone, not uncommon among his fictional progeny, could guarantee neither a psychological nor an aesthetic clean, well-lighted place. A careful and conscious ordering of disparate material was also required in order to fill the Void of nothing (the blank page) with an enduring something. Thus, the characteristic Hemingway style: the clean, precise, scrupulously ordered prose that so often serves to illuminate shimmering individual objects against a dark background of chaos. As for his old waiter figures, the actual places that inspired the author's descriptions pale against the deftly constructed "places" that *are* the descriptions; because the latter are no longer subject to the random, transitory world of fact but rather interiorized and subsequently transmuted into art itself, they are much more secure, and certainly more permanent, strongholds against nothingness.

In spite of the apparent disdain for utilitarian art in the passage from *Death in the Afternoon*, Hemingway also performed some of that function, albeit indirectly, by probing the sources of our well-documented modern malaise and offering at least tentative solutions to it in the form of resolute personal conduct. In this way he too displayed some of the Buberesque qualities of his short story heroes. It should come as no surprise, then, that Granville Hicks' summary of the author's artistic mission has a rather direct applicability to that of the old waiter as well. For in their potential impact on an attentive audience, Hemingway and his extraordinary character are virtually one and the same. Like the latter, "The artist makes his contribution to the salvation of the world by seeing it clearly himself and helping others to do the same."

Perhaps nothing so effectively demonstrates the difficulty of maintaining the clean, well-lighted place than Hemingway's own failure to do so in the years immediately preceding his death. Like so many of his "old man" figures, he never lost sight of *nada* but did lose the essential inner cleanness, without which the light must eventually be overpowered by darkness. With his internal defenses in disarray, Hemingway turned to an old man's despairing act. In effect, in his suicide, he opted for the release from turmoil offered by the metaphorical "opiums" of Mr. Frazer: "He would have a little spot of the giant killer and play the radio, you could play the radio so that you could hardly hear it."

ALFRED KAZIN

Hemingway the Painter

*Our people went to America because that was the place for them to go
then. It had been a good country and we had made a bloody mess of
it and I would go, now, somewhere else as we had always the right
to go somewhere else and as we had always gone. . . . Let the others
come to America who did not know that they had come too late. Our
people had seen it at its best and fought for it when it was well
worth fighting for. Now I would go somewhere else.*

— HEMINGWAY, *Green Hills of Africa*

One of the last photographs of Hem-
ingway shows him wandering a road in Idaho and kicking a can. He is
surrounded by grim mountains. He looks morose, he is evidently in his
now-usual state of exasperation, and he is alone. The emptiness of Idaho
is the only other presence in the picture.

With his gift for locating the most symbolic place for himself,
Hemingway was bound to end up in Idaho. And not just for the hunting
and fishing. At every stage of his life he found himself a frontier appropriate to his fresh needs as a sportsman and his ceremonial needs as a writer.
Only Henry James among his significant predecessors made such a literary
cult of travel. James even in his sacred Europe never went very far. He
certainly never sought the last possible frontier.

Most American writer-wanderers, like Melville the sailor, Mark
Twain the mobile printer, correspondent, and lecturer, went where they
were forced to go to make a living. Hemingway for the most part chose

where he wanted to go. That was the impression he managed to leave. He did spend his early summers "up in Michigan" because his family summered there. Right after the First World War he was sent by the *Toronto Star* to report still more fighting between Turks and Greeks. But his conjunction of Michigan and the Balkans in *In Our Time* made these startling stories read as if *he* had chosen these experiences. There was a point to being Ernest Hemingway and to writing like Ernest Hemingway. Everything was under control like one of his sentences. He was an entirely free man. He had shaped his own career.

To summer up in Michigan was wonderful. It was also wonderful to sit in a café when Paris was "the best town for a writer to be" and, nursing a single *café crème*, to write the first Nick Adams stories in a blue-backed notebook with the stub of a pencil you shaved with a little pencil sharpener as you went along. Sharpening a pencil with a knife was too wasteful. Remembering how poor you had been, thirty years later in *A Moveable Feast*, you also made the point that "wasteful" referred to other people's prose, not E. Hemingway's. And when and where else was poverty so easy to bear that a young couple with baby could live on five dollars a day and go skiing in Austria when a story was finished? It also helped to skip lunch because on an empty stomach all sorts of hidden details in the Cézannes in the Luxembourg became sharper, easier to grasp for your writing when you were learning "to do the country like Cézanne."

Any place Hemingway sojourned in, any place he passed through, somehow took on Hemingway's attributes as an artist. He was the most extraordinary appropriator. He learned to omit many things for his famous style, but a trout stream in Michigan or a street in Paris came rhythmically to belong to Hemingway alone. Michigan became all primitive, brutish, but above all naked, like the starkness of a Hemingway story. Paris was electric, crowded, but above all derisory like *The Sun Also Rises*. No one after Maurice Utrillo established such an intimacy with Paris streets as Hemingway the foreigner did just by the loving repetition of certain names—Rue du Cardinal-Lemoine, Place de la Contrescarpe. And there were always the knowing little references—"The dancing-club was a *bal musette* in the Rue de la Montagne Sainte Geneviève"—that established Hemingway's ability to make a part of his page anything that he had first absorbed as a stranger in Paris.

He was ambitious, he was shrewd, he seemed to have worked out in advance just what he needed to get from a place, and he became contemptuous of others as soon as he had learned it. So much command of experience belonged to an imperial race. Defying his Victorian parents, and a year out of high school, he put himself on the line, went to the

Italian front as a Red Cross volunteer and got himself gloriously wounded. What other solidly middle-class boy from one of "our best families in Oak Park" could at nineteen have won for himself such lasting images of war, fright, and death? And who but Hemingway would have so indelibly recorded his wounding as his moment of truth?

> Then there was a flash, as when a blast-furnace door is swung open, and a roar that started white and went red and on and on in a rushing wind. I tried to breathe but my breath would not come and I felt myself rush bodily out of myself and out and out and out and all the time bodily in the wind. I went out swiftly, all of myself, and I knew I was dead and that it had all been a mistake to think you just died.

From now on it was his war, war was his. Reading Tolstoy's Sebastopol stories while hunting in *Green Hills of Africa* made him think of riding a bicycle down the Boulevard de Sébastopol in the rain:

> And I thought about Tolstoy and about what a great advantage an experience of war was to a writer. It was one of the major subjects and certainly one of the hardest to write truly of and those writers who had not seen it were always very jealous and tried to make it seem unimportant, or abnormal, or a disease as a subject, while, really, it was just something quite irreplaceable that they had missed.

His wounding was a shock that went straight into Hemingway's early stories and fables of the war. *In Our Time* taught him to make set passages out of the body's response to a particular blow. Mastery lay in the moment's triumph over danger; in life as in art, Hemingway needed one deliberate trial of himself after another. He made a point of seeking out violence. Clearly accident-prone, he retained his ability to turn every new accident into the confrontation of something or someone. In his bilious last years he was to say that it was good for a writer in despair to hang himself and "then be cut down without mercy and forced by his own self to write as well as he can for the rest of his life. At least he will have the story of the hanging to commence with."

This need of risk, of the ultimate challenge, became something that only an international sportsman could buy for himself. In *Green Hills of Africa* (1935) he was still boasting to a chance acquaintance:

> "And you know what you want?"
> "Absolutely, and I get it all the time."

This was the mark of a special time and a particular ego. Only the florid buccaneers of the age of enterprise had talked that way. Hemingway's crushing sense of self sought not wealth but fame—absolute distinction, to be top dog, the undoubted original and pacemaker for literary prose in his time. Writing was everything. And the journey that Hemingway undertook, the journey into the country of the dead that Ezra Pound idly and occasionally thought he was writing in the *Cantos*, made possible that extraordinary concentration of line and progression of effect that no matter how often we reread "The Battler," "Fifty Grand," "Big Two-Hearted River," can still make us hold our breath. No other American "in our time" so captured the actual physical element. No one else so charged up the reader, for no one else was so charged up by the act of writing itself.

> Nick walked back up the ties to where his pack lay in the cinders beside the railway track. He was happy. He adjusted the pack harness around the bundle, pulling straps tight, slung the pack on his back, got his arms through the shoulder straps and took some of the pull off his shoulders by leaning his forehead against the wide band of the tump-line. Still, it was too heavy. It was much too heavy.

So Hemingway caused "real" and "concrete" to become the first essentials in the act of writing. He put life back on the page, made us see, feel, and taste the gift of life in its unalloyed and irreducible reality. It may be that all we really have and know is our consciousness, that the alternative is something we know nothing about, that the livingness of being alive is the inescapable drama of our existence. Not many writers have incarnated this in their work, have emphasized the angle of their particular consciousness so that our experience of their work becomes as elemental as their own grasp of existence. To read Hemingway was always to feel more alive. The spontaneous reaction was pleasure from the cunning way sentences fall, from the bright echoing separateness of the words, from every picture a passage put into the mind. One was brought close to some exceptional vividness.

Of all the many things Hemingway appropriated, the most celebrated was his own experience. How he hammered any triviality into place, kept it luminous with his particular gift for shining in his own light! This was what he hungered for beyond anything else, what he kept from dying. With his particular talent for saving and treasuring his experiences, for turning life into the economy of art, he brought into his sacred circle many small things insubstantial and fugitive. It was typical of him to call them "rain" and to celebrate "rain" as what did not vanish when secured in the style of Ernest Hemingway.

His minute details bring us into a world dense but never thick like that of the great nineteenth-century novels—a world stark, each detail oddly magnified, so that the bombardment gives us a sense of being violated. Like many startling achievements of modernism, this can be felt first as pain. In A *Farewell to Arms* there is the confrontation on the bank of the Isonzo between the Italian battle police and the officers separated from their troops in the retreat at Caporetto. The scene excites a quiver of terror when the questioning of the hapless officers is followed by their immediate execution. It is night. The lights being flashed by the battle police into face after face bring to mind the unnaturally bright faces of the condemned being shot by the light of torches in Goya's *Disasters of War*.

> They took me down behind the line of officers below the road toward a group of people in a field by the river bank. As we walked toward them shots were fired. I saw flashes of the rifles and heard the reports. We came up to the group. There were four officers standing together, with a man in front of them with a carabiniere on each side of him. A group of men were standing guarded by carabinieri. Four other carabinieri stood near the questioning officers, leaning on their carbines. They were wide-hatted carabinieri. The two who had me shoved me in with the group waiting to be questioned. I looked at the man the officers were questioning. He was the fat gray-haired little lieutenant-colonel they had taken out of the column. The questioners had all the efficiency, coldness and command of themselves of Italians who are firing and are not being fired on.
>
> "Your brigade?"
> He told them.
> "Regiment?"
> He told them.
> "Why are you not with your regiment?"
> He told them.
> "Do you know that an officer should be with his troops?"
> He did.
> That was all. Another officer spoke.
> "It is you and such as you that have let the barbarians onto the sacred soil of the fatherland."
> "I beg your pardon," said the lieutenant-colonel.
> "It is because of treachery such as yours that we have lost the fruits of victory."
> "Have you ever been in a retreat?" the lieutenant-colonel asked.
> "Italy should never retreat."
> We stood there in the rain and listened to this. We were facing the officers and the prisoner stood in front and a little to one side of us.
> "If you are going to shoot me," the lieutenant-colonel said, "please shoot me at once without further questioning. The questioning is stupid." He made the sign of the cross. The officers spoke together. One wrote something on a pad of paper.
> "Abandoned his troops, ordered to be shot," he said.

The "picture" is certainly very distinct—and so is the paragraphing. The "fat gray-haired little lieutenant-colonel" is on that page forever, saying with perfect contempt, "Please shoot me at once without further questioning. The questioning is stupid." Hemingway certainly learned to parody Italian, Spanish, and French with affection and respect. *Stupido* is a word of perfect contempt. Generations of students, brought up on modernism as the latest (but not the last) academic tradition, have by now learned to speak of *reduction, foreshortening, irony* in order to indicate that Hemingway makes us see, brings us close to, that scene by the river. The *seeing* is all-important; Hemingway learned many things from painters and from extraordinarily visual war scenes in Stendhal, Tolstoy, Crane, that enabled him to get Caporetto just right. But the key to the scene is Hemingway's need to show that while the questioning and the shooting are mistaken, totally unjust, as hideously wrong as anything can be, this is what stoical men "in our time," like the fat little lieutenant-colonel, accept—because they will always be superior to the stupido.

Hemingway had many gifts. His greatest gift, the foundation of all his marvellous pictorial effects, was his sense of some enduring injustice, of some fundamental wrongness at the heart of things, to which an American can still rise, and which he will endure (and describe) as a hero. "There is a great disorder under heaven," the Chinese say. Today they draw political cheer from this, since masses oppressed for centuries learn resignation. Hemingway was an American from the Middle West, "the valley of democracy." He was brought up on the old American religion of the self-sufficient individual. He knew that the public world was pushing him and everyone else toward an abyss. But he still had a private code in the twenties that, as Lady Brett said in *The Sun Also Rises* about "deciding not to be a bitch," sort of replaced one's religion. When repeated often enough in the same tone of discovery, the code became one's politics. Of course the code did not survive into the thirties, the Hitler-Stalin era, and still another world war. What in the twenties was pronounced with so much startled self-approval as a form of conduct was really a lean, wary style of writing, Hemingway's style. This style thrived on "the disasters of war" but somehow saved a few exceptional people from destruction. It was all the law and all the prophets.

Hemingway's great teacher in Paris, Gertrude Stein, was as resentful of him when he became famous as he was of her for condescending to him as she did to everybody else. Unlike Hemingway, whose sense of himself was so imperious that he became violent when he felt himself slighted in the least, Stein was never "insecure." For the most part she operated so much on a personal and domestic level that even her early writing became as indistinct as the message from the other side at a séance. Unlike Hemingway, who always conflated the personal and the political, *his* style and *the* world, Stein talked with an aphoristic brilliance that she disdained to put into her writing. Better, much better, than her taking from a French garage owner (contemptuous of his mechanics) the saying that Hemingway put at the head of *The Sun Also Rises*—"You are all a lost generation"—was her saying that in the twentieth century nothing is in agreement with anything else.

Hemingway was born near the close of the old century and was fated to become one of the great expressers of enduring disorder in this century. His sense of incongruity was everything to him and came out as an uncanny intuition of stress, of the danger point, of the intolerable pressure level in life, personal and political. Women have their bodily fears and men have theirs; both relate to the sexual organs, to sexual vulnerability and respect. Perhaps Hemingway himself did not know just where and how a famously rugged, fearless, sometimes madly aggressive sportsman developed that special fear of violation and of mutilation—it is hinted at in the encounter with a hobo in "The Battler"—that he was able to project back on the world with a burning intuition of the *world's* inherent cruelty, danger, injustice. Sexual vulnerability is a universal condition that only a Hemingway could have concealed and yet mythologized in *The Sun Also Rises* and *Death in the Afternoon*. But in the mysteriously transforming interaction between Hemingway's bruised psyche and his masculine need always to sound *positive*—something extraordinary did result. His self-disapproval at being vulnerable at all had to be hidden, but his shock at not being allowed always to have his own way made him see the world as inherently treacherous. His easy American claim to power—especially over his own life—was constantly being limited and denied. The self remained intact. But wary, very wary, it had premonitions of war after war. Hemingway was not just being cocky when he put down writers who had not seen battle. Phlegmatic types never suffered and understood as he did. (Gertrude Stein was so vain that, living under Nazi occupation in France, she felt mysteriously protected—and she was.) Responding bitterly to accusations that he was "indifferent," Hemingway memorably responded in a letter, "These little punks who have never seen men street fighting, let alone a revolution . . . Listen—they never even heard of the events that produced the heat of rage, hatred, indignation, and disillusion that formed or forged what they call indifference."

II

Society, the body politic, the "world" that makes continually for war and social disorder, works as fiercely on people's unconscious and becomes their true intuitions. This often unhinges them without their recognizing the cause as politics or common fate.

Hemingway's attraction to violence, to hunting and fishing, to war—he saw a lot of war but was never a soldier—was not just a form of hell-raising and self-testing in the usual masculine way. It was a way of coming close to certain ordeals fundamental to his generation. From the beginning, because of his upbringing as a young Christian gentleman in a suffocatingly proper suburb of Chicago—Oak Park, "where the saloons end and the churches begin"—violences fascinated him as clues to what he graphically called "in our time." Like so many great modern writers, he was of solid bourgeois background and therefore knew that, morally, the bourgeois world was helpless.

Confronting danger everywhere, he made himself one with his time by running full tilt into everything that would bring a fresh emergency into his life. And everything certainly did. Gertrude Stein laughed in *The Autobiography of Alice B. Toklas* that for a man so professionally virile and athletic, Hemingway was certainly fragile. John Dos Passos was to say in *The Best Years* that Hemingway was always having to go to bed to recuperate from his many injuries. When he did not seek damage, it sought him. From boyhood on he suffered accidents that were grotesque in their violence toward this body they did not kill. As a boy, he fell and had a stick driven into the back of his throat, gouging out part of both tonsils. In 1918, when he was a Red Cross worker in Italy distributing supplies to soldiers, a mortar shell exploded more than twenty fragments into his legs; he was then hit twice by machine-gun bullets while carrying a more seriously injured man to the rear. As a young writer in Paris during the twenties, he was clipped on the forehead by pieces of a skylight that fell just as he was standing under it. In Wyoming in 1930, his car turned over and his right arm was pinned back by the top of the windshield and badly fractured, the bone sticking through the muscle. At another time, his brother Leicester reports, Hemingway shot a shark with a rifle, but the bullets split into several small pieces of hot lead that ricocheted into the calves of both his legs. In 1949, while duck shooting in the marshes near Venice, he got a bit of shell wadding blown into his eye, and a serious infection developed; in 1953 he crash-landed in Africa, and the rescue plane that picked him up crashed and burned; when he reached medical aid at Nairobi (just in time to read his obituaries), his internal organs had been wrenched out of place, his spine was injured, and he was bleeding from every orifice.

It is absurd to separate Hemingway from his work. He pushed his life at the reader, made his fascination with death and danger the central theme in his many pages about bullfighting, sport, and war, brought the reader closer to his own fascination with violence and terror as a central political drama. His great gift was to locate repeated episodes of violence (so linked by some profound compulsion that we anticipated the shotgun suicide) in the Turks expelling the Greeks in the lacerating inter-chapters of *In Our Time*, in the horns perforating the bullfighter (so that all the internal organs were sliced through at once) in *Death in the Afternoon*, in the very impotence of Jake Barnes in *The Sun Also Rises* and Colonel Cantwell in *Across the River and into the Trees*.

One could go on, as Hemingway certainly did, from the early story "Indian Camp," in which the Indian husband in the upper bunk cuts his throat as the doctor in the bunk below performs a cesarian on his wife with a jackknife and sews her up with nine-foot tapered gut leaders, to the ridiculously inflated episodes in the posthumous *Islands in the Stream*, where Hemingway talks of going after German submarines all by himself. The point is that Hemingway was a soul at war. He wins our assent, perhaps now more than ever, because it is the "outside" world that is increasingly violent today. Hemingway may have been as big a braggart and egotist as ever lived, but he had the stamp of the true artist. His emotions were prophetic, his antennae were out to the truth. He knew that destruction is a god over our lives, that the fear of death shapes us, that without any belief in immortality there can be no expectation of justice, so that the whole ghastly century is beginning to look like one unending chain of murder and retribution.

Hemingway's greatest gift was to identify his own capacity for pain with the destructiveness at large in our time. The artist works by locating the world in himself. Hemingway did something more: he located in himself his century's infatuation with technology, technique, instruments of every kind. Hemingway was recognized as an original, he fascinated and magnetized, because his theme was the greatest possible disturbance. His own sense of this was cold, proud know-how, professionally detached and above all concerned with applying a systematic, consistent *method* to everything he described. Obviously one attraction of sport, war, bullfighting was that each called for the maximum concentration of technique. Hemingway was clever and informed and quick to tell you what he knew. He always made a point of giving you in the midst of a story the exact name of a wine, the exact horsepower of a machine, even the exact moment in Paris—remember Lady Brett's entrance in *The Sun Also Rises*—when a woman appeared in a tight sweater and skirt so that she looked like the sides of a yacht. "She started all that."

Hemingway liked to write, as Nick Adams liked to make camp in "Big Two-Hearted River," from technical detail to detail. He had grown up in a world where men still travelled by horse, took care of their horses, repaired things themselves, walked everywhere, often grew or shot their own food. He believed in the work of one's own hands even to the point of usually writing by hand. It was this that led him to his great discovery of what painting could do for writers. Newspapers work for the *Kansas City Star* and the *Toronto Star* had taught him the first basic: to write professionally is to write *to* somebody else's mind, and you have to lay out all the facts in an assured, flat, knowing manner without the slightest suggestion or indecision or demonstrative emotion about what you know. You have to "reach the reader," said managing editors, to write for a newspaper so that said reader will distinguish Ernest M. Hemingway from a dozen other newswriters.

The paintings young Hemingway saw in France, most intimately at Gertrude Stein's flat, 27 Rue de Fleurus, were spellbindingly the work of an artist's own hand, of new theories of perception, of common physical materials. Nothing could have been more instantly pleasing to his imagination and his native sense of things. Painting was the decisive experience for an American abroad; "Europe" could seem one great painting. Painting stimulated a young reporter, already shrewdly aware of war and sport as the stuff of literature, to think of writing as a method. Painting was to do more for Hemingway than it was to do even for Stein, who in the end cared for painters more than for painting. "Genius" and "personality" were to become her topics. Stein could not draw at all and in fact had to leave Johns Hopkins medical school because of this and other failures in observation. Her famous Cézannes had been discovered and bought by her erratic brother Leo, her Matisses by Michael and Sally Stein. She kept the family collection when Leo became infuriated by cubism and stopped buying paintings. She depended on painting for the mental impressions that were her specialty. Unlike Hemingway, she had little feeling for the sensuous world. Her great interest was psychology, the "bottom truth" about anybody she met. Proceeding from psychology to composition, she became fascinated by what she felt to be the human mind as its own self-sufficient subject. "The human mind writes what it is. . . . The human mind consists only in writing down what is written and therefore it has no relation to human nature."

Stein was a profoundly clever theoretician, a great aphorist and wit, and a true inventor of composition based on what she called "the continuous present." Without seeing her paintings, without listening to the infatuated conversation about painting at 27 Rue de Fleurus, Hemingway might not have become Hemingway at all. As *she* was jealously to charge in *The Autobiography of Alice B. Toklas*, Hemingway was a sedulous ape, an all-too-adept pupil of other people's ideas and methods. But her comparative indifference to the subject matter of painting and the way she took off *from* painting to emphasize for psychological purposes the authority of the eye gave Hemingway the advantage over her.

Stein was fascinated by the small particular difference that distinguished identically made objects, like her Ford car, from each other. Sentences were all sentences, but each sentence was itself. She believed that the single sentence is the key to writing, and she certainly practiced what she preached: "in composition one thing is as important as another thing." As Kenneth Burke was to say, we have been sentenced to the sentence. It was *sentences* she heard from her family's black retainers. As a very bright student in William James's psychology courses, she was on the track of the individual, self-contained statement as disclosure. She was to see the sentence as orphic revelation: hers! So a sentence could become the glowing unit of a page, the building block of literature. But she was arrogant, she saw herself as a sibyl without fear of reproach, and writing through the night (in the morning Toklas would worshipfully pick up and type the scattered scrawled sheets) she heedlessly wrote straight from the ear to the paper. Her last books, like Hemingway's last books, showed the expansion and disintegration of a style founded on conversation.

Stein's genius was for conversation and especially for listening to other people's conversation. What fascinated her in the "new" painting by Cézanne and Matisse was the fact that something, anything, could be done by a temperament sufficiently self-willed—the slashing lines and thickly encrusted colors, Matisse in particular with his use of color *as* line, the thick, joyously rhythmical color building up an impression totally sufficient to the design that would satisfy the eye. Every image is made up of minute particulars. Every particular is realized through the maximum concentration and toil. The world is built up from such particulars. As the cubists soon proved, an object is a form made up of inherent forms. We go from cube to cube, atom to atom, as nature did in the long creation of every living thing that makes up the whole.

Hemingway's approach to painting was more diffident but actually closer to its sensuous content and to his own delight in method. The difference between Stein and Hemingway can be seen even in their handwriting. Her letters were tall, sprawling, arrogantly sloppy, with the large telltale spaces between words that were characteristic of her reflective mind. His letters were close, carefully and slowly shaped. They remind me of Nick Adams making camp in "Big Two-Hearted River," another demonstration of Hemingway's own planned, anxiously careful, tidy assemblage of words as objects.

> He started a fire with some chunks of pine he got with the ax from a stump. Over the fire he stuck a wire grill, pushing the four legs down into the ground with his boot. Nick put the frying pan on the grill over the flames. He was hungrier. The beans and spaghetti warmed. Nick stirred them and mixed them together. They began to bubble, making little bubbles that rose with difficulty to the surface. There was a good smell. Nick got out a bottle of tomato catchup and cut four slices of bread. The little bubbles were coming faster now. Nick sat down beside the fire and lifted the frying pan off.

Of course the great precedent to all this, Hemingway acknowledged, was *Huckleberry Finn*. The passage in which Nick Adams packs his captured trout between layers of fern reminds one of Huck planning to escape his father. He methodically lists the things he has, the things he has gained, the things he is sure of.

> The old man made me go to the skiff and fetch the things he had got. There was a fifty-pound sack of corn meal and a side of bacon, ammunition, and a four-gallon jug of whiskey and an old book and two newspapers for wadding besides some tow. I toted up a load, and went back and sat down on the bow of the skiff to rest. I thought it all over and I reckoned I would walk off with the gun and some lines and take to the woods, when I run away. I guessed I wouldn't stay in one place but just tramp right across the country, mostly nighttimes, and hunt and fish to keep alive and so get so far away that the old man nor the widow wouldn't ever find me any more.

Hemingway was naturally drawn to painting in France because it celebrated homely natural materials—like the world he knew and wanted to write about. Although he had seen the pioneer collections of the Art Institute in Chicago, it was the double experience of writing English in France and of being daily stimulated by the streets, the bridges, the museums, by meeting Gertrude Stein, Ezra Pound, James Joyce, Ford Madox Ford, that helped to form this cunningly obedient listener into the powerfully undercutting stylist that he became. Stein said: "One of the things I have liked all these years is to be surrounded by people who know no English. It has left me more intensely alone with my eyes and my English." That is what Hemingway felt; it is his marvellous representation of this vital early experience that makes his Paris in A Moveable Feast so beautiful, though the book is wicked in its attempt to destroy Stein, Ford, and Fitzgerald and a downright lie in its underhanded description of the collapse of his marriage to Hadley. He does not say that when he became famous he became insupportably arrogant. He was unknown, "poor and happy," in A Moveable Feast, but he became ferocious in the days of fame. Fame inflamed him more than liquor and turned Stein's obedient little "ape" into an inferno of unrelenting ego. It did not make him happy. Painting at least took him out of himself.

French painting did more for Hemingway than reinforce his American passion for technique, for method, for instruments, for utensils. It gave him, as it did a whole generation of foreign artists in Paris, a sense of what Baudelaire called luxe, calme et volupté. Marc Chagall, another foreigner in Paris, said: "These colors and these forms must show, in the end, our dreams of human happiness." Hemingway lived a life of danger, near-catastrophe, and was inwardly ravaged by his attraction to danger and the boozy life he led in the company of sycophants all over the world; he became a victim of his own celebrity. He was attracted to the harmony in painting as he was influenced by the direction it gave his imagination.

One of the recurrent themes in his work is the rallying from discomfort to comfort, from danger to safety, from death to life, from ordeal to escape. He was as much a romantic about himself as he was a cold-eyed observer of the world at large. In fact, he was so savagely competitive and such a brutal antagonist to other people that the pastoral, harmonious, cuddly sensations he described were as vital to his existence as the seeking of danger. Painting, even the most violent-looking painting by those whom the French once called les fauves, wild beasts, usually subsides into a source of peace. You can look at a Cézanne in 1906 and walk away from it disturbed, but in 1926 you will not remember what once jarred you. When Leo Stein first went to the picture dealer Ambrose Vollard to look at the Cézannes that Bernard Berenson told him about, he had to turn them up, one after another, from a dusty pile. Leo and Gertrude Stein, usually Leo, had to talk night and day to their friends to make them see these paintings. When the great Stein collection was exhibited at the Museum of Modern Art in New York, the room seemed to blaze with sunlight.

Painting far more than writing suggests the actual texture of human happiness. Hemingway understood that; what excited him, as a writer, about painting was a promise of relief from civilization, a touch of the promised land. The Hemingway hero is usually alone in nature, and the landscape he sees (and will bring back in words) is in minute particulars unseen by anyone but him. Again and again in his work this often cruel writer shows himself to be an unabashed American romantic positively melting in the presence of BEAUTY. The opening lines of A *Farewell to Arms* cast a spell. They do not altogether make sense except as pure visual impressionism, repeated and echoing Hemingway's own effort to get these "impressions" down.

> In the late summer of that year we lived in a house in a village that looked across the river and the plain to the mountains. In the bed of the river there were pebbles and boulders, dry and white in the sun, and the water was clear and swiftly moving and blue in the channels. Troops went by the house and down the road and the dust they raised powdered the leaves of the trees. The trunks of the trees too were dusty and the leaves fell early that year and we saw the troops marching along the road and the dust rising and leaves, stirred by the breeze, falling and the soldiers marching and afterward the road bare and white except for the leaves.

If Cézanne's greatness lay in the removal of his subjects from the contingent world, this opening paragraph is an imitation of that removal. It is exclusively an impression from the outside, it rests within the eye of the beholder. As an impression it is static, for it calls attention to the beholder's effort to capture one detail after another rather than to the scene of war. As so often happens in Hemingway's prose forays into war, bullfighting, marlin fishing, hunting, there is an unnatural pause in the last sentence—"leaves, stirred by the breeze"—a forced transition made necessary by "painting" the scene in words. We positively see the writer at his easel.

What Stein caught from painting—it was a literary idea—was the ability of the writer to call attention to each stroke. Hemingway said that writing is architecture, not interior decoration. When he turned from the obedient pupil into the world-famous Ernest Hemingway, he made a great point, in talking about his own writing through his contempt for other people's writing, of saying that they were "unreadable." *Readable* meant the reduction of the world to a line of glitteringly clear sentences. Ironically, Stein criticized his first writings as being *inaccrochable*, not hangable on a wall, not ready to be looked at. It was she, with her thousand-page soliloquies and meanderings, who turned out to be *inaccrochable*. She longed to have a great public, like Hemingway. When she and the GIs discovered each other in 1944, she would not let a single Brewsie or Willie go.

Hemingway had the magnetic gift of fame, of arousing attention with every word, that Stein bitterly missed. He had learned his lesson from her all too well. He had in fact learned to lasso the reader, to become his eyes and ears exactly as a Cézanne or a Matisse rivets attention, obliterates everything around it. This works better in Hemingway's marvellous stories, which are consistent, all "composition," every inch of the canvas filled, than in his novels. There he often stops the action to do some scene painting and is swaggeringly self-indulgent, both in self-portraiture and as a maker of beautiful effects.

A picture is an action that must fill up its available space. Stein was fascinated by the concentration that is behind all true painting. She was always telling Hemingway: "concentrate." He certainly learned to concentrate. The inter-chapters of In Our Time, which tell of condemned men being carried to the gallows in a chair because they have lost control of their sphincter muscles and German soldiers climbing over a wall and being potted one two three—"We shot them just like that"—showed that Hemingway was concentrating all right, concentrating on the reader. Hemingway influenced a whole generation of journalists to become pseudoartists, especially around Time, where every little article was called a "story" and was rewritten and rewritten as if it were a paragraph by Flaubert instead of the usual Luceite's overemphasized account of the personal characteristics of some big shot who had made the week's cover.

Eventually, Hemingway's influence began to influence him too much. The famous brushwork became bloated and sometimes suggested the relaxed intention that all good American writers seek after writing. But Hemingway at his best understood that a short story by its very compressiveness comes nearest a lyric poem or haiku in its total intactness. A novel is by tradition too discursive, epic, and widespread. Of all Hemingway's novels, The Sun Also Rises has the best chance of surviving, for it is more consistent in its tone, its scene, and even Hemingway's scorn than A Farewell to Arms, which veers between the sheerest personal romanticism and Hemingway's desire to give an essentially lyric cast to his observations of the Italian-Austrian front in World War I.

More and more in his big books Hemingway, for all his genius at intuiting the trouble spots and danger points in human existence, used his well-developed style as a lyric diversion from his increasing sense of being closed in. The old rugged individualist had somehow known from the beginning that the coming century was going to be war on the individual. That was the dark and even ominous climate of feeling—achieved in the fewest, somehow punitive words—he got so unforgettably into his great stories, especially "Big Two-Hearted River." This story sums up the Hemingway hero's courage and despair, his furthest need and his deepest fear, in a way that also sums up the Western American's virtually sexual encounter with Nature, his adoration and awe, his sense of being too small for it, his abrupt, unfulfilled confrontation with what once seemed the greatest gift to man, but somehow always threw *him* off.

Hemingway was always a deeply personal writer. The immediacy, sometimes the deliberate brutality, but above all his vulnerability to anxiety, rage, frustration, and despair, gave him a masterful closeness to his kaleidoscope of emotions. He was by turns so proud yet so often stricken a human creature that the reader again and again surrenders to him. For Hemingway makes you feel in painfully distinct human detail how much the world merely echoes the endless turmoil in the human heart.

> Ahead the river narrowed and went into a swamp. The river became smooth and deep and the swamp looked solid with cedar trees, their trunks close together, their branches solid. It would not be possible to walk through a swamp like that. The branches grew so low. . . .
> . . . He did not feel like going on into the swamp. He looked down the river. A big cedar slanted all the way across the stream. Beyond that the river went into the swamp.
> Nick did not want to go in there now. He felt a reaction against deep wading with the water deepening up under his armpits, to hook big trout in places impossible to land them. In the swamp the banks were bare, the big cedars came together overhead, the sun did not come through, except in patches; in the fast deep water, in the half light, the fishing would be tragic. In the swamp fishing was a tragic adventure. Nick did not want it. He did not want to go down the stream any further today.

Hemingway was a painfully complex man who was indeed as gifted and, yes, as "brave" as he claimed to be. He did his work. He hauntingly intimated on paper some fundamental conflicts that like all of us he did not resolve in the flesh. Especially not in the flesh. Nor did he realize these conflicts in his novels as the great novelists have done. He was too immature and self-absorbed, in the fashion of so many gifted Americans maddened by the gap between their talent and their vulnerability. What made Hemingway important, what will keep his best work forever fresh, was his ability to express a certain feeling of hazard that men in particular do not suffer any less because they go out of their way to meet it. Who is to say how much this sense of hazard, peril, danger, with its constant rehearsal of the final and perhaps only real battle—with death as the embodiment of a universe that is not ours alone, that may not be ours at all—who is to say how much Hemingway sought it out for his natural subject matter as much as it constantly whipped *him* to prove himself again and again? In Gregory Hemingway's memoir, he says that he felt:

relief when they lowered my father's body into the ground and I realized that he was really dead, that I couldn't disappoint him, couldn't hurt him anymore. . . .

I hope it's peaceful, finally. But oh God, I knew there was no peace after death. If only it were different, because nobody every dreamed of, or longed for, or experienced less peace than he.

This is the truth about Hemingway that all the carousing and boasting could not conceal. Yet it is a truth that every reader recognizes with gratitude as being at the heart of the darkness that Hemingway unforgettably described: the sense of something irremediably *wrong*. Against this, Hemingway furiously put forth his dream of serenity, of Nature as the promised land, for which composition—the painter's word that he picked up as his ideal—suggested the right order of words in their right places. As Ford Madox Ford put it so beautifully in his introduction to A *Farewell to Arms*, "Hemingway's words strike you, each one, as if they were pebbles fetched fresh from a brook. They live and shine, each in its place. So one of his pages has the effect of a brook-bottom into which you look down through the floating water."

Nature as a nonhuman ideal has always been an American's romantic dream. All the great American landscape painters have always portrayed Mother Nature as too big for the solitary man on the cliff looking down. By contrast, as Malraux wrote in *Man's Fate*, painting to Orientals has been the practice of "charity." Charity is hardly what Hemingway found in the world or what he sought from painting. There is no charity in his writing at all, serenity on occasion, a rally, a promise of peace. He was a tough, sharp realist about other people, for in portraying himself so exhaustively, he portrayed us and the pitiless century into which we were born.

JOHN HOLLANDER

Hemingway's Extraordinary Actuality

Of all the Hemingway material to be posthumously unveiled, short stories dating from before World War II would surely be the most welcome. This awkward volume *The Fifth Column and the First Forty-Nine Stories* brings together four previously uncollected stories mostly set in Madrid during the siege, with *The Fifth Column*, Hemingway's play set in the same scene. This last is already familiar to us through inclusion in the canonical old Modern Library Giant edition of forty-nine short stories (until Scribner's removed it, for undisclosed reasons when they took over the collected stories reprint again in the Fifties). These four stories are all a bit long-winded: they are not of the genre of the World War I sketches. They propound a world of desperation, military blunders, a senseless slaying of a civilian in a café, the necessary dirtiness of turning in a spy, and the crippling aspect of the International presence on the Loyalist side. Within that world, familiar Hemingwayan acts of grace occur, in a kind of low-keyed way, and the genuine people are mostly being hurt. The Spaniards all speak the patented Hemingway dialect, no contractions and *muy formal*. But the stories are authentic enough, and are quite better than the worst of those in the collected volume. It only seems a pity that these were not included in it, instead of appearing in this somewhat artificial format: "The Denunciation," "The Butterfly and the Tank," "Night Before Battle," and "Under the Ridge" together take up 62 pages. In any event, once the publishers were committed to such a presentation, they might at least have included a note on the publishing history of its contents. But such a selection does cause us to reflect on the nature of his best stories. They belong to what may turn out to have been, save for *The Sun Also Rises*, his

First published in this volume. Copyright © 1985 by John Hollander. Parts of this essay appeared in *Harper's Magazine*.

major genre. Hemingway's marvelous delicacy, his wielding of the powerful right cross, as it were, of nuance after so many jabs of apparent bald
presentation of fact, his deployment of the resonances of a conversational
phrase that remains unmatched—except in Joyce's *Dubliners*—by all of his
followers, including the frequently formidable John O'Hara, are all more
clearly manifest in his sketches than in his *grandes machines*. His best
stories reveal a narrator who is a much greater figure and more clearly
touched by a bit of nobility than any of his fictional heroes, whether
earlier anti-heroes or later naively sentimental ones to whom we cannot
help but condescend. It is not only the celebrated tone of voice of the
narration (troped, as always, by a palpable style—but what else is new?)
enabling it to personify itself so well, which accounts for these stories'
peculiarly lyrical power. (And even Nick Adams is characterized by the
sensibility which is internal monologue in, say, the "Big Two-Hearted
River" stories, and so which he shares with the putatively more distanced
narration). It is the very fabric of what some Frenchified critics would call
the narratology, the very telling of the tale of telling, which itself pitches
these accounts of episodes and moments at, and not above, the tension of
the lyre.

Wallace Stevens wrote of Hemingway in 1942 as a poet; "the most
significant of living poets, so far as the subject of extraordinary actuality is
concerned." In one of his *Adagia* Stevens observed that "In the poem of
extraordinary actuality, consciousness takes the place of imagination," and
he might as well have been characterizing not only the stories themselves,
but the pregnant parataxis which forever refuses to allow of trivial connections, and which marks several levels of Hemingway's writing. The cursive
sentence structure manifests a refusal to subordinate clauses, not out of
fake naïveté, nor out of a weak misconstruction of Gertrude Stein, but
rather, in a language supremely conscious of persons in places, in order to
avoid the reductiveness that exposition and description, in their zeal to
account for the way things seem to be, often effect. A certain kind of
trivial literary history would link Hemingway's manner to another sort of
reduction, the stripping of the rhetorical varnish demanded by the aesthetic programs of Continental modernism. But any serious reader knows
such rhetoric to be of the nature of the wood itself, and that varnish,
stain, paint, raw creosoted surfaces, or whatever, merely represent differ-
ing rhetorical projections.

Yet beyond the styling of the prose, Hemingway's parataxis stands
between larger elements, full of possibility and silence like the white
spaces between printed stanzas of verse. The impossibility of allegorizing
the italicized interchapters (those beautifully crafted lyrical vignettes—or

are they more like dramatic monologues?) placed between the reminiscent stories in *In Our Time* in order to make them fit the stories they precede or follow, marks the effect of another level of poetical parataxis. Insofar as they act like macaronic refrains in some other language, placed between stanzas of a ballad, they seem to connect in one way while (or, perhaps, *by*) palpably disconnecting even further. Insofar as they present an unmeditative present in narrowed vignette, and a more fully realized past, they mediate between the opening of Wordsworth's "Tintern Abbey," say, and the standard vulgar cinematic dissolve into flashback.

Nowhere is Hemingway's poetry of "extraordinary actuality" more fully realized, perhaps, than in a story which he once declared to be a favorite, the one from *Men Without Women* called "Hills Like White Elephants." In this sketch, which Dorothy Parker rightly perceived as "delicate and tragic," an American couple waiting for a train at a small station in Spain are overheard, in about six pages of dialogue, while a bout of what must be a continuing disagreement about an abortion (the young man keeps maintaining that "It's perfectly simple;" the young woman knows that it, and much else, is not) gradually decays. The dialogue is framed by bits of description—rather like stage directions in their length and frequency of occurrence, but also unlike them, for the most part, in that they keep cutting away from the dialogue to describe a passage of scenery, or to recall such a passage previously invoked. The story opens with an observation of a bit of the landscape: "The hills across the Ebro were long and white," and the ellipsis of the more epistemologically plausible example—"Seen from the small railroad station in Castile on a hot afternoon, the extensive ridge of hills across the valley of the Ebro looked white"—moves the sentence from the rhetoric of novelistic point of view into that of lyrical trope. After some preliminary dialogue about ordering drinks, the narration observes that the girl "was looking off at the line of hills. They were white in the sun and the country was brown and dry."

> "They look like white elephants," she said.
> "I've never seen one," the man drank his beer.
> "No, you wouldn't have."

Even were it not for the synecdochal title, the apparent-white-elephantness of the hills has become a counter in their conversation, and leads to the first indication of the trouble between them, the passage from disillusion to dissolution which the vignette of talk and scene embraces:

> "Well, let's try and have a fine time."
> "All right. I was trying. I said the mountains looked like white elephants. Wasn't that bright?"

"That was bright."

"I wanted to try this new drink. That's all we do, isn't it—look at things and try new drinks?"

"I guess so."

The girl looked across at the hills.

"They're lovely hills," she said. "They don't really look like white elephants. I just meant the coloring of their skin through the trees."

The girl's *looking* at the hills describes a totally different act from the disaffected sightseeing of the "look at things and try new drinks," of course, and the hills have been privileged by the narration to begin with. Even when she retracts her formulation about the white elephants, in the interests of maintaining the surface of the "fine time," she cannot abandon her observation entirely. What for the reader of novels constitutes her slip about the "skin" of the hills, operates in the poem of the sketch to reaffirm the truth and rightness and brightness of the original and originating trope: The ridge of hills, low peaked and undulant, lined up in circus fashion, trunk to tail, parade across the middle-high horizon, calm, beneficent, reaffirming the health of distant vision. The narration, and the girl, both know this. But this image of possibility and delight is tragically and inevitably linked, by the ways of the world, to a darker, narrower emblem, and as soon as the conversation moves to the matter of the abortion, the girl's pregnancy itself becomes part of the matter. Proverbially, the "white elephant" of unwanted possession, the objectified burden (which comes, as *Brewer's Dictionary of Phrase and Fable* elegantly puts it, from the story of a Siamese king who "used to make a present of a white elephant to courtiers he wished to ruin"), the ugly and useless bric-a-brac, gets allusively stuck to that pregnancy, even as the girl's momentarily repressed sense of her body (what will she look like to herself in her ninth month?) may perhaps be reflected as well.

And it is this touch of a more narrowed emblem which darkens the long, white *symbole* of the hills. After a later turn of unsatisfactory false resolution (she agrees to the operation, he returns with "I don't want you to do it if you feel that way") the narration again cuts away (and again, one can hardly avoid the cinematic verb) to what is there:

> The girl stood up and walked to the end of the station. Across, on the other side, were fields of grain and trees along the banks of the Ebro. Far away, beyond the river, were mountains. The shadow of a cloud moved across the field of grain and she saw the river through the trees.
>
> "And we could have all this," she said. "And we could have everything and every day we make it more impossible."

This is a more pictorial landscape now, and less of a visionary one. And yet, its mode of accessibility to the reading eye, the nearby growth of grain and tree, the promise of plenitude and the promise of continuity in the glimpse of the river—all of these lost before to the beyondness of the elephantine hills—now comprise a full figure of what the girl calls "all this." The parataxis of what should in more expository narrative be the adduced moral, and which is here replaced by the girl's statement, seems far more delicate than another famous moment of cutting from dialogue to glimpse of scene in American literature. The cloud about to pass in front of the moon in Robert Frost's "The Death of the Hired Man" fills in a few minutes of the wife's waiting for her husband to report on the condition of the old man who, it will turn out, has died. The wife says:

> "I'll sit and see if that small sailing cloud
> Will hit or miss the moon."
> It hit the moon.
> Then there were three there, making a dim row,
> The moon, the little silver cloud, and she.

The *ad hoc omen* ("It hit the moon") decays into a schematic trope in the last line, explicitly connecting the phenomenon and the interpeting observer. But Hemingway's glimpse is more elusively parabolic than this, and certainly more Wordsworthian in one mode even as it is less so in another.

In general, the riddling power of a figure like that of the hills lies in the way Hemingway's narrative controls the mode of figuration. The hills are, at the outset, simply *there*, as given as given can be; then they are grasped by the girl, become more and more rhetorically problematic as the brief dialogue unrolls, and finally vanish behind a later, sadder kind of landscape. And yet their beauty is nobler than their narrowed emblematic meaning, and that beauty calls up a wider and stronger evocation (like that of, say, the shadow of the distant poplar tree falling across the face of Tennyson's sleeping Mariana). I have twice used the term "cut" to describe the movement away from dialogue to glimpse of scene in this story. I should not have thought that early readers of it would have felt anything cinematic about it—indeed, what became momentarily celebrated about the story was the girl's string of seven *please*s in her request, at the end of all their discourse, that the young man stop talking. (Virginia Woolf, in a singularly obtuse review of *Men Without Women* in 1927, expresses nothing but impatience with the dialogue, and sneers; "At last we are inclined to cry out with the little girl 'Would you please . . .' How she can call the quite grown-up young woman, fully equipped with a dose of *Weltschmerz*, a "little girl" is most curious and suggests that she thinks the operation in question to be a tonsillectomy.) It would not be until the days of 1960's Italian cinema that the amazing resemblance of this story to an Antonioni shooting script—in the relation of dialogue and shots of landscape cut away to as a move in the dialogue itself, rather than as mere punctuation, and ultimately in the way in which dialogue and uninterpreted glimpse of scene interpret each other—would become apparent. But the poetics of that kind of film, and the poetics of extraordinary actuality in Hemingway, are connected by more than analogy, for the literary-historical line from Hemingway to the novels of Pavese and on to the films of Antonioni is quite clear.

In stories like this one, like "God Rest You Merry, Gentlemen," like "The Light of the World" and, inevitably, like "A Clean, Well-Lighted Place," the unfolding of the central tropes has the kind of power of lyrical movement and tells a tale of the genesis of complex meaning which the more familiar chronicling of the longer stories may not be able to achieve. They may make even the Kilimanjaro and Macomber stories seem, some day, like anecdotes.

Chronology

1899	Born July 21 in Oak Park, Illinois.
1917	Works as reporter on *Kansas City Star*.
1918	Service in Italy as ambulance driver for Red Cross; wounded on July 8 near Fossalta di Piave.
1920	Reporter for *Toronto Star*.
1921	Marries Hadley Richardson; moves to Paris.
1922	Reports Greek-Turkish war for Toronto *Star*.
1923	*Three Stories and Ten Poems* published in Paris.
1924	*In Our Time* published in Paris.
1925	*In Our Time*, which adds fourteen short stories to the earlier vignettes, is published in America, Hemingway's first American book.
1926	*Torrents of Spring* and *The Sun Also Rises* published.
1927	*Men Without Women* published. Marries Pauline Pfeiffer.
1928	Moves to Key West.
1929	*A Farewell to Arms* published.
1932	*Death in the Afternoon* published.
1933	*Winner Take Nothing* published.
1935	*Green Hills of Africa* published.
1937	*To Have and Have Not* published. Returns to Spain as war correspondent on the Loyalist side.
1938	Writes scripts for the film, *The Spanish Earth*. *The Fifth Column and the First Forty-Nine Stories* published.
1940	Marries Martha Gellhorn. *For Whom the Bell Tolls* published. Buys house in Cuba, where he lives throughout most of the 40s and 50s.
1942	Edits *Men at War*.
1944	Takes part in Allied liberation of Paris with partisan unit.
1946	Marries Mary Welsh.
1950	*Across the River and into the Trees* published.
1952	*The Old Man and the Sea* published.
1954	Receives Nobel Prize for Literature.
1960	Returns to United States and settles in Ketchum, Idaho.
1961	Suicide on July 2, in Ketchum.
1964	*A Moveable Feast* published.

Contributors

HAROLD BLOOM, Sterling Professor of the Humanities at Yale University, is the author of *The Anxiety of Influence*, *Poetry and Repression*, and many other volumes of literary criticism. His forthcoming study, *Freud: Transference and Authority*, attempts a full-scale reading of all of Freud's major writings. A MacArthur Prize fellow, he is general editor of five series of literary criticism published by Chelsea House.

LIONEL TRILLING's critical writings include studies of Matthew Arnold (1939), E. M. Forster (1943), and collections of literary essays, among them *The Liberal Imagination* (1950), *The Opposing Self* (1955), and *Beyond Culture* (1965). He is also the author of *Freud and the Crisis of Our Culture* (1955).

EDMUND WILSON was literary editor of The New Republic (1926–31), and his wide-ranging writing and criticism includes *Axel's Castle* (1931), *To the Finland Station* (1940), *Memoirs of Hecate County* (1946), *The Dead Sea Scrolls* (1969), and *Patriotic Gore* (1962).

ROBERT PENN WARREN's literary achievements include the poetry *Promises* (1957), *The Cave* (1959), *Incarnations* (1968), *Audubon: A Vision* (1969), *Now and Then* (1976–79), *Chief Joseph of the Nez Perce* (1983), and the prose works *World Enough and Time* (1950), *Band of Angels* (1955), and *Democracy and Poetry* (1975). He has taught at colleges throughout the South and in the Northeast.

HARRY LEVIN has written widely on Joyce, Marlowe, Hawthorne and Shakespeare, and is the author of *Contexts of Criticism* (1957), *Refractions* (1966), *Grounds for Comparison* (1972) and *Memories of the Moderns* (1980).

CARLOS BAKER, Hemingway's official biographer, has also written on Shelley (1948), and is the author of the novels *A Friend in Power* (1958), *The Land of Rumbelow* (1963), and *The Gay Head Conspiracy* (1973).

MARK SPILKA is Professor of English at Brown University and author of *The Love Ethic of D. H. Lawrence* (1955), *Dickens and Kafka* (1963), and *Virginia Woolf's Quarrel with Grieving* (1980).

GEORGE PLIMPTON, editor-in-chief of *The Paris Review*, has published numerous articles and books on sports, and is the author of *Rabbit's Umbrella* (1956), *Paper Lion* (1966), *The Bogey Man* (1968), *Shadow Box* (1976), and most recently *Fireworks* (1984).

REYNOLDS PRICE, novelist, poet, and playwright is Professor of English at Duke University. Among his works are *A Long and Happy Life* (1962), *The Names and Faces of Heroes* (1963), *A Generous Man* (1966), *Things Themselves* (1972), *The Source of Light* (1981), and *Vital Provisions* (1982).

MALCOLM COWLEY was editor of *The New Republic* and has written widely on American literature. His literary achievements include *Blue Juanita* (1929), *Exile's Return* (1934), *The Dry Season* (1941), *Think Back On Us* (1967), and *The Dream of the Golden Mountains* (1980).

STEVEN K. HOFFMAN is Assistant Professor of English at Duke University. He has written on Emily Dickinson, Robert Lowell, Shirley Jackson, and on confessional poetry.

ALFRED KAZIN is Professor on English at Hunter College and is the author of *On Native Grounds* (1942), *A Walker in the City* (1951), *The Inmost Leaf* (1955), and *New York Jew* (1978).

JOHN HOLLANDER is Professor of English at Yale University and has written several collections of poetry, including *The Unturning of the Sky* (1961), *Visions from the Rambler* (1965), *Types of Shape* (1968), and most recently *Powers of Thirteen* (1983).

Bibliography

Baker, Carlos. *Ernest Hemingway: Critiques of Four Major Novels.* New York: Scribner's, 1962.

————. *Ernest Hemngway: A Life Story.* New York: Scribner's, 1969.

————. *Hemingway, The Writer As Artist.* Princeton, New Jersey: Princeton University Press, 1972.

————,ed. *Ernest Hemingway, Selected Letters.* New York: Granda, 1981.

Benson, Jackson J. *Hemingway: The Writer's Art of Self-Defense.* Minneapolis: The University of Minnesota Press, 1969.

Brenner, Gerry. *Concealments in Hemingway's Works.* Columbus: Ohio State University Press, 1983.

Broer, Lawrence R. *Hemingway's Spanish Tragedy.* University: University of Alabama Press, 1973.

Bruccoli, Matthew J. *Scott and Ernest: The Authority of Failure and the Authority of Success.* New York: Random House, 1978.

Buckley, Peter. *Ernest.* New York: Dial Press, 1978.

Burgess, Anthony. *Ernest Hemingway and His World.* New York: Scribner's 1978.

Cowley, Malcolm, ed. *Hemingway,* New York: The Viking Press, 1944.

Donaldson, Scott. *By Force of Will: The Life and Art of Ernest Hemingway.* New York: Viking, 1977.

Falco, Joseph M. *The Hero in Hemingway's Short Stories.* Pittsburgh: University of Pittsburgh Press, 1968.

Fenton, Charles Andrews. *The Apprenticeship of Ernest Hemingway: The Early Years.* New York: Farrar, Straus and Young, 1954.

Flora, Joseph M. *Hemingway's Nick Adams.* Baton Rouge: Louisiana State University Press, 1982.

Gajdusek, Robert E., ed. *Hemingway's Paris.* New York: Scribner's, 1978.

Gellens, Jay. *Twentieth Century Interpretations of "A Farewell to Arms."* Englewood Cliffs, N.J.: Prentice-Hall, 1970.

Gurko, Leo. *Ernest Hemingway and The Pursuit of Heroism.* New York: Crowell, 1968.

Hemingway, Ernest. *Men without Women.* New York: Scribner's, 1927.

————. *Death in the Afternoon.* New York: Scribner's, 1932.

————. *Green Hills of Africa.* New York: Scribner's, 1935.

————. *To Have and Have Not.* New York: Scribner's, 1937.

————. *The Fifth Column, and the First Forty-nine Stories.* New York: Scribner's, 1938.

————. *For Whom the Bell Tolls.* New York: Scribner's, 1940.

————. *Across the River and Into the Trees.* New York: Scribner's, 1950.

————. *The Old Man and the Sea.* New York; Scribner's, 1952.

————. *The Sun Also Rises.* New York: Scribner's, 1954.

————. *A Farewell to Arms.* New York: Scribner's, 1957.

————. *In Our Time.* New York: Scribner's 1958.

————. *A Moveable Feast.* New York: Scribner's, 1964.

————. *The Snows of Kilimanjaro, and Other Stories.* New York: Scribner's, 1970.

————. *Islands in the Stream.* New York: Scribner's, 1970.

————. *The Nick Adams Stories.* New York: Scribner's, 1972.

————. *Winner Take Nothing.* New York: Scribner's, 1983.

Hemingway, Gregory. *Papa: A Personal Memoir.* Boston: Houghton Mifflin, 1976.

Hemingway, Leicester. *My Brother Ernest Hemingway.* Cleveland: World Publishing, 1962.

Hermann, Lazar. *Hemingway: A Pictorial Biography.* New York: Viking, 1961.

Hotchner, A. E. *Papa Hemingway: A Personal Memoir.* New York: Random House, 1966.

Hovey, Richard Bennett. *Hemingway: The Inward Terrain.* Seattle: University of Washington Press, 1968.

Jobes, Katherine T., ed. *Twentieth Century Interpretations of "The Old Man and the Sea."* Englwood Cliffs, N.J.: Prentice-Hall, 1968.

Killinger, John. *Hemingway and the Dead Gods: A Study in Existentialism.* Lexington: Univeristy of Kentucky Press, 1960.

Lee, A. Robert, ed. *Ernest Hemingway: New Critical Esssays.* Totowa, N.J.: Barnes and Noble, 1983.

McCaffrey, John K. *Ernest Hemingway: The Man and His Work.* New York: Cooper Square Publishers, 1969.

Meyers, Jeffrey, ed. *Hemingway: The Critical Heritage.* Boston: Routledge and Kegan Paul, 1982.

Montgomery, Constance Cappel. *Hemingway in Michigan.* New York: Fleet Publishing Corp., 1966.

Nagel, James, ed. *Ernest Hemingway, The Writer in Context.* Madison: University of Wisconsin Press, 1984.

Nahal, Chaman Lal. *The Narrative Pattern in Ernest Hemingway's Fiction.* Rutherford, N.J.: Fairleigh Dickinson University Press, 1971.

Nelson, Raymond S. *Hemingway: Expressionist Artist.* Ames: Iowa State University Press, 1979.

Oldsey, Bernard Stanley. *Hemingway's Hidden Craft: The Writing of "A Farewell to Arms."* University Park: Pennsylvania State University Press, 1979.

Pearsall, Robert Brainard. *The Life and Writings of Ernest Hemingway.* Amsterdam: Rodopi, 1973.

Raeburn, John. *Fame Became of Him: Hemingway as a Public Writer.* Bloomington: Indiana University Press, 1984.

Reynolds, Michael S. *Hemingway's First War: The Making of "A Farewell to Arms."* Princeton: Princeton University Press, 1976.

————. *Critical Essays on Ernest Hemingway's "In Our Time."* Boston: G.K. Hall, 1983.

Rovit, Earl. *Ernest Hemingway.* New York: Twayne Publisher, 1963.

Ryan, Frank L. *The Immediate Critical Reception of Ernest Hemingway.* Washington, D.C., University Press of America, 1980.

Sanderson, Stewart, *Ernest Hemingway.* New York: Grove Press, 1961.

Scribner, Charles, Jr., ed. *The Enduring Hemingway.* New York: Charles Scribner's Sons, 1974.

Svoboda, Frederic Joseph. *Hemingway and "The Sun Also Rises": The Crafting of a Style.* Lawrence: The University of Kansas Press, 1983.

Wagner, Linda Wilshimer. *Five Decades of Hemingway Criticism.* East Lansing: Michigan State University Press, 1974.

White, William, ed. *By-Line: Hemingway, Selected Articles and Dispatches of Four Decades.* New York: Scribner's 1967.

Williams, Wirt. *The Tragic Art of Ernest Hemingway.* Baton Rouge: Louisiana State University Press, 1981.

Young, Philip. *Ernest Hemingway: A Reconsideration.* 2nd ed. University Park; Pennsylvania State University Press, 1966.

Acknowledgments

"Hemingway and His Critics" by Lionel Trilling from *Partisan Review* 6 (Winter 1939), copyright © 1939 by Lionel Trilling. Reprinted by permission of Harcourt, Brace Jovanovich Inc.

"Hemingway: Gauge of Morale" by Edmund Wilson from *The Wound and the Bow* by Edmund Wilson, copyright © 1939 by Edmund Wilson. © renewed 1968 by Edmund Wilson. Reprinted by permission of Farrar, Straus and Giroux, Inc.

"Ernest Hemingway" by Robert Penn Warren from *Robert Penn Warren: Selected Essays* by Robert Penn Warren, copyright © 1966 by Robert Penn Warren. Reprinted by permission of Charles Scribner's Sons.

"Observations on the Style of Ernest Hemingway" by Harry Levin from *Contexts of Criticism* by Harry Levin, © 1957 by Harry Levin. Reprinted by permission.

"The Way It Was" by Carlos Baker from *The Writer as Artist* by Carlos Baker, copyright © 1952, 1956, 1963, 1972, 1980, by Carlos Baker. Reprinted by permission.

"The Death of Love in *The Sun Also Rises*" by Mark Spilka from *Twelve Original Essays on Great American Novels*, edited by Charles Shapiro, copyright © 1958 by Mark Spilka. Reprinted by permission of the Wayne State University Press.

"An Interview with Ernest Hemingway" by George Plimpton from *Writers At Work: The Paris Review Interviews*, edited by George Plimpton, copyright © 1963 by The Paris Review. Reprinted by permission of Viking Penguin Inc.

"For Ernest Hemingway" by Reynolds Price from *Things Themselves*, edited by Stephen Berg, copyright © 1972 by Reynolds Price. Reprinted by permission of Atheneum Publishers, Inc.

"Mr. Papa and the Parricides" by Malcolm Cowley from *And I Worked at the Writer's Trade* by Malcolm Cowley, copyright © 1963, 1964, 1965, 1967, 1968, 1971, 1972, 1975, 1976, 1977, 1978 by Malcolm Cowley. Reprinted by permission of Viking Penguin Inc.

Index